THE NEW CULTURAL ATLAS OF

EGYPT

Edited by Leon Gray

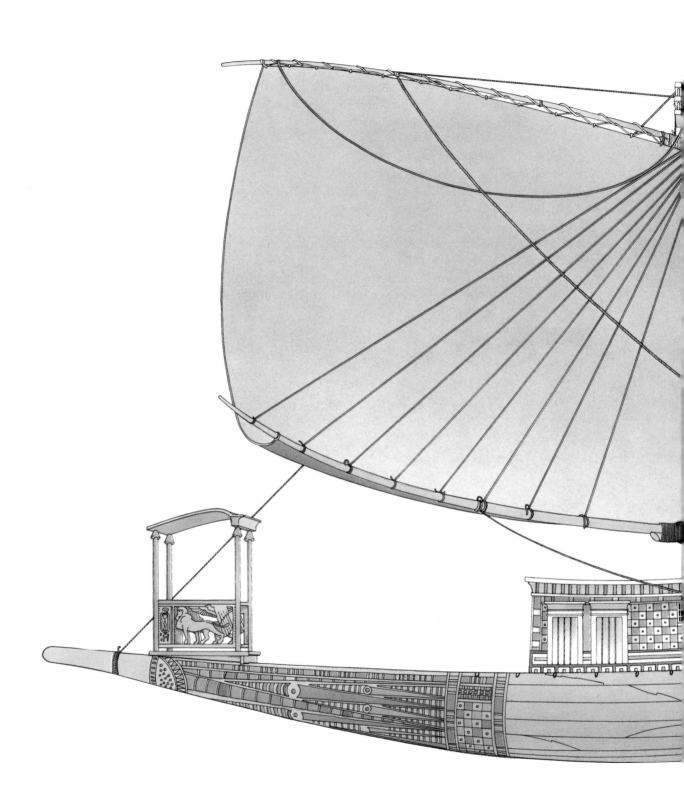

THE NEW CULTURAL ATLAS OF
EGYPT

Edited by Leon Gray

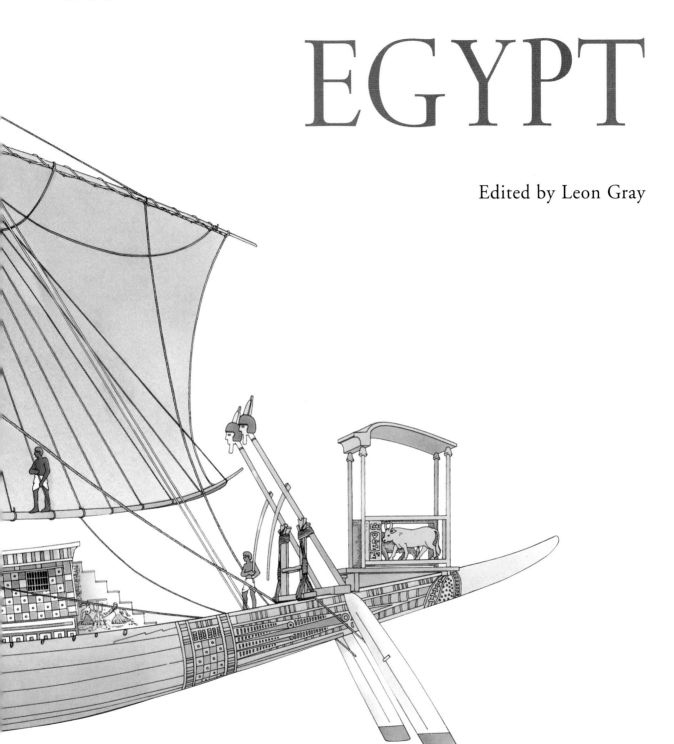

Marshall Cavendish
Reference
New York

This edition first published in 2010 in the United States of America by Marshall Cavendish.

Marshall Cavendish
99 White Plains Road
Tarrytown, New York 10591-9001

Library of Congress Cataloging-in-Publication Data

Marshall Cavendish Corporation
  The new cultural atlas of Egypt.
     p. cm.
  Includes bibliographical references and index.
  ISBN 978-0-7614-7877-5 (alk. paper)
  1. Egypt--Civilization--Maps. 2. Egypt--History--Maps. 3. Egypt--Antiquities--Maps. I. Title.
  G2491.E6M3 2009
  911'.32--dc22
                     2009005904

Printed and bound in Singapore

For the Brown Reference Group Ltd:
Editorial Director: Lindsey Lowe
Senior Managing Editor: Tim Cooke
Editor: Leon Gray
Design Manager: David Poole
Designer: Kim Browne
Indexer: Indexing Specialists (UK) Ltd.
Picture Manager: Sophie Mortimer
Production Director: Alastair Gourlay

Text adapted from the *Cultural Atlas of the World: Ancient Egypt*, revised edition, 1990, Checkmark Books (Facts On File), New York. Original text by John Baines and Jaromír Málek.

Contents

Timeline

		4500 BCE	3500 BCE	3000 BCE	2500

EGYPTIAN HISTORY		Predynastic Badarian/Tasian culture, Nile valley c.4500–4000. Merimda cultures, Delta c.4800–4100. Faiyum culture c.5400–4400.	Predynastic Naqada I, Nile valley c.4000–3500. Naqada II–III, Nile valley c.3500–3100. Invention of writing.	Foundation of Egyptian state c.3100. Trade with Mesopotamia. Early Dynastic Period c.2920–2575. 1st–3rd Dynasties. First mining expeditions to Sinai.	Old Kingdom c.2575–2134. 4th–6th Dynasties. Raids on Libya, Palestine, and Lower Nubia. Trade with Upper Nubia. First Intermediate Period c.2134–2040. 7th–11th Dynasties. Rival dynasties and civil wars.

Hunters from stone palette, c.3000 BCE

Tomb stela of King Wadj from Abydos, c.2980 BCE

Statue of King Khephren from Giza, c.2495 BCE

ARCHITECTURE AND TOMBS		Reed huts. Graves under hut floors at Merimda Beni Salama.	Mud-brick "funerary palaces" at Abydos. Mud-brick mastaba tombs at Saqqara. First stone buildings.	Mud-brick "funerary palaces" at Abydos. Mud-brick mastaba tombs at Saqqara. First stone buildings.	Massive stone pyramids and stone mastaba tombs at Giza, Saqqara, and Abusir. Stone sun temples and obelisks at Abu Ghurab and Abusir.

Painted terra-cotta figurine of a dancer, c.4000 BCE

Step pyramids at Saqqara.

Painting of geese from a tomb at Maidum, c.2560 BCE

Step Pyramid of King Djoser at Saqqara, c.2560 BCE

ART AND CRAFTS		Fine pottery vessels, clay figurines, objects carved from ivory.	Painted pottery, stone palettes and vessels, terra-cotta and ivory figurines. First wall paintings and stone statuettes.	Large stone statues. First reliefs in wood and stone. First stone stelae. Gold jewelry. Faience figurines.	Painted tomb reliefs of daily life. Royal statues in hard stones or in copper. Private statues in stone or wood. Furniture in wood and decorated sheet gold.

...e Kingdom c.2040–1640.
...3th Dynasties.

...on of Egypt under Theban
...ty. Trade with Syria and
...tine. Occupation of Lower
...a.

...d Intermediate Period
...–1532. 14th–17th Dynasties.

...pation of Delta by Hyksos
...Syria/Palestine. Kerma
...re occupies Lower Nubia
...etween the Hyksos and
...an kings.

...ue of King Senwosret III from
...r el-Bahri, c.1850 BCE

Early New Kingdom 1550–1307.
17th–18th Dynasties.

Egypt reunited under
Theban dynasty.

Conquest of Lower and
Upper Nubia.

Rise of Egyptian empire in
Syria and Palestine.

Gold mask from the mummy of
King Tutankhamun, c.1325 BCE

Late New Kingdom c.1307–1196.
19th–20th Dynasties.

Wars against the Hittites in
Syria. Depopulation of Lower
Nubia. Wars against the Sea
Peoples. Gradual loss of Near
Eastern empire.

Colossal statue at the Great Temple
of Abu Simbel, c.1270 BCE

Third Intermediate Period
c.1070–712. 21st–25th Dynasties.

Egypt divided. Kings ruling
Delta and High Priests ruling
Thebes. Rise of Nubian Kingdom
of Napata. Civil wars among
petty rulers.

Late Period 712–332. 25th–30th
Dynasties

Egypt reunited by Nubian
kings. Conquest of Egypt by the
Assyrians and by the Persians.
Periods of native rule between
conquests.

Kneeling
Egyptian from
statue base
of a Persian
king, c.500 BCE

Greco-Roman Period. 332 BCE–395
c.e. Greek rule
332–30 BCE

Egypt ruled by Ptolemies. Many
Greek immigrants. Some
Egyptian rebellions.

Roman rule 30 BCE–395 c.e.

Egypt becomes part of the
Roman Empire. Most of Nubia
ruled by Kings of Meroe.

Head of a priest in green schist,
c.75 BCE

...e mortuary temple of
...uhotep III at Deir el-Bahri.

...brick pyramids in Middle
...t and at Dahshur.

...cut tombs in Middle Egypt.

...in Nubia.

...ooden figurine
...a servant from
...Theban tomb,
...2020 BCE

Terraced temple of Hatshepsut
at Deir el-Bahri.

Rock-cut royal tombs in the
Valley of the Kings.

Temples of Amon at Karnak
and Luxor.

Palaces and Aten temples at
el-Amarna.

Relief from a vizier's tomb
at Thebes, c.1360 BCE

Mortuary temples of Ramesses II
(The Ramesseum) and Ramesses
III (Medinet Habu) at Thebes.

Great Hypostyle Hall at Karnak,
Ramesses II.

Great Temple of Abu Simbel and
other rock-cut and freestanding
temples in Nubia.

Relief of a blind harpist from a
Saqqara tomb, c.1300 BCE

Temple of Amon at Tanis with
underground royal tombs.

Large tombs with mud-brick
pylons at Thebes.

Shaft tombs at Saqqara.

Granite temple of Isis at Behbeit
el-Hagar.

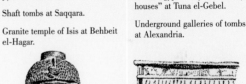

Inlaid bronze figure of a
high priestess, c.850 BCE

Great Egyptian-style temples at
Philae, Kom Ombo, Edfu, Esna,
and Dendara.

Greco-Egyptian style "funerary
houses" at Tuna el-Gebel.

Underground galleries of tombs
at Alexandria.

Facade of the temple of Hathor
at Dendara, c.34 c.e.

...l portrait sculpture.

...b paintings of daily life.

...ted wooden models of
...life.

...jewelry in gold and
...precious stones.

Temple reliefs with royal and
religious scenes.

Monumental sculpture.

Tomb paintings and painted
reliefs of daily life.

Decorated pottery / faience vessels.

Colossal stone statues.

Temple reliefs with battle and
hunting scenes.

Illustrated "Books of the Dead."

Tomb paintings of religious
scenes.

Faience bowls and chalices.

Bronze figurines.

Private sculpture in hard stones.

Decorated cartonnage coffins and
stone sarcophagi.

Portrait sculpture in hard stones.

Temple reliefs of religious
scenes.

Faience and terra-cotta figurines.

Painted "mummy portraits."

Introduction

The monuments—pyramids, temples and tombs, statues and stelae—represent the most valuable source for our knowledge of ancient Egypt. A study of Egyptian monuments, either those still at various sites all over Egypt, or those in their new locations in museums and collections, is a happy hunting-ground of specialists and non-specialists. No special knowledge is required in order to be impressed by the grandeur and technical accomplishment of the Great Pyramid at Giza, to be enchanted by paintings in the Ramessid private tombs at Deir el-Medina, or be left dumbfounded by the opulence and—rather erratic—taste shown in the objects from the tomb of Tut'ankhamun. Nonetheless, knowledge may add to our appreciation and enjoyment.

So the aim of this book is easily defined: to provide a systematic survey of the most important sites with ancient Egyptian monuments, an assessment of their historical and cultural importance, and a brief description of their salient features, based on the most up-to-date Egyptological knowledge. Further chapters and special features deal with general aspects of Egyptian civilization. These enable the reader quickly to find his or her bearings in the bewildering mass of names of palaces, gods, and kings, and at the same time help to understand the broader issues of Egyptian society, and provide a background to the fluctuating fortunes of Egyptian towns and temples.

Geographically the basic limits of the book are set by the frontiers of Egypt along the Nile, at the first cataract of the Nile, and at the sea; the main exception is Egypt's traditional imperial extension of Lower Nubia. The maps present much of the book's content topographically, and supplement the information in the text at many points. Those in Part One are organized by theme and period. In Part Two, the maps for each section present a detailed, large-scale view of the successive stages of our journey, including both ancient and modern features.

The period covered by the native Egyptian dynasties of kings (with the brief interruptions of foreign rule), about 2920 to 332 BCE, provides the temporal setting. But some knowledge of the Predynastic Period is essential for understanding the earliest stages of Egyptian dynastic history, while for centuries the culture of the Greco-Roman Period remained largely Egyptian; these two phases, sometimes referred to as separate units, are referred to and discussed where appropriate.

THE CULTURAL SETTING

Ancient Egypt was exceptional in its setting and unique in its continuity. The setting is the extreme case among several cultural and physical oases which were the great states of antiquity. It is almost impossible for us to recapture a feeling for this situation, with its mixture of geographical and human elements, just as we find it difficult to comprehend the time-span involved, half as long again as the Christian era. The position of the designer of the first pyramid, who created the earliest stone building on its scale in the world and lived in the only large, united state of the time, can never be recaptured. Any understanding of ancient Egypt must include an awareness of these and other enormous differences between antiquity and our own times. Yet humankind is the same everywhere, and much of our detailed knowledge of other civilizations will include material as ordinary as any in our own lives. When approaching an ancient civilization we need knowledge about both the ordinary and the exotic. Both are affected by the constraints of the environment. One exploits it in a routine fashion, the other more creatively; neither is independent of it.

The Geography of Ancient Egypt

In its geographical context Egypt is part of the larger area of northeastern Africa, and within this wider region its proximity to the heartlands of agricultural development in western Asia was initially of great significance. Dynastic Egypt was largely self-contained at most periods, but this was only because its economy was very heavily agricultural; for many important raw materials and for the requirements of high civilization foreign trade or travel into the desert was necessary, so that the perspective of the wider region is essential for understanding Egyptian culture. The same is true of the population of the country, which probably came from all the surrounding areas, and was not racially heterogeneous.

The boundaries of ancient Egypt

A definition of the boundaries of Egypt in antiquity is not simple. The basic areas of the country—the Nile valley, the delta, and the Faiyum—were supplemented by parts of the surrounding regions over which the Egyptians exerted particular rights, such as those of mining. The southern frontier, traditionally at the first cataract of the Nile at Aswan, moved farther south in some periods; New Kingdom texts sometimes use words for Egypt to refer also to parts of Nubia, which were then part of the state. Apart from these extensions of Egyptian territory, the line of oases that runs from Siwa in the north to el-Kharga in the south, approximately parallel to the Nile and about 120 miles (200 km) west of it, was settled and governed by Egyptians during most of the Dynastic Period, reaching the peak of its prosperity during the Roman occupation.

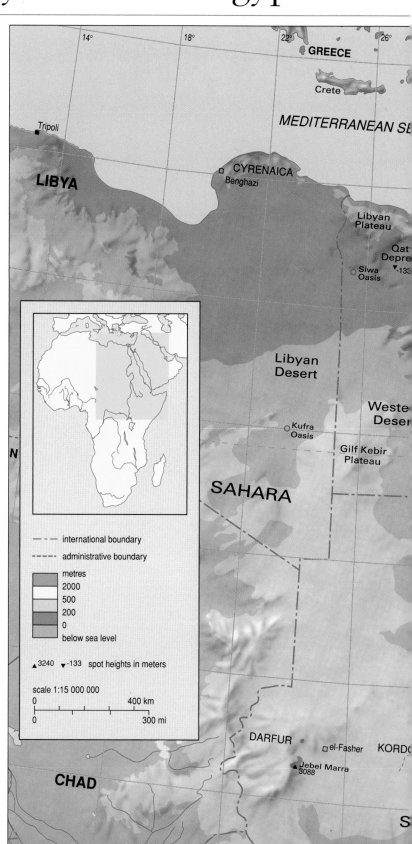

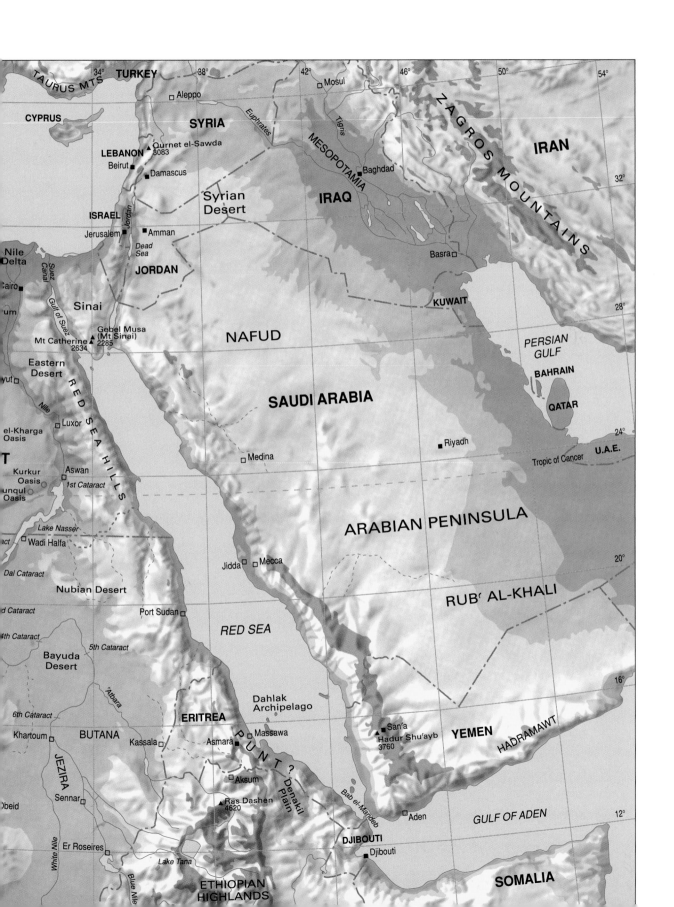

◀ *(pages 10–11) Tourists are dwarfed by the pyramids of Giza. The three structures have become a powerful symbol of the achievement of the ancient Egyptians.*

◀ *(pages 12–13) Egypt's position makes it a natural bridge between Africa and Asia, and between temperate and tropical climates.*

▶ *A map showing the nomes of Upper Egypt, whose origins go back to the Early Dynastic Period. The divisions shown are based on a Middle Kingdom list. The nome capitals are shown by a solid black square. Where more than one square is present, the capital shifted or the nome division changed in some period; where none is given, the capital is uncertain.*

The Nile Valley and Agriculture

Without the Nile, agriculture would be impossible in Egypt, except perhaps on the Mediterranean coast. In antiquity, the annual floodwaters between July and October covered most of the land in the Nile valley and the delta—with careful management the water deposited produced an abundant crop.

The waters of the Nile come from the Blue Nile, which rises in the Ethiopian highlands, and the White Nile, which rises south of Lake Victoria in central Africa and receives water from many smaller rivers in southern Sudan. The White Nile is fed by the rains of the tropical belt and provides a constant supply throughout the year, mediated by the great marshes of the Sudd in southern Sudan, which absorb much water during the rainy season. The Blue Nile and the 'Atbara, which flows into the Nile some way north of Khartoum, bring vast quantities of water from the Ethiopian summer monsoon (which forms part of the Indian Ocean monsoon system), and provide almost all the water in the river from July to October (earlier in Sudan itself). This period corresponds to the time of the rains on the savanna in central Sudan. In

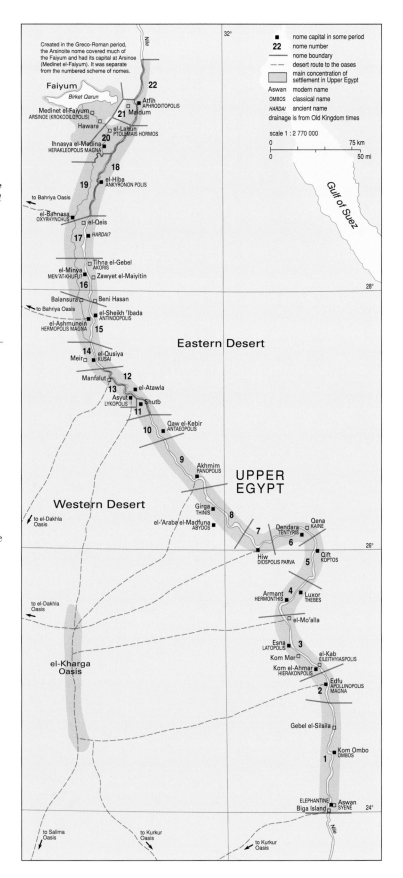

Egypt, the water in the river was at its lowest from April to June. The level rose in July and the flood normally began in August, covering most of the valley floor from mid-August to late September, washing salts out of the soil and depositing a layer of silt, which built up at the rate of several inches per century. After the water level fell, the main crops were sown between October and November, ripening from January to May according to variety. In antiquity, agriculture was possible over much of the Nile valley and the delta, the chief exceptions being tracts of swamp.

Agriculture involved leveling the floodplain and forming it into a series of large basins that "terraced" the land for irrigation in stages both down river and away from the banks. Each terrace was only just lower than the last: the drop in river level from Aswan to the sea is no more than 280 feet (85 m). Effective groups of basins would have been about the size of the ancient provinces or nomes, of which there were just over 20 from the first cataract to south of Memphis. In the Dynastic Period, the irrigated area in the valley increased through the reclamation of low-lying and swampy land, and to some extent through improved water-lifting technology that seems mostly to have been introduced from the Near East.

▼ A map showing the nomes of Lower Egypt. The definitive number of 20 nomes was not established until the Greco–Roman Period. Many nome boundaries were formed along the branches of the Nile whose ancient course is tentative.

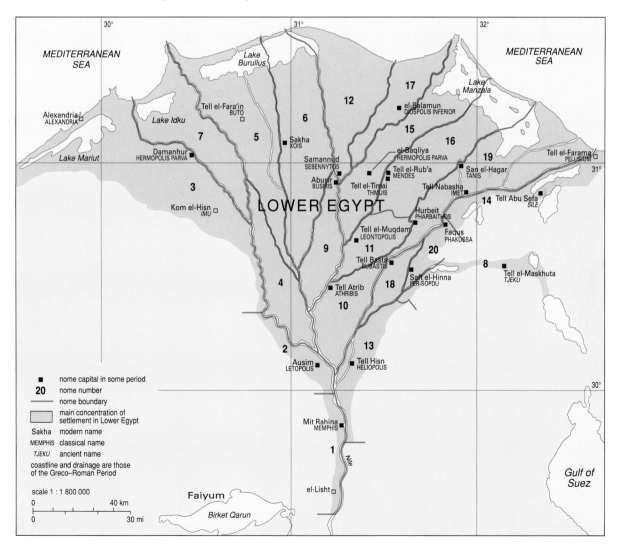

15

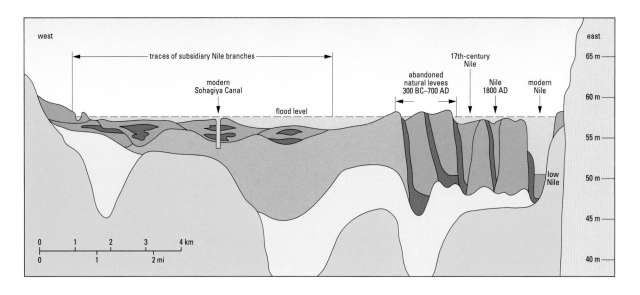

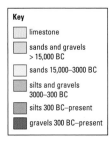

Key

- limestone
- sands and gravels > 15,000 BC
- sands 15,000–3000 BC
- silts and gravels 3000–300 BC
- silts 300 BC–present
- gravels 300 BC–present

▲ *A generalized cross-section through the Nile valley between Sohag and Asyut. Over time, the main watercourse has migrated eastward, leaving traces of its earlier raised banks. The vertical scale is greatly exaggerated.*

The main crops were cereals—emmer (*Triticum dicoccum*) for bread and barley for beer. (Wheat [*Triticum durum*] came later, in the Greco–Roman Period.) In addition to these there were pulses such as lentils and chickpeas; vegetables—lettuces, onions, and garlic; fruit, especially dates; fodder crops for animals, which were needed for hides as well as meat and other products; and plants grown for oil, such as sesame. Honey was the chief sweetener, and bee keeping was important. Meat was a luxury. Herds probably grazed on swampy, marginal land, especially in the delta. Beef, mutton, pork, and goat were eaten, as well as the flesh of various species of antelope. Wealthy Egyptians ate fowl such as ducks, geese, and various game birds. Chickens were unknown before the New Kingdom. Finally, two very important plant crops were papyrus, swamp areas of which were actively managed, and flax, which was used for clothing and for sails and ropes (and possibly linseed oil).

The Delta

The delta presents a similar picture to the Nile valley but must have been a harder challenge for reclamation for agriculture.

Land reclamation was probably significant for development in all periods. Through its agricultural strength, the delta increasingly dominated Egyptian economic and political life from about 1400 BCE on. The potential amount of usable land in the delta was double that in the Nile valley, and it was closer to the agriculturally advanced societies of West Asia, contacts with which played an ever-greater part in later Egyptian history.

The delta was created by interplay between the sea, in periods of high sea levels in earlier geological ages, and the mud deposited by the Nile. The areas most suitable for permanent settlement were sandy ridges, or turtlebacks, between the Nile branches and other water channels. Some of these were probably occupied from the beginning of the Predynastic period. The land around the ridges could be used for crops or grazing. The swamps contained far more wildlife, fish, and papyrus than those in the Nile valley. The agricultural exploitation of the two main regions evidently differed, and there is evidence for trade between them. No large cities of earlier periods have been found in the delta.

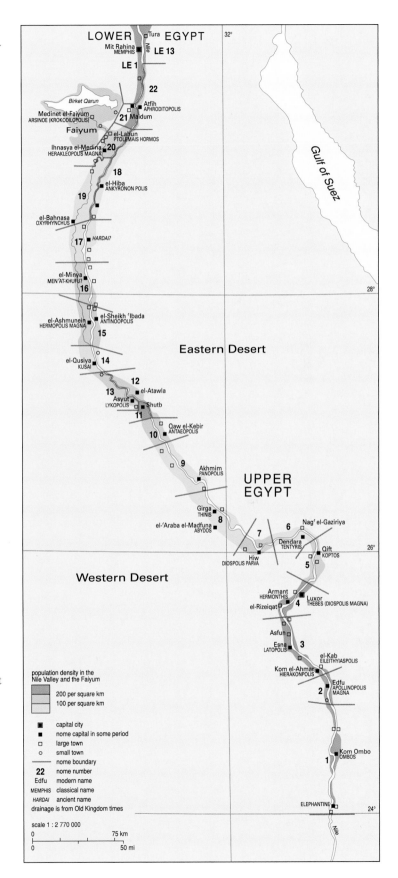

The Faiyum

The third sizable area of ancient settlement was the Faiyum. This is a lakeside oasis west of the Nile valley and south of Memphis, which is fed by the Bahr Yusuf, a branch of the Nile that diverges westward north of Asyut and terminates in the Birket Qarun (Lake Moeris of Classical antiquity). Intensive exploitation of the area depended on lowering the lake level to reclaim land, using the water that would otherwise have filled it to irrigate both above and below the natural level. Major works were undertaken by 12th-Dynasty kings, who won back about 170 square miles (450 km^2) for cultivation. Later the Ptolemies made it into one of the most prosperous and heavily populated parts of the country, with about 460 square miles (1,200 km^2) of agricultural land, much of it settled by the ethnic Greek population. A different form of irrigation is required in the Faiyum from the rest of Egypt, relying on large amounts of labor rather than any advanced techniques. In lower-lying areas it would have been possible to produce two major crops per year, and there is evidence for this in the Greco–Roman Period.

An area analogous to the Faiyum but much less significant is the Wadi el-Natrun, a natural oasis that lay close to the delta, northwest of Cairo and south of Alexandria. The word *Natrun* in its name refers to the salt lakes there. These were the chief ancient source of natron (sodium carbonate/bicarbonate), which was used for cleaning,

▶ *This map shows the estimated population densities in the nomes of the Nile valley during Dynastic times. The densities are higher near the capital and in narrow parts of the valley, most probably because these areas were fully settled at an earlier date; the narrow parts may also have been easier to exploit.*

ritual purposes such as mummification, and in the manufacture of Egyptian faience and of glass.

The Western Desert

The remaining areas to be discussed were more peripheral and could be held only when Egypt was powerful.

The oases of the Western Desert produced valuable crops, such as grapes and the best dates, and were vital links in trade with more remote areas. From south to north four main oases were governed by Egypt: el-Kharga, el-Dakhla (west of el-Kharga), Farafra, and Bahariya. The more remote westerly oasis of Siwa was incorporated into Egypt only in the Late Period. There are various smaller oases west of the Nile; the more southerly—Kurkur, Dunqul, and Salima—were important staging posts on long-distance caravan routes

but have not produced any significant ancient remains.

For most of Egyptian history the oases were an Egyptian outpost against the Libyans. (*Libya* was the name for the entire region west of the Nile valley.) In early periods, some Libyans were culturally similar to the Egyptians and may have spoken a similar language, but contacts during the Dynastic Period were mostly hostile.

From the western oases, a trail now called the Darb el-Arba'in ("40-day track") leads to el-Fasher, the capital of Darfur province in western Sudan.

The Eastern Desert

To the east of Egypt were a number of important sources of minerals. The northernmost is the Sinai peninsula, which supplied turquoise, mined by the Egyptians

▼ *The topography of the Delta c. 4000 BCE compared to the present day. The northern delta was formerly lagoon and swamp and was gradually coated with layers of Nile silt, slowly increasing the area of land that was seasonally above water.*

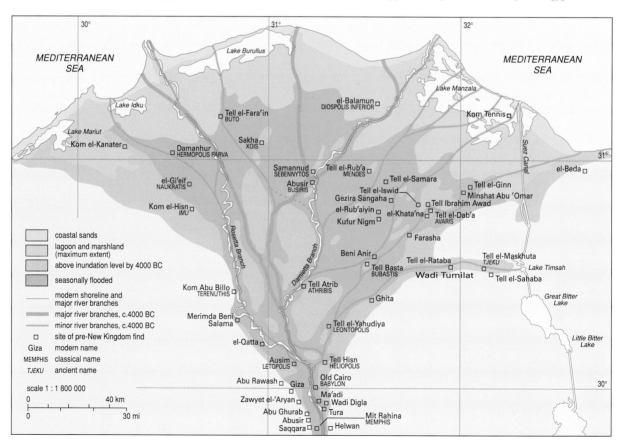

from the 3rd Dynasty to the end of the New Kingdom, but not later. Sinai is also a source of copper, and copper mines contemporary with the Egyptian 18th–20th Dynasties have been excavated at Timna near Eilat; these were probably worked by locals under Egyptian direction.

The eastern desert of Egypt yielded many stones for building and statuary, as well as semiprecious stones, and was the route to the Red Sea. Some quarries were near the Nile valley, such as Gebel Ahmar for quartzite and Hatnub for calcite (Egyptian alabaster or travertine), but others required significant expeditions. They could not have been exploited without Egyptian domination of, or collaboration with, the local nomadic

population. The Egyptians also needed control to use the three main routes to the Red Sea. These run by way of the Wadi Gasus to Safaga, the Wadi Hammamat to Quseir, and the Wadi Abbad to Berenike.

Nubia

South of Gebel el-Silsila was the first Egyptian nome or province, the main towns in which were Aswan and Kom Ombo. Its early separate status was recorded in its name *Nubia*. Between the first and second cataracts lay Lower Nubia, which was Egypt's main target for conquest. This acquisition of territory was significant later, when an Egyptian-influenced civilization arose and established its center at Napata, the capital of

▲ *A view near the edge of Luxor, showing the Red Sea hills in the distance. Throughout the Nile valley, fertile land, irrigated over many centuries, is rarely far from the barren soils of the desert.*

19

Upper Nubia, producing the 25th Egyptian Dynasty and the state of Napata–Meroe, which survived into the 4th century CE.

Lower Nubia seems to have been regarded as being Egyptian by right and was vital for access to raw materials, principally hard stones and gold, in the desert to either side of the Nile. Agriculture could never have been that important, because the cultivable area is no more than a narrow strip on either side of the river. However, it was the route through which came many of the southern products the Egyptians prized. These included spices, ivory, ebony, ostrich feathers, and certain species of baboon. It is difficult for us to evaluate the importance of these products for the Egyptians, which was often religious, but they were made into a focus for prestige comparable to precious stones and rare exotica in the modern world.

Palestine and Syria

Contacts between Egypt and the Near East are attested from Predynastic times, and the name of Na'rmer, the latest king of Dynasty 0, has been found at many sites in Palestine. Trade in lapis lazuli, whose main ancient source was Badakshan in Afghanistan, flourished from still earlier, and Egypt may already have been importing metal from Asia. Connections between Egypt and Byblos in Lebanon are attested in the Old Kingdom, and the funerary boat of Khufu, the builder of the Great Pyramid, was made of Lebanese cedar. Egyptian wood is sparse and generally of poor quality, so that good timber always had to be imported from the Near East. The Middle Kingdom saw an intensification of these links, while in the New Kingdom the Egyptians conquered large parts of the area and held them for more than two centuries, exploiting vassal city-states and trading with

neighbors. During resurgences of Egyptian power in the 22nd and 26th Dynasties, parts of Palestine were again conquered, as they were also in the Ptolemaic Period. The possession of part of Syria–Palestine was a natural goal for a strong regime in Egypt, but its achievement was far more difficult than in Nubia.

Many advances in Egyptian material culture came from the Near East. In return for these "invisible" imports, and for wood, copper, possibly tin, silver, precious stones, wine, and oil, the Egyptians could offer four main resources: gold, linen, food surpluses, and, particularly in later periods, papyrus. Trade in gold and the bartering of African goods imported into Egypt are well known, but exports of food and other non-prestige products can be proved only in exceptional cases. They leave little or no mark in the archaeological record and are almost never mentioned in texts. But Egyptian agriculture was far more productive than any in Syria–Palestine, and just as Rome's granary in imperial times was Egypt, so may the Near East's have been in some earlier periods. Grain was very important in Late Period foreign relations, especially with the states of the Aegean.

In various periods, Egypt also developed relations with a number of more remote areas, including Mesopotamia, Anatolia, Iran, Arabia, the Aegean, Cyprus, Rome, and India. Whereas earlier Egypt was rather self-contained in culture, politics, and economy, from the mid-second millennium BCE onward it was increasingly integrated into the Near East and the Mediterranean world. Both its naturally well defined boundaries, and its position at the bridge between Africa and Asia, the tropics and the temperate zone, are vital to understanding its civilization.

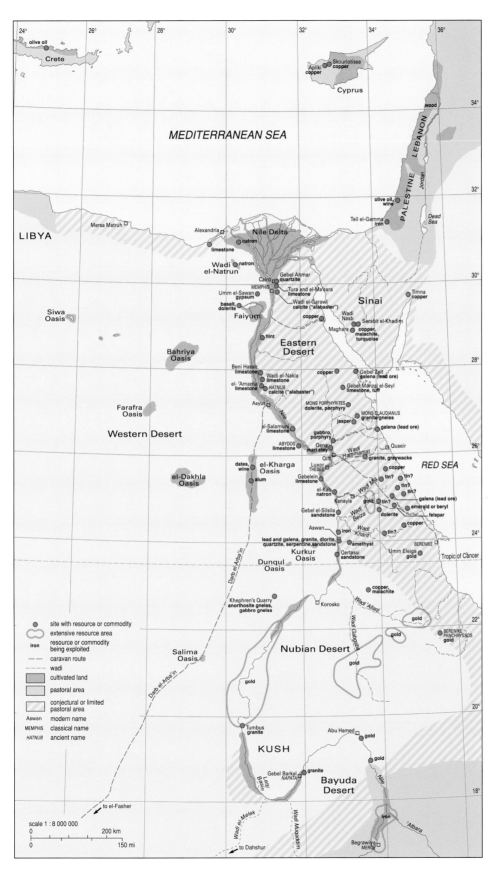

◄ The sites shown on this map are places where there are ancient workings of the minerals named. It is often impossible to date workings precisely, but several are exclusively Greco–Roman, such as the sources of emerald or beryl, porphyry, and the granite of Mons Claudianus. The area under cultivation varied from season to season, especially within the Delta.

olive oil
Crete

MEDITERRANEAN SEA

Skouriotissa
copper

Apliki
copper

Cyprus

wood

PALESTINE

LEBANON

olive oil,
wine

Tell el-Gamma
iron

Dead
Sea

Jordan

Mersa Matruh

Alexandria

Nile Delta

natron

LIBYA

limestone

Wadi
el-Natrun

natron

Cairo

Gebel Ahmar
quartzite

MEMPHIS

Sinai

Timna
copper

Umm el-Sawan
gypsum

Tura and el-Ma'sara
limestone

Wadi el-Garawi
calcite ("alabaster")

Siwa
Oasis

basalt,
dolerite

copper

Wadi
Nasb

Serabit el-Khadim

Faiyum

Eastern
Desert

Maghara

copper,
malachite,
turquoise

flint

Bahriya
Oasis

Beni Hasan
limestone

Wadi el-Nakla
limestone

copper

Gebel Zeit
galena (lead ore)

el-'Amarna
limestone

HATNUB
calcite ("alabaster")

Gebel Manzal el-Seyl
limestone, tuff

Farafra
Oasis

Asyut

MONS PORPHYRITES
dolerite, porphyry

MONS CLAUDIANUS
granite gneiss

jasper

Western Desert

el-Salamuni
limestone

galena (lead ore)

gabbro,
porphyry

ABYDOS
limestone

Qena
marl clay

Wadi
Hammamat

Quseir

RED SEA

el-Dakhla
Oasis

dates,
wine

el-Kharga
Oasis

Luxor
THEBES

granite, graywacke

copper

tin?

tin?

tin?

Gebelein
limestone

alum

tin?

galena (lead ore)

el-Kab
natron

Kanayis

gold

tin?

emerald or beryl

Gebel el-Silsila
sandstone

Wadi
Beiza

dolerite

felspar

copper

Aswan

iron

Wadi
Kharit

tin?

copper

lead and galena, granite, diorite,
quartzite, serpentine, sandstone

amethyst

Kurkur
Oasis

Qertassi
sandstone

Umm Eleiga
gold

BERENIKE

Tropic of Cancer

Darb el-Arba'in

Dunqul
Oasis

Korosko

Wadi 'Allaqi

copper,
malachite

Khephren's Quarry
anorthosite gneiss,
gabbro gneiss

gold

gold

● site with resource or commodity

⬭ extensive resource area

iron resource or commodity being exploited

– – – caravan route

– · – wadi

▨ cultivated land

▨ pastoral area

▨ conjectural or limited pastoral area

Aswan modern name

MEMPHIS classical name

HATNUB ancient name

Salima
Oasis

BERENIKE
PANCHRYSSOS
gold

Nubian Desert

gold

Wadi Gabgaba

gold

Darb el-Arba'in

gold

to el-Fasher

scale 1 : 8 000 000

0   200 km

0   150 mi

Tumbus
granite

KUSH

Gebel Barkal
NAPATA

granite

Abu Hamed

gold

Bayuda
Desert

Leiti
Basin

Nile

gold

Wadi el-Melek

Wadi Muqadim

iron

to Dahshur

Begrawiya
MEROE

'Atbara

24° 26° 28° 30° 32° 34° 36°

34°

32°

30°

28°

26°

24°

22°

20°

18°

The Study of Ancient Egypt

Egypt has been of continual interest to people of other cultures, from the ancient Greeks onward. When it could no longer be an object of contemporary study, it was remembered throughout the Middle Ages for its monuments, notably the pyramids.

Interest in Mediterranean antiquity revived in the Renaissance, and the late 16th and early 17th centuries brought the first visitors to Egypt in search of antiquities. Pietro della Valle (1586–1652) traveled all over the eastern Mediterranean from 1614 to 1626, bringing Egyptian mummies and Coptic manuscripts back to Italy. The manuscripts were in the latest form of the Egyptian language, written in Greek letters, which was regularly learned by priests in the Coptic Church in Egypt. It was also the initial study of the great Jesuit polymath Athanasius Kircher (1602–1680), who was one of the first to attempt a decipherment.

A byway in the development of European knowledge of Egypt is revealed in a text that records the travels of an unidentified Venetian in 1589 through Upper Egypt and Lower Nubia. His is one of dozens of similar accounts, but the only one to proclaim a disinterested fascination for the ancient monuments. The author stated that he "did not travel for any useful purpose, but only to see so many superb edifices, churches, statues, colossi, obelisks, and columns."

Travelers and antiquaries

The earliest explorations cannot be termed archaeological. The word can, however, be applied to John Greaves (1602–1652), an English astronomer who published his *Pyramidographia, or a Discourse of the Pyramids in Aegypt* in 1646. Greaves visited Giza in 1638–1639, measured the pyramids, and made a critical analysis of ancient writings about them. The resulting work was more penetrating than any other of its time on ancient Egypt; a notable feature is its use of medieval Arabic sources.

From the later 17th century onward, the number of travelers to Egypt rose gradually. The most significant advance in knowledge was made by Claude Sicard (1677–1726), who was commissioned by the French regent to investigate ancient monuments. His studies were never completed and survive mainly in the form of letters and a map. He visited Upper Egypt four times and was the first modern traveler to identify Thebes, and to attribute correctly the colossi of Memnon and the Valley of the Kings—on the basis of Classical descriptions. His most important successor was the Dane Frederik Ludwig Norden (1708–1742), who visited Egypt in 1737–1738, and whose posthumous volume of travels appeared in various editions from 1751 to the end of the 18th century.

The increase in the numbers of visitors to Egypt went together with an improvement in the treatment of Egyptian artifacts—and of antiquity as a whole—in major 18th century works, of which the most important are the works of Bernard de Montfaucon (published in 1719–1724) and the Comte de Caylus (1752–1764). Both devoted a notable amount of space to Egypt.

Deciphering hieroglyphics

The hieroglyphic script continued to be studied in the 18th century, although little progress was made toward a decipherment.

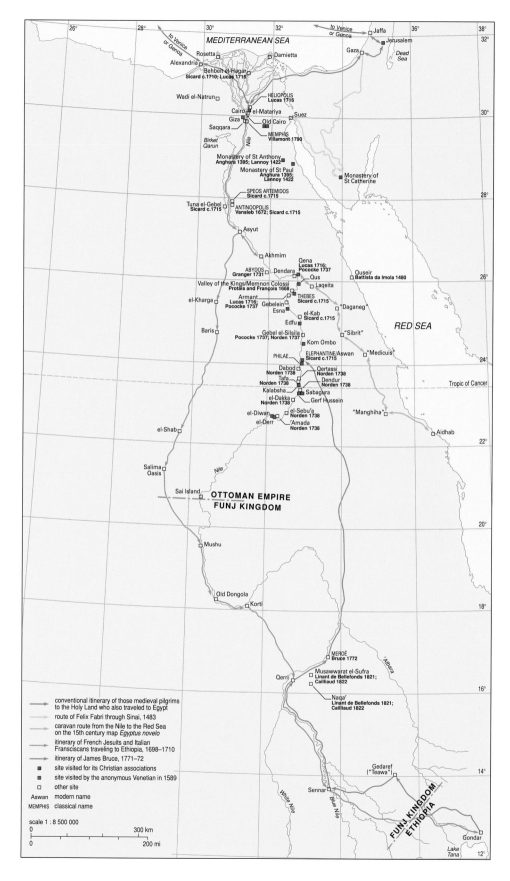

◀ *A map showing the travelers to Egypt and Sudan before 1800. The sites and towns marked are prominent in the records of explorers prior to Napoleon's expedition in 1798. The names of the explorers, and the dates of their expeditions, are given in bold typeface.*

MEDITERRANEAN SEA

to Venice or Genoa
Jaffa
to Venice or Genoa
Gaza
Jerusalem
Dead Sea

Rosetta
Damietta
Alexandria
Behbeit el-Hagar
Sicard c.1710; Lucas 1716
Wadi el-Natrun
HELIOPOLIS
Lucas 1716
Cairo el-Matariya
Giza
Old Cairo
Suez
Saqqara
MEMPHIS
Villamont 1790
Birket Qarun
Monastery of St Anthony
Anghura 1395; Lannoy 1422
Monastery of St Paul
Anghura 1395; Lannoy 1422
Monastery of St Catherine
SPEOS ARTEMIDOS
Sicard c.1715
Tuna el-Gebel
Sicard c.1715
ANTINOOPOLIS
Vansleb 1672; Sicard c.1715
Asyut
Akhmim
Qena
Lucas 1716; Pococke 1737
ABYDOS
Granger 1731
Dendara
Qus
Quseir
Battista da Imola 1480
Laqeita
Valley of the Kings/Memnon Colossi
Protais and François 1668
THEBES
Sicard c.1715
el-Kharga
Armant
Lucas 1716; Pococke 1737
Gebelein
Esna
"Daganeg"
el-Kab
Sicard c.1715
Baris
Edfu
Gebel el-Silsila
Pococke 1737; Norden 1737
Kom Ombo
"Sibrit"
RED SEA
PHILAE
ELEPHANTINE/Aswan
Sicard c.1715
"Medicuis"
Dabod
Norden 1738
Qertassi
Norden 1738
Tafa
Norden 1738
Dendur
Norden 1738
Kalabsha
Sabagura
el-Dakka
Norden 1738
Gerf Hussein
el-Diwan
el-Sebu'a
Norden 1738
el-Derr
'Amada
Norden 1738
el-Shab
"Manghiha"
Aidhab
Tropic of Cancer
Salima Oasis
Nile
Sai Island
OTTOMAN EMPIRE
FUNJ KINGDOM
Mushu
Old Dongola
Korti
MEROË
Bruce 1772
Qerri
Musawwarat el-Sufra
Linant de Bellefonds 1821; Cailliaud 1822
Naqa'
Linant de Bellefonds 1821; Cailliaud 1822
Gedaref ("Teawa")
Sennar
White Nile
Blue Nile
FUNJ KINGDOM
ETHIOPIA
Gondar
Lake Tana

conventional itinerary of those medieval pilgrims to the Holy Land who also traveled to Egypt
route of Felix Fabri through Sinai, 1483
caravan route from the Nile to the Red Sea on the 15th century map *Egyptus novelo*
itinerary of French Jesuits and Italian Fransciscans traveling to Ethiopia, 1698–1710
itinerary of James Bruce, 1771–72
■ site visited for its Christian associations
■ site visited by the anonymous Venetian in 1589
□ other site
Aswan modern name
MEMPHIS classical name

scale 1 : 8 500 000
0   300 km
0   200 mi

Antiquarian and linguistic interest in Egypt culminated with the Dane Georg Zoëga (1755–1809), whose two major works, a treatise on obelisks, which includes a section on the hieroglyphic script, and a catalog of Coptic manuscripts in the collections of the Vatican, are of lasting value. The 1797 work on obelisks marks a peak in Egyptian studies before Napoleon's expedition in 1798.

Napoleon's expedition was accompanied by a vast team of scholars who were sent to study and record all aspects of Egypt. The Rosetta Stone, discovered by soldiers repairing a fort, soon passed into British hands, but the team produced a multivolume work, *Description de l'Egypte*, first published in 1809–1830. This was the last and most important such work produced before the decipherment of the script by Jean-François Champollion le Jeune (1790–1832) in 1822–1824, which signals the beginning of Egyptology as a distinct subject. Champollion and the Pisan Ippolito Rosellini (1800–1843) mounted a joint expedition to record monuments in Egypt in the late 1820s, but they were latecomers. In the previous twenty years numerous travelers had visited Egyptian and Lower Nubian sites and had rifled them for antiquities, written books about them, or both.

By 1840, the first generation of Egyptologists was already dead, and the subject retained a precarious existence in France, Holland, and especially in Prussia.

The growth of Egyptology

In the mid-19th century the Prussian Carl Richard Lepsius (1810–1884), Heinrich Brugsch (1827–1894), and a few other scholars continued to advance the subject, while the Frenchman Auguste Mariette (1821–1881) placed work in Egypt on a permanent footing. Mariette entered the service of the Khedive Said in 1858, excavated at many sites before and after that date, and founded the Egyptian Museum and Antiquities Service (now the Supreme Council of Antiquities).

From about 1880 to 1914, there was much archaeological work in Egypt. Sir William Matthew Flinders Petrie (1853–1942) first went to Egypt in 1880 to measure the Great Pyramid. He went on to excavate at sites all over Egypt. Sites in Nubia also came into prominence with the completion and subsequent raising of the first Aswan Dam (1902 and 1907). The end of the 19th century saw major advances in the understanding of Egyptian language and chronology, made in Berlin by Adolf Erman (1854–1937) and Eduard Meyer (1855–1930) respectively.

Excavation in the 20th century

The public image of 20th century excavation was dominated by a few spectacular discoveries and by the salvage campaigns in Nubia occasioned by the second raising of the first Aswan dam in the 1930s and the construction of the High Dam in the 1960s.

Foremost in popular attention has been exploration in the Valley of the Kings at Thebes. The first find of royalty was the discovery in the 1870s of the pit containing the mummies of a majority of the New Kingdom kings. Then, in 1898, Victor Loret (1859–1946) discovered the tomb of Amenhotep II in the Valley of the Kings, which proved to contain the mummies of most of the kings missing from the earlier find. Work in the valley continued almost without interruption until 1932. The most methodical examination was by Howard Carter (1874–1939), under the patronage of Lord Carnarvon. Carter's main discovery was

the tomb of Tut'ankhamun, which he found in 1922 and worked on for ten years.

Several other royal burials or cemeteries were excavated in Egypt in the 20th century. Reisner's discovery of the funerary deposit of Hetepheres at Giza in 1925 is the only major find of Old Kingdom jewelry and furniture. In the 1940s, Pierre Montet (1885–1966) excavated several intact tombs of the 21st- and 22nd-Dynasty kings and royal family at Tanis, producing rare examples of art in precious materials from a period that has left rather few significant remains.

The most important excavated settlement sites, el-'Amarna and Deir el-Medina, have been extensively studied. After the discovery of the el-'Amarna cuneiform tablets in the 1880s, Urbain Bouriant (1849–1903) worked there. A German expedition in 1913–1914, under Ludwig Borchardt (1863–1938), unearthed the house compound of the sculptor Thutmose. This contained the world-famous bust of Nefertiti among other masterpieces.

In the 1920s and 1930s, several seasons of British excavations contributed to the history of the 18th Dynasty. Since the 1960s, standards of excavation and survey have risen greatly and the range of sites studied has increased. Because of high population levels and alterations to the environment, much fieldwork is now rescue archaeology, especially in the delta.

Surveys and publications

In the 1890s, the Egypt Exploration Fund (later Society) began an "Archaeological Survey of Egypt" to record standing monuments. The project was unrealistically ambitious, but it initiated the work of Norman de Garis Davies (1865–1941), the most prolific copyist of Egyptian monuments.

◀ Napoleon with military staff during his 1798 campaign in Egypt (Jean-Leon Gerome, 1863, on display at the State Hermitage Museum, St. Petersburg). Napoleon brought a vast team of scholars and scientists to Egypt, marking the start of Egyptology as a science.

He published more than 25 volumes on tombs alone, almost always presenting a complete record of their decoration; his wife Nina and others made colored reproductions of selected scenes.

The most important epigraphic venture to follow Davies was the foundation of Chicago House, a field station of the Oriental Institute of the University of Chicago at Luxor, in 1924. The Oriental Institute itself was the creation of James Henry Breasted (1865–1935), the virtual founder of American Egyptology, who gained the support of John D. Rockefeller.

Egyptology outside Egypt

Indispensable though it is, fieldwork is only a very small part of the total activity of Egyptologists, who also rely on publications of the monuments, more detailed studies on texts—hieroglyphic, hieratic, and demotic—and numerous reference works. In these areas Kurt Sethe (1869–1934) was perhaps the leading scholar and the most prolific editor of texts. Sir Alan Gardiner (1879–1963), who began his career as a grammarian, was the leading editor of papyrus texts who, with the papyrus conservator Hugo Ibscher (1874–1943), set new standards in the treatment of the papyri themselves and in their presentation.

Today, Egyptology is pursued in academic institutions in more than 25 countries. The work cover fields—from art to archaeology and language to literature—that would normally be separate in the study of more recent civilizations. The advances in archaeology outlined above have also played their part in this more thorough integration of Egyptology among the humanities and social sciences. These developments are beneficial, because no subject can be autonomous.

27

The Historical Background

Predynastic Egypt

Predynastic cultures are named for the places where a certain type of settlement was first located. On the delta margins, Merimda Beni Salama provides evidence of two phases of a Neolithic culture dating to perhaps 5000 BCE. In the Nile valley, the earliest Neolithic cultures are the Tarifian in the Theban area, the Tasian, and the Badarian, in an area south of Asyut. Several Neolithic cultures are also known from the second cataract area.

Naqada I (or Amratian) is a prelude to the more expansive phase of Naqada II (or Gerzean), which gradually spread over the entire Nile valley and into the delta. During this time, the cultural demarcation with the Nubian culture to the south led to emergence of complex society in Egypt and the definition of a political frontier. This process led into Naqada III (the latter phase of which is often termed Dynasty 0), the latest predynastic phase, and the Early Dynastic Period, when Egypt was united under one ruler, within boundaries comparable to those of later periods. The rulers in Naqada III, centered on Abydos, seem to have controlled most of the emerging country.

Early Dynastic Period

The 1st Dynasty begins with the legendary Menes, whose name occurs in later Egyptian king lists and in Classical sources. Both the identification and the existence of Menes are disputed, but he was perhaps King 'Aha, to whose reign dates the earliest tomb at Saqqara, the elite necropolis of the recently founded Memphis. The duration of the 1st Dynasty is estimated at about 150 years. Large cemeteries of the period, with rich burials, have been found in many parts of the country, including the delta. The kings were buried at Abydos in Umm el-Qa'ab, a cemetery set well back in the desert.

Hotepsekhemwy, the first king of the 2nd Dynasty, moved the royal necropolis to Saqqara. After the third king, Ninetjer, the record is uncertain.

The first king of the 3rd Dynasty (c. 2650–2575), Djoser, is known above all as the builder of the Step Pyramid at Saqqara. The time of Djoser was later looked back upon as a golden age of achievement. The name of Imhotep, the probable architect of the Step Pyramid, came to be venerated, and in the Greco-Roman Period he was a popular deity, associated with healing.

The still larger monument of the next king, Sekhemkhet, scarcely progressed beyond ground level, and his reign is followed by an obscure period. But by the end of the Early Dynastic Period, Egyptian cultural, administrative, and technical resources had developed virtually into their classic forms.

Old Kingdom (c. 2575–2150)

The 4th Dynasty (c. 2575–2450) was the time of the great pyramids. Snofru, the first ruler of the dynasty, built the two pyramids at Dahshur and either built or completed the Maidum pyramid. There are also nonroyal mastabas of his reign at Maidum, Dahshur, and Saqqara. The reliefs and paintings in these contain the earliest examples of the repertory of subjects found in later Old Kingdom nonroyal tombs.

During the reign of Snofru there were major campaigns to Nubia, which are recorded in the fragmentary royal annals

▶ *This map shows the sites of a number of Predynastic and Early Dynastic cultures.*

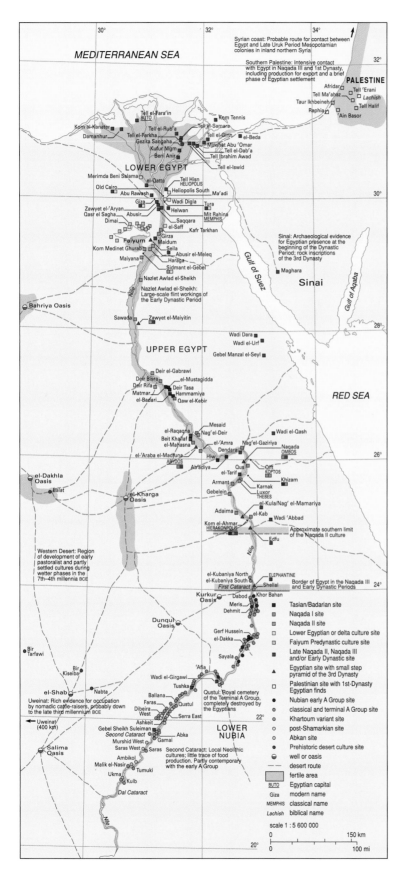

The following labels appear on the map:

MEDITERRANEAN SEA

Syrian coast: Probable route for contact between Egypt and Late Uruk Period Mesopotamian colonies in inland northern Syria

Southern Palestine: Intensive contact with Egypt in Naqada III and 1st Dynasty, including production for export and a brief phase of Egyptian settlement

PALESTINE

Afridar
Tell 'Erani
Tell Ma'ahaz
Lachish
Taur Ikhbeineh
Tell Halif
Raphia
'Ain Basor

Tell el-Fara'in
BUTO
Kom el-Kanater
Kom Tennis
Tell el-Rub'a
Tell el-Samara
Damanhur
Tell el-Ferkha
Tell el-Ginn
el-Beda
Gezira Sangaha
Kufur Nigm
Minshat Abu 'Omar
Tell el-Dab'a
Beni Anir
Tell Ibrahim Awad
Tell el-Iswid

LOWER EGYPT

Merimda Beni Salama
Tell Hisn
HELIOPOLIS
el-Qatta
Heliopolis South
Old Cairo
Abu Rawash
Ma'adi
Giza
Wadi Digla
Zawyet el-'Aryan
Helwan
Qasr el Sagha
Abusir
Tura
Dimai
Saqqara
Mit Rahina
MEMPHIS
el-Saff
Kafr Tarkhan
Faiyum
Girza
Kom Medinet Ghurab
Maidum
Seila
Maiyana
Abusir el-Meleq
Harага
Sidmant el-Gebel
Nazlet Awlad el-Sheikh

Nazlet Awlad el-Sheikh: Large-scale flint workings of the Early Dynastic Period

Bahriya Oasis

Sawada
Zawyet el-Maiyitin

UPPER EGYPT

Gulf of Suez

Sinai

Maghara

Sinai: Archaeological evidence for Egyptian presence at the beginning of the Dynastic Period; rock inscriptions of the 3rd Dynasty

Gulf of Aqaba

Wadi Dara
Wadi el-Urf
Gebel Manzal el-Seyl

RED SEA

Deir el-Gabrawi
Deir Bisra
el-Mustagidda
Deir Rifa
Deir Tasa
Matmar
Hammamiya
el-Badari
Qaw el-Kebir

Mesaid
el-Raqaqna
Nag' el-Deir
Wadi el-Qash
Beit Khallaf
el-'Amra
el-Mahasna
Nag' el-Gaziriya
el-'Araba el-Madfuna
Hiw
Dendara
Naqada
ABYDOS
OMBOS
Ab'adiya
el-Tarif
Qus
Orff
KOPTOS
Khizam
Armant
Karnak
Gebelein
Luxor
THEBES
el-Kula/Nag' el-Mamariya
Adaima
el-Kab
Kom el-Ahmar
Wadi 'Abbad
HIERAKONPOLIS
Edfu

Approximate southern limit of the Naqada II culture

el-Dakhla Oasis

el-Kharga Oasis
Balat

Western Desert: Region of development of early pastoralist and partly settled cultures during wetter phases in the 7th–4th millennia BCE

el-Kubaniya North
ELEPHANTINE
el-Kubaniya South
Shellal
First Cataract

Border of Egypt in the Naqada III and Early Dynastic Periods

Kurkur Oasis
Dabod
Khor Bahan
Meris
Dehmit
Bir Tarfawi
Dunqul Oasis
Gerf Hussein
el-Dakka
Bir Kiseiba
Sayala
'Afia
el-Shab
Nabta
Wadi el-Girgawi
Tushka
Ballana
Qustul: Royal cemetery of the Terminal A Group, completely destroyed by the Egyptians
Faras
Qustul
Dibeira West
Serra East
Ashkeit
Gebel Sheikh Suleiman
Abka
LOWER NUBIA
Second Cataract
Murshid West
Gamai
Salima Oasis
Saras West
Saras
Second Cataract: Local Neolithic cultures; little trace of food production. Partly contemporary with the early A Group
Ambikol
Malik el-Nasir
Tumuki
Ukma
Kulb
Dal Cataract

Uweinat: Rich evidence for occupation by nomadic cattle-raisers, probably down to the late third millennium BCE

Uweinat (400 km)

Legend:
- Tasian/Badarian site
- Naqada I site
- Naqada II site
- Lower Egyptian or delta culture site
- Faiyum Predynastic culture site
- Late Naqada II, Naqada III and/or Early Dynastic site
▲ Egyptian site with small step pyramid of the 3rd Dynasty
□ Palestinian site with 1st-Dynasty Egyptian finds
◉ Nubian early A Group site
◉ classical and terminal A Group site
○ Khartoum variant site
○ post-Shamarkian site
○ Abkan site
⊖ Prehistoric desert culture site
⊖ well or oasis
--- desert route
fertile area
BUTO Egyptian capital
Giza modern name
MEMPHIS classical name
Lachish biblical name

scale 1 : 5 600 000
0 — 150 km
0 — 100 mi

(the Palermo Stone) and may be linked with rock inscriptions in Nubia itself. An Egyptian settlement was founded at Buhen and lasted for around 250 years, probably as a base for mining expeditions and trade with regions farther south.

A major factor in 4th- and 5th-Dynasty history was solar religion. The true pyramid is most probably a solar symbol, so that Snofru himself was a solar innovator. The compounding of royal names with the Sun god Re' and the use of the royal epithet "Son of Re'" are found from the reign of Re'djedef onward. It seems that the Sun god's influence and importance grew continuously until the mid-5th Dynasty.

Of the remaining rulers of the 4th Dynasty, Khufu and Khephren stand out through their pyramids. Shepsekaf built himself a massive mastaba instead, and this almost unique departure may be reflected in the practice of kings of the 5th Dynasty (c. 2450–2325). The first of these, Userkaf, built a small pyramid at Saqqara, east of the Step Pyramid, as well as a solar temple near Abusir; this latter practice was followed by five successors. These temples were separate from the pyramids but were closely associated with the kings who built them.

The last kings of the 5th Dynasty did not build separate solar temples, which may imply a lessening in the importance of solar religion or of its role in the king's destiny in the next world. Wenis appears to be a transitional figure, heralding the 6th Dynasty (c. 2325–2175). His pyramid complex, with its small pyramid, is of great interest both for the reliefs on its long causeway and for the texts on the walls of the internal chambers.

▶ *This map shows Egypt in the Old Kingdom and First Intermediate Period.*

More is known of the political history of the 6th Dynasty than of earlier periods, but still only a random spread of information; much of what is regarded as typical of it could have happened at other times, too. This applies particularly to military campaigns, such as those to the northeast—perhaps in southern Palestine—recorded by the high official Weni. Even if the import of these campaigns is unknown, their occurrence is attested. Campaigns recorded in royal mortuary reliefs, however, have no simple relationship with fact. A campaign to Libya depicted in the complex of Sahure' was repeated on monuments of Neuserre', Pepy I, Pepy II, and finally Taharqa (690–664 BCE); this ritual event probably corresponded with a real campaign before the time of Sahure', but with no other specific happening.

Occasional archaeological evidence highlights our ignorance of Egyptian relations with West Asia. Some 5th-Dynasty goldwork has appeared in Anatolia, while stone vases of Khephren and Pepy I have been excavated at Ebla in Syria, the capital of a state that fell around 2250 BCE. Such objects might have been either diplomatic gifts or exotic trade goods. As in the Middle Kingdom, the main channel of communication was no doubt Byblos on the Lebanese coast, where Old Kingdom objects have been found.

The biographical inscriptions of expedition leaders in their tombs opposite Aswan give much information about trade to the south in the 6th Dynasty. Among other events, the biographies show the settling of the C Group in Nubia—first in three princedoms, and later in a single political unit, with which Egypt's relations gradually deteriorated.

The deterioration in relations was probably an aspect of Egypt's declining power during the more than 50 years of Pepy II's reign.

▶ *(overleaf, page 32) A map showing Egypt in the Middle Kingdom and Second Intermediate Period.*

▶ *(overleaf, page 33) This colossal portrait of King Ramesses II of the 19th Dynasty stands at the Temple in Luxor.*

The decline can be seen in nonroyal tombs in the Memphite area, whose decoration is much more modest than hitherto. But although details of this sort are significant, nothing prepares for the eclipse of royal power and the poverty that came after Pepy II. The numerous kings of the next 20 years (late 6th and 7th–8th Dynasties) were accepted in the whole country, but central control was only nominal. Provincial notables had become hereditary office-holders and treated their nomes virtually as their own domains, whose interests they defended, often by force, against their neighbors.

First Intermediate Period and reunification

In the 1st Intermediate Period (c. 2125–1975), rulers from Herakleopolis (Ihnasya el-Medina) claimed the kingship, forming the 9th dynasty. After a generation or two, a rival dynasty, the 11th, was proclaimed in Thebes. From that time the Herakleopolitan line is conventionally termed the 10th Dynasty. The power of the two dynasties increased and there were frequent clashes at the border, mostly north of Abydos. Both sides used Nubian mercenaries in their armies.

The Herakleopolitan Dynasty suffered frequent changes of ruler and is little known because few monuments survive from it. The most important king of the Theban Dynasty was the fourth, Nebhepetre' Mentuhotep (called I or II, c. 2010–1960), who defeated the northern dynasty and reunited the country. During his reign, there was also activity in Lower Nubia, and a landscaped mortuary complex of novel type was built at Deir el-Bahri. The artistic style of its reliefs is a refined version of 1st Intermediate Period work more than a resumption of Old Kingdom traditions, emphasizing, like the

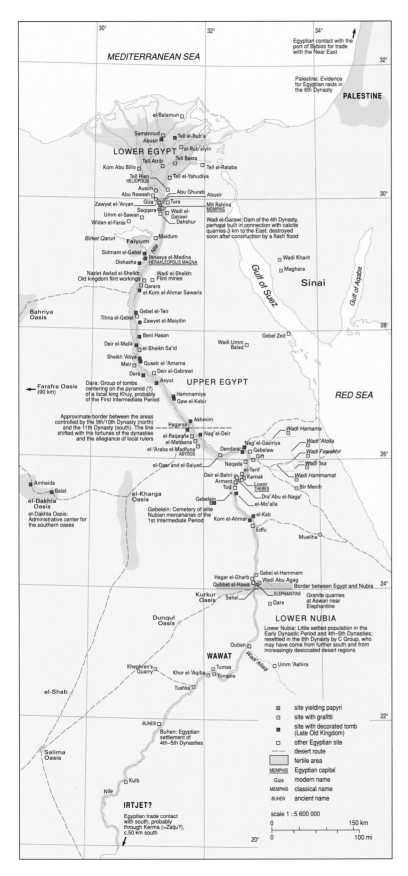

Theban location, the local base of the king's power. Mentuhotep was later venerated as one of the founders of Egypt; part of this prestige may go back to his own self-glorification, for he was depicted in a form more nearly divine than that of most Egyptian kings.

Middle Kingdom

The last two kings of the 11th Dynasty retained Thebes as their capital. Both built widely, and the route to the Red Sea was revived. This indicates that Egypt was strong, but the political order did not last. The second king, Nebtawyre' Mentuhotep, is absent from later lists, which record seven blank years; he was probably viewed retrospectively as an illegitimate ruler. Amenemhet, his vizier, was the first king of the 12th Dynasty.

The most important political act of Amenemhet I (c. 1938–1908) was to move the royal residence from Thebes to near Memphis where, perhaps late in his reign, he founded a place called Itjtawy. The main center of population remained at Memphis, so that the capital was located where it had been in the Old Kingdom. This move was thus both an innovation and a return to older traditions. The nomarchs in Middle Egypt, who had been virtually independent, were left in office but made to display loyalty to the new regime, while the central administration acquired increasing authority.

The 12th dynasty kings maintained a sizable standing army. In foreign policy, Amenemhet I built on the work of Nebhepetre' Mentuhotep in Nubia, and in several campaigns late in his reign conquered as far as the second cataract. The leader of the campaigns was probably Senwosret I (c. 1918–1875), who acted for his father and may have been his coregent for ten years, in a new development in patterns of rule. Senwosret I built widely in Egypt and began the great series of forts in Lower Nubia. The literary works and the material and intellectual achievements of the dynasty made it classical in later Egyptian and in modern eyes. Despite the achievements of the first 12th-dynasty rulers, far more archaeological material is preserved from its later kings.

The 12th-Dynasty king with the most lasting reputation was Senwosret III (c. 1878–1841). He is noted especially for his Nubian campaigns, in which the frontier was moved south to Semna at the southern end of the second cataract, and for the establishment of new forts and the extension of others. In later times he was worshiped there as a god. During his reign, there was also a campaign to Palestine, which marked a period of Egyptian influence there. Palestine may have been seminomadic, becoming settled around the end of the 12th Dynasty.

Senwosret III made important reforms in administration, which seem to have finally removed power from the nomarchs. The country was organized into four "regions," each of which corresponded to roughly half the Nile valley or the delta. Titularies of officials and documents of the late 12th and 13th Dynasties give the impression of a pervasive bureaucracy that came to run the country under its own momentum.

Within Egypt the most striking visible legacy of Senwosret III is his royal statuary, which breaks earlier conventions in showing an aging, careworn face, perhaps

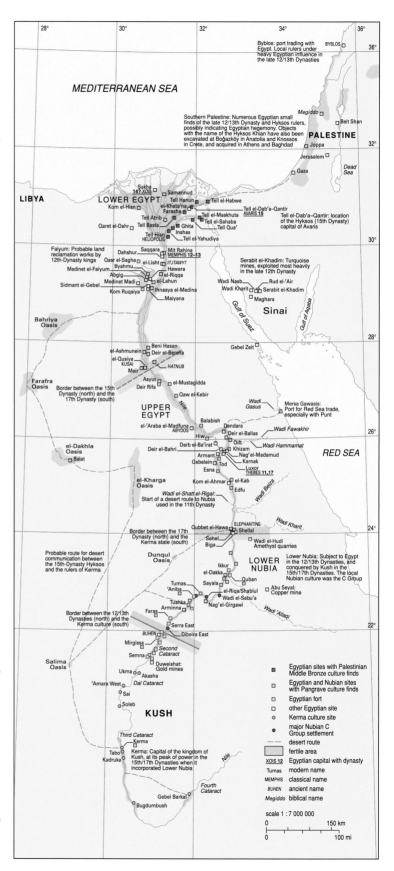

KINGS OF EGYPT

A king's full titulary consisted of five main elements. These are (1) Horus, (2) Two Ladies, and (3) Golden Horus, all of which are epithets evoking how the king manifested a deity or deities; (4) the first cartouche, prefaced by two words for king that were identified with the two halves of the country, which contains a statement about the Sun god Re' in relation to the king; (5) the second cartouche, which contains the king's own birth name preceded by "Son of Re'."

Since the pronunciation of names is uncertain, Greek forms from the history of Manetho (3rd century BCE) are used for some kings. The birth name is generally placed first, followed by the first cartouche (in italics). The 20th Dynasty kings used Ramesses as a dynastic name in their second cartouches; Ptolemaic kings were called Ptolemy.

Overlapping dates within dynasties indicate coregencies. Precise dates are marked *. Female kings are marked Q.

LATE PREDYNASTIC c. 3100

"Dynasty 0"	Several kings; Iryhor(?); Ka(?); Na'rmer

EARLY DYNASTIC PERIOD c. 2950–2575 BCE

1st Dynasty c. 2950–2775	Menes (= 'Aha?); Djer; Wadj; Den; 'Anedjib; Semerkhet; Qa'a
2nd Dynasty c. 2775–2650	Hotepsekhemwy; Re'neb; Ninetjer; Peribsen; Kha'sekhem(wy)
3rd Dynasty c. 2650–2575	Djoser (Netjerykhet); Sekhemkhet; Zanakht (= Nebka?); Kha'ba; Huni(?)

OLD KINGDOM c. 2575–2150 BCE

4th Dynasty c. 2575–2450	Snofru; Khufu (Cheops); Re'djedef;Khephren (Re'kha'ef); Menkaure' (Mycerinus); Shepseskaf
5th Dynasty c. 2450–2325	Userkaf; Sahure'; *Neferirkare'* Kakai; *Shepseskare'* Ini; Re'neferef; *Neuserre'* Izi; Menkauhor; *Djedkare'* Izezi; Wenis
6th Dynasty c. 2325–2175	Teti; Pepy I (*Meryre'*); *Merenre'* Nemtyemzaf; Pepy II (*Neferkare'*)
7th/8th Dynasty c. 2175–2125	Numerous ephemeral kings, including Neferkare'

1st INTERMEDIATE PERIOD c. 2125–1975 BCE

9th Dynasty c. 2125–2080	(Herakleopolitan)
10th Dynasty c. 2080–1975	(Herakleopolitan); Several kings called Khety; Merykare'; Ity
11th Dynasty c. 2080–1975	(Theban); Inyotef I (Sehertawy); Inyotef II (Wah'ankh); Inyotef III (Naktnebtepnufer); *Nebhepetre'* Mentuhotep

MIDDLE KINGDOM c. 1975–1640 BCE

11th Dynasty c. 1975–1940	(all Egypt); *Nebhepetre'* Mentuhotep c. 2010–1960; *S'ankhkare'* Mentuhotep c. 1960–1948; ; *Nebtawyre' Mentuhotep* c. 1948–?
12th Dynasty c. 1938–1755	Amenemhet I (*Sehetepibre'*) c. 1938–1908; Senwosret I (*Kheperkare'*) c. 1918–1875; Amenemhet II (*Nubkaure'*); c. 1876–1842; Senwosret II (*Kha'kheperre'*) c. 1842–1837; Senwosret III (*Kha'kaure'*) c. 1836–1818; Amenemhet III (*Nima'atre'*) c. 1818–1770; Amenemhet IV (*Ma'akherure'*) c. 1770–1760; Nefrusobk (*Sebekkare'*) c. 1760–1755
13th Dynasty c. 1755–1630	About 70 kings; better-known ones are listed (numbers are their approximate positions in a complete list); Wegaf (*Khutawyre'*) 1; Amenemhet V (*Sekhemkare'*) 4; Harnedjheriotef (*Hetepibre'*) 9; Amenyqemau 11b; Sebekhotep I (*Kha'ankhre'*) 12; Hor (*Awibre'*) 14; Amenemhet VII (*Sedjefakare'*) 15; Sebekhotep II (*Sekhemre'*-

khutawy) 16; Khendjer (*Userkare*) 17; Sebekhotep III (*Sekhemre'-swadjtawy*) 21; Neferhotep I c. 1710–1700 (*Khasekhemre*) 22; Sebekhotep IV c. 1700–1690 (*Kha'neferre*) 24; Sebekhotep V c. 1690–1685 (*Kha'hotepre*) 25; Aya c. 1685–1670 (*Merneferre*) 27; Mentuemzaf (*Djed'ankhre*) 32c; Dedumose II (*Djedneferre*) 37; Neferhotep III (*Sekhemre'-s'ankhtawy*) 41a

14th Dynasty	**Minor kings who were probably all contemporaneous with the 13th or 15th Dynasties**

2nd INTERMEDIATE PERIOD c. 1630–1520 BCE

15th Dynasty (Hyksos) c. 1630–1520

	Salitis; Sheshi; Khian; Apophis c. 1570–1530; Khamudi c. 1530–1520
16th Dynasty	**Minor Hyksos rulers, contemporaneous with the 15th Dynasty**
17th Dynasty c. 1630–1540	**Numerous Theban kings; numbers give positions in a complete list; Inyotef V (*Nubkheperre*) 1; Sebekemzaf I (*Sekhemre'-wadjkha'u*) 3; Nebireyeraw (*Swadjenre*) 6; Sebekemzaf II (*Sekhemre'-shedtawy*) 10; Ta'o (or Djehuti'o) I (*Senakhtenre*) 13; Ta'o (or Djehuti'o) II (*Seqenenre*) 14; Kamose c. 1545–1539 (*Wadjkheperre*) 15**

NEW KINGDOM c. 1539–1075 BCE

18th Dynasty c. 1539–1292	'Ahmose c. 1539–1514 (*Nebpehtire*); Amenhotep I c. 1514–1493 (*Djeserkare*); Thutmose I c. 1493–? (*'Akheperkare*); Thutmose II c. ?–1479 (*'Akheperenre*); Thutmose III c. 1479–1425 (*Menkheperre*); Hatshepsut c. 1473–1458 (*Ma'atkare*) Q; Amenhotep II c. 1426–1400 (*'Akheprure*); Thutmose IV c. 1400–1390 (*Menkheprure*); Amenhotep III c. 1390–1353 (*Nebma'atre*); Amenhotep IV/Akhenaten (*Neferkheprure' wa'enre*) c. 1353–1336; Smenkhkare' c. 1335–1332 (*'Ankhkheprure*); Tut'ankhamun c. 1332–1322 (*Nebkheprure*); Aya c. 1322–1319 (*Kheperkheprure*); Haremhab c. 1319–1292 (*Djeserkheprure*)
19th Dynasty c. 1292–1190	Ramesses I c. 1292–1290 (*Menpehtire*); Sety I c. 1290–1279 (*Menma'atre*); Ramesses II c. 1279–1213 (*Userma'atre' setepenre*); Merneptah c. 1213–1204 (*Baenre' hotephirma'at*); Sety II c. 1204–1198 (*Userkheprure' setepenre*); Amenmesse (*Menmire*), usurper during reign of Sety II; Siptah c. 1198–1193 (*Akhenre' setepenre*); Twosre c. 1198–1190; (*Sitre' meritamun*) Q
20th Dynasty c. 1190–1075	Sethnakhte c. 1190–1187 (*Userkha'ure' meryamun*); Ramesses III c. 1187–1156 (*Userma'atre' meryamun*); Ramesses IV c. 1156–1150 (*Heqama'atre' setepenamun*); Ramesses V c. 1150–1145 (*Userma'atre' sekheperenre*); Ramesses VI c. 1145–1137 (*Nebma'atre' meryamun*); Ramesses VII c. 1137–1129 (*Userma'atre' setepenre' meryamun*); Ramesses VIII c. 1129–1126 (*Userma'atre' akhenamun*); Ramesses IX c. 1126–1108 (*Neferkare' setepenre*); Ramesses X c. 1108–1104 (*Kheperma'atre' setepenre*); Ramesses XI c. 1104–1075 (*Menma'atre' setepenptah*)

3rd INTERMEDIATE PERIOD c. 1075–715 BCE

21st Dynasty c. 1075–945	Smendes c. 1075–1050 (*Hedjkheperre' setepenre'*); Amenemnisu c. 1050–1040 (*Neferkare'*); Psusennes I c. 1040–995 (*'Akheperre' setepenamun*); Amenemope c. 994–985 (*Userma'atre' setepenamun*); Osorkon I c. 985–978 (*Akheperre' setepenre'*); Siamun c. 978–960 (*Netjerkheperre' setepenamun*); Psusennes II c. 960–945 (*Titkheprure' setepenre'*)
22nd Dynasty c. 945–715	Shoshenq I c. 945–925 (*Hedjkheperre' setepenre'*); Osorkon II c. 925–910 (*Sekhemkheperre' setepenre'*); Takelot I c. 910–? (*Userma'atre' setepenamun*); Shoshenq II ?–c. 885 (*Heqakheperre' setepenre'*); Osorkon III c. 885–855 (*Userma'atre' setepenamun*); Takelot II c. 860–835 (*Hedjkheperre' setepenre'*); Shoshenq III c. 835–785 (*Userma'atre' setepenre'/amun*); Pami c. 785–775 (*Userma'atre' setepenre'/amun*); Shoshenq V c. 775–735 (*'Akheperre'*); Osorkon V c. 735–715 (*'Akheperre' setepenamun*)
23rd Dynasty c. 830–715	Various contemporaneous lines of kings recognized in Thebes, Hermopolis, Herakleopolis, Leontopolis, and Tanis; arrangement and order are disputed; Pedubaste I c. 830–805; Osorkon IV c. 775–750; Peftjau'awybast 740–725 (*Neferkare'*)
24th Dynasty (Sais) c. 730–715	(Tefnakhte (*Shepsesre'*?)); Bocchoris (*Wahkare'*) c. 722–715
25th Dynasty c. 770–715	(Nubia and Theban area); Kashta (*Nima'atre'*) c. 770–750; Piye c. 750–715; (*Userma'atre'* and others)

LATE PERIOD c. 715–332 BCE

25th Dynasty c. 715–657	(Nubia and all Egypt); Shabaka (*Neferkare'*) c. 715–700; Shebitku (*Djedkaure'*) c. 700–690; Taharqa c. 690–664 (*Khure'nefertem*); Tantamani c. 664–657 (*Bakare'*); (possibly later in Upper Nubia)
26th Dynasty *664–525	(Necho I *672–664); Psammetichus I *664–610 (*Wahibre'*); Necho II *610–595 (*Wehemibre'*); Psammetichus II *595–589 (*Neferibre'*); Apries (*Ha'a'ibre'*) *589–570; Amasis (*Khnemibre'*) *570–526; Psammetichus III *526–525 (*'Ankhkaenre'*)
27th Dynasty *525–404 (Persian)	Cambyses *525–522; Darius I *521–486; Xerxes I *486–466; Artaxerxes I *465–424; Darius II *424–404
28th Dynasty *404–399	Amyrtaios *404–399
29th Dynasty *399–380	Nepherites I *399–393 (*Baenre' merynetjeru*); Psammuthis *393 (*Userre' setepenptah*); Hakoris *393–380 (*Khnemma'atre'*); Nepherites II *380

30th Dynasty *380–343	Nectanebo I *380–362 (*Kheperkare'*); Teos *365–360 (*Irma'atenre'*); Nectanebo II *360–343 (*Senedjemibre' setepenanhur*)
2nd Persian Period *343–332	Artaxerxes III Ochus *343–338; Arses *338–336; Darius III Codoman *335–332; Period interrupted by an indigenous ruler Khababash (*Senentanen setepenptah*)

GRECO-ROMAN PERIOD *332 BCE–395 CE

Macedonian Dynasty *332–305	Alexander III the Great *332–323; Philip Arrhidaeus *323–316; Alexander IV *316–305
Ptolemaic Dynasty *305–30	Ptolemy I Soter I *305–284; Ptolemy II *285–246; Philadelphus; Ptolemy III Euergetes I *246–221; Ptolemy IV Philopator *221–205; Ptolemy V Epiphanes *205–180; Ptolemy VI *180–164, *163–145;Philometor; Ptolemy VIII *170–163, *145–116; Euergetes II (Physkon); Ptolemy VII *145; Neos Philopator; Cleopatra III Q and *116–107; Ptolemy IX Soter II (Lathyros); Cleopatra III Q and *107–88; Ptolemy X Alexander I; Ptolemy IX Soter II *88–81; Cleopatra Berenice Q *81–80; Ptolemy XI Alexander II *80; Ptolemy XII Neos *80–58, *55–51; Dionysos (Auletes); Berenice IV Q *58–55; Cleopatra VII Philopator Q *51–30; Ptolemy XIII *51–47; Ptolemy XIV; *47–44; Ptolemy XV Caesarion *44–30 Further coregencies with queens called Arsinoe, Berenice, and Cleopatra, who had no independent reigns. Native usurpers: Harwennofre (205–199), 'Ankhwennofre (199–186), Harsiese (131)
Roman emperors *30 BCE–395 CE	(names attested in hieroglyphic and demotic texts, down to the tetrarchy of 284–305) Augustus *30 BCE–14 CE; Tiberius*14–37; Gaius (Caligula) *37–41; Claudius *41–54; Nero *54–68; Galba *68–69; Otho*69; Vespasian *69–79; Titus *79–81; Domitian *81–96; Nerva *96–98; Trajan *98–117;xz Hadrian *117–138; Antoninus Pius *138–161; Marcus Aurelius *161–180; Lucius Verus *161–169; Commodus *180–192; Septimius Severus 193–211; Caracalla *198–217; Geta *209–212; Macrinus *217–218; Diadumenianus *218; Severus Alexander *222–235; Gordian III *238–244; Philip *244–249; Decius *249–251; Gallus and Volusianus *251–253; Valerian *253–260; Gallienus *253–268; Macrianus and Quietus *260–261; Aurelian *270–275; Probus *276–282; Diocletian *284–305; Maximian *286–305; Galerius *293–311

symbolizing the burdens of kingship depicted in the period's literature. The same style was used in statues of his successor Amenemhet III (c. 1818–1770), whose long reign seems to have been peaceful. Amenemhet III was deified later in the Faiyum, where he may have begun a land reclamation scheme, changing the area from a huntsman's marshy paradise into productive arable land.

Egypt remained prosperous under Amenemhet IV (c. 1770–1760) and the female king Nefrusobk (c. 1760–1755), but the presence of a woman on the throne suggests that the ruling family was dying out.

In about 150 years, some 70 kings of the 13th Dynasty came and went. The country seems to have been stable, although there was no acknowledged means of replacing

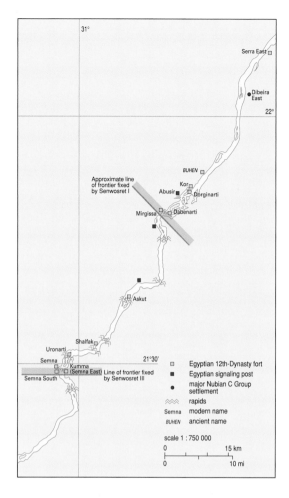

▶ A map showing the second cataract forts of the Middle Kingdom (now submerged under Lake Nasser). The forts to the north were begun under Senwosret I; those south of Mirgissa were added by Senwosret III.

31°

Serra East ☐

• Dibeira East

22°

BUHEN ☐

Approximate line of frontier fixed by Senwosret I

Kor ☐
Abusir ■ ☐ Dorginarti

Mirgissa ☐ ◢ ☐ Dabenarti

■

◢ Askut

Shalfak ◢

Uronarti
Semna   21°30'
☐ ☐ Kumma
☐ ☐ (Semna East) Line of frontier fixed
Semna South   by Senwosret III

☐   Egyptian 12th-Dynasty fort
■   Egyptian signaling post
•   major Nubian C Group
    settlement
〜〜〜 rapids
Semna   modern name
BUHEN   ancient name

scale 1 : 750 000
0   15 km
0   10 mi

▶ A map showing Egypt in the New Kingdom and Third Intermediate Period.

kings in rapid succession. Stable authority seems instead to have rested with the viziers, the highest officials, of whom a family is known that spanned a large part of the 18th century BCE. Official titles of all ranks proliferated, possibly because of an increase in the size of the bureaucracy.

As late as 1700, Egypt appears to have lost little power or prestige at home or abroad. If the number of nonroyal monuments is any guide, prosperity may even have increased. Many immigrants came from Palestine, who were absorbed into the lowest levels of Egyptian society, but at least one of whom, Khendjer, became king. They probably came as a result of shifts of population in West Asia after 1800, and were earlier members of the movement that was to bring foreign rule

in the 2nd Intermediate Period. Areas of the eastern delta were heavily settled by Asiatics; notable among these was Tell el-Dab'a–Qantir, which became the Hyksos capital of Avaris and much later the Ramessid capital Pi-Ri'amsese. Egypt retained control of Lower Nubia, probably until the later 13th Dynasty, but the local army contingents became increasingly independent and some settled, staying behind after the area was overrun by the Kerma state around the beginning of the 15th/17th Dynasties. At about the time of the loss of Nubia, the capital of the 13th Dynasty may have moved from the Memphite area to Thebes; the latest kings of the dynasty are attested only from there.

Second Intermediate Period

Around 1630, kingship in Lower Egypt was taken over by a group usually called the Hyksos—a Greek form derived from an Egyptian phrase for "ruler of foreign lands." The Hyksos, the 15th Egyptian Dynasty, seem to have been recognized as the chief line of kings in the whole country, but they tolerated other dynasties. The 13th Dynasty may have continued in existence, as may also the 14th, a line of rulers in the northwestern delta. The most important of the concurrent dynasties was the 17th, a line of native Egyptians who ruled from Thebes, holding the Nile valley from the first cataract north as far as Kusai (el-Qusiya). The area that had been held by the 12th–13th Dynasties was thus divided between the Kerma rulers in the south, the Theban 17th Dynasty, and the Hyksos in the north. For nearly a century they appear to have coexisted more or less peacefully.

Names of 15th-Dynasty kings have been found on objects from widely separated sites in West Asia, showing that they had diplomatic or trading relations over a vast area. Contact abroad brought technical innovations that were important in later periods. Among the new techniques were bronzeworking; an improved potter's wheel and the vertical loom; hump-backed cattle (zebu) and new vegetable and fruit crops; the horse and chariot; composite bows and other weapons. New musical instruments were also introduced.

With Seqenenre' Ta'o II of the 17th Dynasty, the Thebans began to campaign against the Hyksos. The first episode is known only from a New Kingdom tale, but Seqenenre''s mummy supports the reality of conflict since it shows that he died violently. Two stelae of his successor, Kamose, describe skirmishes between Thebes and the Hyksos, who were allied with the Nubian kings. Kamose nearly reached Avaris, the Hyksos capital, and campaigned in the south as far as Buhen.

New Kingdom

'Ahmose (c. 1539–1514), Kamose's successor, finally drove out the Hyksos rulers around 1520, many years after Kamose's attempts. After the victory, 'Ahmose campaigned in Palestine for some years. In Nubia, he fought as far south as the island of Sai, near the third cataract; he also suppressed rebellions in Egypt or Lower Nubia.

'Ahmose left a unified state that stretched from south of the second cataract to Palestine and was the chief power in West Asia. His son Amenhotep I (c. 1514–1493) may have extended Egyptian influence farther south. In the late

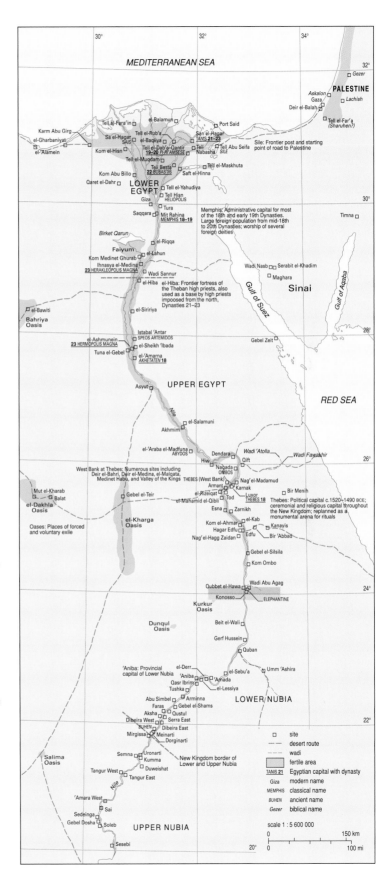

39

18th–20th Dynasties, Amenhotep and his mother were revered by the inhabitants of Deir el-Medina, possibly because he had founded the institutional complex to which they belonged, which built the royal tombs. The Valley of the Kings and the site of the village itself, however, appear not to have been used until rather later.

The campaigns of Thutmose I (from c. 1493) extended farther than those of any Egyptian king. Early in his reign, he reached the Euphrates in the north and Kurgus, far upstream of the fourth cataract, in the south. Either Amenhotep I or he destroyed the Kerma state in Upper Nubia. These feats define the limits of territory ever conquered by Egypt but may not have been such a leap forward as they seem. In Syria–Palestine there may have been preparatory campaigns in previous reigns, and the Egyptians seem not to have had another major power as an opponent at the time. During the reign of Amenhotep I, the kingdom of Mitanni, Egypt's chief northern rival for a century, formed in Syria; this new polity was Thutmose I's adversary on the Euphrates.

The rulers of the petty states of Palestine and Syria that formed the Egyptian "empire" were bound to the Egyptian king by oaths of allegiance and paid him tribute, but remained self-governing. Egyptian presence was maintained by relatively small army detachments and a few high officials. Nubia, in contrast, was treated as a colonial land and administered directly by a viceroy who was responsible to the king of Egypt. Both areas included territories that formed part of the endowment of Egyptian institutions such as temples, but the harsher Nubian system seems to have contributed to widespread depopulation in the 19th–20th Dynasties. Both in West Asia and in Nubia, a prime motive for Egyptian expansion was to secure the routes for long-distance trade and access to raw materials; defense was probably a secondary consideration. Trade and gold, much of it from Nubia, enhanced the country's wealth and international standing.

Thutmose II, whose reign has left little trace, was succeeded by his young son, Thutmose III (c. 1479–1425), for whom Hatshepsut, Thutmose II's sister and widow, acted initially as regent. There seems to have been little military activity in the first 20 years of Thutmose III's reign, and Egypt lost some ground in Asia. Around Thutmose III's seventh year, Hatshepsut proclaimed herself "king" and ruled as the dominant partner in a coregency with her nephew until her death around his year 22.

No campaign to Asia is attested from the time of Hatshepsut. At her death, Thutmose III assumed sole role and launched a series of campaigns to the Near East, starting by reconquering territory in Palestine that had recently rejected allegiance to Egypt. In the next 20 years, the Egyptians fought mainly in Syria, where the Mitanni successfully resisted, and Thutmose could not maintain his farthest points of expansion on the Euphrates. This conflict was to last for another generation. Thutmose III was also active in Nubia late in his reign and established the provincial capital of Napata at the downstream end of the fourth cataract.

In the last years of his reign, Thutmose took his son Amenhotep II (c. 1426–1400) as coregent. Amenhotep, like other kings, faced the problem that vassal rulers owed allegiance to a king rather than to Egypt in general. New kings often needed to assert their authority afresh. His military exploits were parades of strength, not strategically significant campaigns. The parades had a

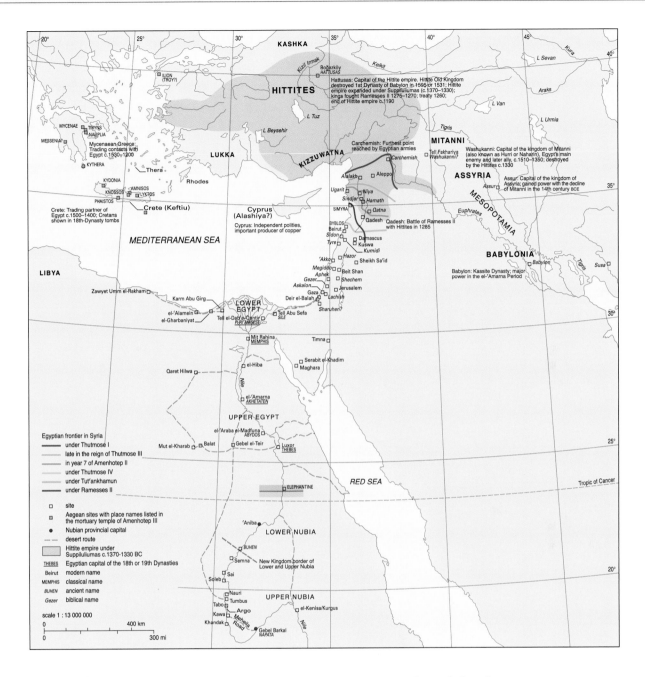

Map labels (reproduced as shown):

KASHKA

ILION (TROY)

Boğazköy HATTUSAS

Kizil Irmak

Kelkit

HITTITES

Hattusas: Capital of the Hittite empire. Hittite Old Kingdom destroyed 1st Dynasty of Babylon in 1595 or 1531; Hittite empire expanded under Suppiluliumas (c.1370–1330); kings fought Ramesses II 1275–1270; treaty 1260; end of Hittite empire c.1190

L Tuz

L Sevan

Kura

Araks

L Van

L Urmia

MYCENAE   TIRYNS
NAUPLIA

MESSENIA

Tigris

MITANNI

Washukanni: Capital of the kingdom of Mitanni (also known as Hurri or Naharin), Egypt's main enemy and later ally, c.1510–1350; destroyed by the Hittites c.1330

Mycenaean Greece: Trading contacts with Egypt c.1530–1200

KYTHERA

Thera

LUKKA

KIZZUWATNA

Tell Fakhariya
Washukanni?

Carchemish: Furthest point reached by Egyptian armies

Carchemish

ASSYRIA

Assur: Capital of the kingdom of Assyria; gained power with the decline of Mitanni in the 14th century BCE

KYDONIA

AMNISOS

KNOSSOS   LYKTOS

PHAISTOS

Rhodes

Crete (Keftiu)

Crete: Trading partner of Egypt c.1500–1400; Cretans shown in 18th-Dynasty tombs

Cyprus (Alashiya?)

Cyprus: Independent polities, important producer of copper

Alalakh   Aleppo

Ugarit

Niya

Sindjar   Hamath

SIMYRA   Qatna

BYBLOS

Beirut

Sidon   Damascus

Tyre   Kuswa

Kumidi

Qadesh

Qadesh: Battle of Ramesses II with Hittites in 1285

Assur

MESOPOTAMIA

Euphrates

BABYLONIA

Babylon

Babylon: Kassite Dynasty; major power in the el-'Amarna Period

Susa

Tigris

MEDITERRANEAN SEA

'Akko   Hazor

Megiddo   Beit Shan

Aphek   Sheikh Sa'id

Gezer   Shechem

Askalon   Jerusalem

Gaza   Lachish

Deir el-Balah

Sharuhen?

LIBYA

Zawyet Umm el-Rakham

Karm Abu Girg

LOWER EGYPT

el-'Alamein   Tell el-Dab'a–Qantir
PI-RI-AMSESE

el-Gharbaniyat   Tell Abu Sefa
SILE

Mit Rahina
MEMPHIS

Timna

Qaret Hilwa

Serabit el-Khadim
Maghara

el-Hiba

Nile

el-'Amarna
AKHETATEN

UPPER EGYPT

el-'Araba el-Madfuna
ABYDOS

Mut el-Kharab   Balat

Gebel el-Teir

Luxor
THEBES

RED SEA

Tropic of Cancer

ELEPHANTINE

'Aniba

LOWER NUBIA

BUHEN

Semna

New Kingdom border of Lower and Upper Nubia

Sai

Soleb

UPPER NUBIA

Nauri

Tabo   Tumbus

Argo

Kawa   Meroitic
Road

Khandak

Gebel Barkal
NAPATA

Nile

Legend:

Egyptian frontier in Syria
— under Thutmose I
— late in the reign of Thutmose III
— in year 7 of Amenhotep II
— under Thutmose IV
— under Tut'ankhamun
— under Ramesses II

□ site

▪ Aegean sites with place names listed in the mortuary temple of Amenhotep III

● Nubian provincial capital

- - - desert route

▨ Hittite empire under Suppiluliumas c.1370-1330 BC

THEBES Egyptian capital of the 18th or 19th Dynasties
Beirut modern name
MEMPHIS classical name
BUHEN ancient name
Gezer biblical name

scale 1 : 13 000 000
0 .... 400 km
0 .... 300 mi

20° 25° 30° 35° 40° 45°

message for foreign powers; in his year 9 Amenhotep received presentations of gifts (the normal mode of diplomatic contact) from the three major powers of the time, the Hittites, Mitanni, and Babylon.

Both abroad and at home, the reigns of Thutmose IV (c. 1400–1390) and Amenhotep III (c. 1390–1353) form a single phase. Egypt lost more ground to Mitanni, but the two powers made peace before Thutmose IV's

death, sealing their relationship with the gift of a Mitanni princess to the king as a minor wife. In his turn, Amenhotep III married more than one Mitanni princess.

Peace brought a further upsurge in wealth. In the number and size of buildings erected, the reign of Amenhotep III can be compared only with that of Ramesses II, while royal and nonroyal statuary was produced on an unparalleled scale. In a significant

▲ *A map showing Egypt and the Near East from around 1520–1200 BCE. The successive frontiers of Egyptian rule in Syria–Palestine, from north to south and in chronological order, show the limits of expansion under a series of rulers from Thutmose I to Ramesses II.*

41

ideological shift, Amenhotep III was deified in his own lifetime.

Amenhotep IV (c. 1353–1336) became heir after the death of his elder brother Thutmose. At the start of his reign, he gave himself the title of high priest of the Sun god, a role that was traditional for Egyptian kings. He also formulated a new "dogmatic" name for the Sun god, "Re'-Harakhty who rejoices on the horizon in his name of Shu [or: 'light'] which is the Sun disk [Aten]." The god was shown in a new iconography of a disk with rays ending in hands that hold out the hieroglyph for "life" to the king and queen. The new cult left almost no place for traditional deities except for the Sun god. It became the king's main purpose in life; he presented himself as the only person who comprehended the god and also promoted his own godlike status. His queen, Nefertiti, was almost equally prominent in the changes.

Probably in his fifth year, Amenhotep IV changed his name to Akhenaten ("One Beneficial for the Disk") and began a new capital at el-'Amarna, naming it Akhetaten ("Horizon of Aten"). Around year 9, Akhenaten closed all temples for other gods and had the word *Amun,* and sometimes *gods,* hacked out wherever they occurred.

Akhenaten had six daughters but no son by Nefertiti. After his death in his year 17, a woman may have succeeded him briefly, perhaps Meritaten, his eldest daughter. The next ruler may have reigned for only three years. Tut'ankhaten, later Tut'ankhamun, a boy of about nine, then succeeded (c. 1332–1322). He was perhaps the son of Akhenaten's secondary wife, Kiya. Early in Tut'ankhamun's reign, the new religion was abandoned but not suppressed completely until later. Memphis, which had long been the chief city, became the capital.

While Tut'ankhamun was king, executive power lay in the hands of Aya and the general Haremhab (c. 1319–1292). He is normally placed in the 18th Dynasty but was considered by Egyptians of the next century to be the first king of their era, which we call the 19th Dynasty.

Haremhab dismantled the temples of Akhenaten at Karnak and built there extensively himself. He also annexed most of Tut'ankhamun's inscriptions, which may in part have recorded his own exploits. His second successor, Sety I (c. 1290–1279), continued the restoration work, repairing monuments and removing the names of Akhenaten and his successors down to Haremhab from the official record. He also built extensively himself.

Late in his reign, Sety I nominated his son Ramesses II (c. 1279–1213) crown prince. The new king inherited problems in Syria. After a success in year 4 he confronted the Hittite army for the first time in year 5 in an indecisive battle at Qadesh, which Ramesses presented as a great victory. After further engagements there was a truce, followed by a formal treaty in year 21. Peace continued for more than 50 years, reinforced diplomatically by marriages between Ramesses II and Hittite princesses.

Ramesses II built more buildings and had more statues than any other king, as well as having his name or reliefs carved on older monuments. Like Amenhotep III, he was deified in his own lifetime. By his projection of his personality he made his name synonymous with kingship for centuries.

One of the most important undertakings of Ramesses II was the removal of the capital city to a new site in the delta called Pi-Ri'amsese ("Domain of Ramesses"), modern Tell el-Dab'a–Qantir. The royal family came

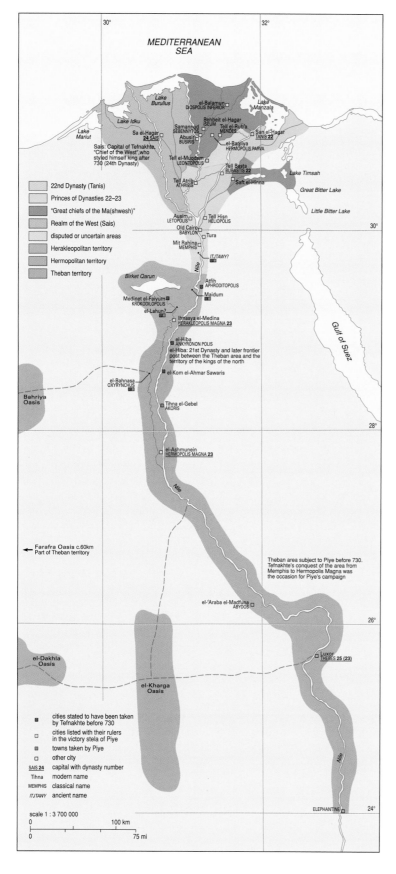

MEDITERRANEAN SEA

Lake Burullus

Lake Idku

Lake Mariut

Lake Manzala

el-Balamun
DIOSPOLIS INFERIOR

Behbeit el-Hagar
ISEUM

Samannud
SEBENNYTOS

Tell el-Rub'a
MENDES

Sa el-Hagar
24 SAIS

Abusir
BUSIRIS

San el-Hagar
TANIS 22

el-Baqliya
HERMOPOLIS PARVA

Sais: Capital of Tefnakhte, "Chief of the West," who styled himself king after 730 (24th Dynasty)

Tell el-Muqdam
LEONTOPOLIS

Tell Atrib
ATHRIBIS

Tell Besta
BUBASTIS 22

Saft el-Hinna

Lake Timsah

Great Bitter Lake

Little Bitter Lake

Ausim
LETOPOLIS

Tell Hisn
HELIOPOLIS

Old Cairo
BABYLON

Tura

Mit Rahina
MEMPHIS

ITJTAWY?

Birket Qarun

Medinet el-Faiyum
KROKODILOPOLIS

Maidum

el-Lahun?

Ihnasya el-Medina
HERAKLEOPOLIS MAGNA 23

el-Hiba
ANKYRONON POLIS

el-Hiba: 21st Dynasty and later frontier post between the Theban area and the territory of the kings of the north

el-Kom el-Ahmar Sawaris

el-Bahnasa
OXYRYNCHUS

Bahriya Oasis

Tihna el-Gebel
AKORIS

Gulf of Suez

el-Ashmunein
HERMOPOLIS MAGNA 23

Farafra Oasis c.60km
Part of Theban territory

el-'Araba el-Madfuna
ABYDOS

Theban area subject to Piye before 730. Tefnakhte's conquest of the area from Memphis to Hermopolis Magna was the occasion for Piye's campaign

el-Dakhla Oasis

Luxor
THEBES 25 (23)

el-Kharga Oasis

ELEPHANTINE

Legend:
- 22nd Dynasty (Tanis)
- Princes of Dynasties 22–23
- "Great chiefs of the Ma(shwesh)"
- Realm of the West (Sais)
- disputed or uncertain areas
- Herakleopolitan territory
- Hermopolitan territory
- Theban territory

- ■ cities stated to have been taken by Tefnakhte before 730
- □ cities listed with their rulers in the victory stela of Piye
- ▣ towns taken by Piye
- □ other city
- SAIS 24 capital with dynasty number
- Tihna modern name
- MEMPHIS classical name
- ITJTAWY ancient name

scale 1 : 3 700 000

0 —— 100 km

0 —— 75 mi

from this area, but the main reason for the move was probably that the economic and international center of the country had shifted into the delta. Relatively few standing monuments are preserved, so less is known of the history of the Late Period than of the New Kingdom.

Ramesses II was succeeded by his 13th son Merneptah (c. 1213–1204). Merneptah fought in the western delta against invading Libyans and "Sea Peoples"—groups with names that suggest origins around the Mediterranean seaboard. The battle went against the invaders: some fled, while others were forcibly settled as prisoners of war.

The first king of the 20th Dynasty, Sethnakhte (c. 1190–1187), referred in an inscription to a period of civil war that lasted into the second year of his own reign and ended with his defeat of the rebels. The next king, Ramesses III (c. 1187–1156), inherited a stable country but was pressed from the west and north by Libyan invasions and by a renewed attack of the Sea Peoples. All of these were defeated, and Egypt also retained control of Sinai and southern Palestine.

The achievements of Ramesses III were not equalled by his successors. In 90 years there were eight more kings called Ramesses, all apparently descended from Ramesses III and all competing for the throne.

Records of the 19th and especially the 20th Dynasty show a significant long-term change: a high proportion of land passed to temples, in particular that of Amon-Re' at Karnak, which eventually acquired virtual control of Upper Egypt. Major priestly offices became hereditary, and largely independent of the king, so the high priests formed a succession that came to rival him.

During the reign of Ramesses XI (c. 1104–1075) the viceroy of Nubia, Panehsy, fought a long battle for the Theban area, which he lost. After his intervention, the previous line of high priests disappeared from office, and a military man, Herihor, replaced them in Ramesses' year 19. Herihor enhanced his status beyond that of his predecessors, having himself portrayed as king in the Karnak temple complex and using an alternative dating system, which probably alludes to the presence of two "kings" in the country. After only five years Herihor died. His successor Pi'ankh also predeceased Ramesses XI, but the virtual partition of the country was established, setting the pattern for the next period.

Third Intermediate Period

Ramesses XI was succeeded by Smendes (c. 1075–1050), the first king of the 21st Dynasty, and Pi'ankh by Pinudjem I. The new dynasty ruled from Tanis in the northeastern delta and controlled the country as far south as el-Hiba.

The Nile valley from el-Hiba to Aswan was controlled by the Theban high priests, who acknowledged the Tanite kings, dated by their regnal years, and intermarried with their family, but ruled a separate domain. The Thebans, many of whom were ethnically Libyan, harked back to their military origins. Libyans were also active in the north—their chief area of settlement—and Osorkon I (c. 985–978), the little-known fifth king of the Tanite Dynasty, bore a Libyan name. The last king, Psusennes II (c. 960–945), probably also held the office of high

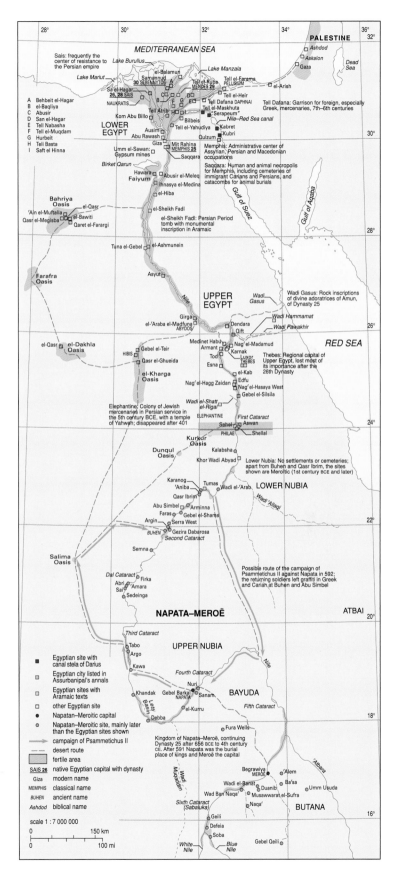

◀ *(page 45) This map shows Egypt in the Late Period (712 BCE–4th century CE). It shows the route of the Nubian campaign under Psammetichus II in 592 BCE and the Nile–Red Sea canal, begun by Necho II and finished by Darius I.*

priest of Amun, uniting the two realms in his person but not making them a single unit.

Shoshenq I (c. 945–925), the first king of the 22nd Dynasty, belonged to a Libyan family from Bubastis (Tell Basta). He exploited the simultaneous extinction of the line of high priests to install his son in Thebes, attempting to centralize Egypt, as did some of his successors. But although there was never a fully independent ruler of Thebes, the region was not integrated with the north for another 300 years. Shoshenq's reign brought an increase in prosperity that is visible in renewed building activity. He also revived relations with Byblos, Egypt's traditional Phoenician trading partner.

After nearly a century of internal peace, the 22nd Dynasty from the reign of Takelot II (c. 860–835) was a period of conflict and decline. The first cause of unrest was the appointment of Takelot's heir, Osorkon, as high priest of Amun. Osorkon was rejected by the Thebans, and a civil war followed.

Beginning with the reign of Shoshenq III (c. 835–785), who may have usurped a throne that had been destined for his brother, the high priest Osorkon, the kingship became split. The first rival was Pedubaste I (c. 830–805) of what is conventionally termed the 23rd Dynasty, who was recognized alongside Shoshenq III. From this time on, the way was open for powerful local rulers to call themselves kings and to be accepted when this suited the local elites. By the late 8th century there were numerous kings in the country, with the 22nd–25th Dynasties ruling simultaneously. After 770 an important force joined the melee. A Nubian king Kashta (c. 770–750), whose capital was at Napata near the fourth cataract, was accepted as a ruler as far north as Thebes, marking the arrival of the 25th Dynasty in Egypt.

While kingship weakened, so also did the high priesthood of Amun. Osorkon IV of the 23rd Dynasty (c. 775–750) installed his daughter Shepenwepet in an old Theban office with the title "Divine Adoratrice of Amun." From this time on the adoratrice, who passed on her office by "adoption," was a member of a royal family and the chief religious figure in the Theban area. The 23rd-Dynasty control of the office was short-lived. Shepenwepet adopted Amenirdis I, a sister of Kashta, who had presumably been imposed on her by Kashta's brother and successor Piye (c. 750–715).

In the late 8th century the most important factions in Egypt were the ancestors of the 24th Dynasty, who were local rulers in Sais in the western delta, and the 25th Dynasty. Around 730 they came into conflict. Piye set out from Napata on a campaign through Egypt as far as Memphis to extract submission from local rulers, in particular Tefnakhte of Sais. Tefnakhte was in theory forced to submit, but he did not come to Piye in person. The affair had little deep impact, because Piye returned to Napata without making himself the sole king of Egypt.

Late Period

At the beginning of the reign of Piye's successor Shabaka (c. 715–700), the conflict between Napata and Sais was renewed. The 24th-Dynasty King Bocchoris (c. 722–715) was killed in battle between the two powers. Shabaka's victory disposed of all the other kings in the country but did not alter the political structure greatly; local rulers remained largely independent and were indeed called "kings" in the records of the Assyrian invasion of Egypt 40 years later. From Shabaka's reign on, the Nubians took a far greater interest in Egypt, making

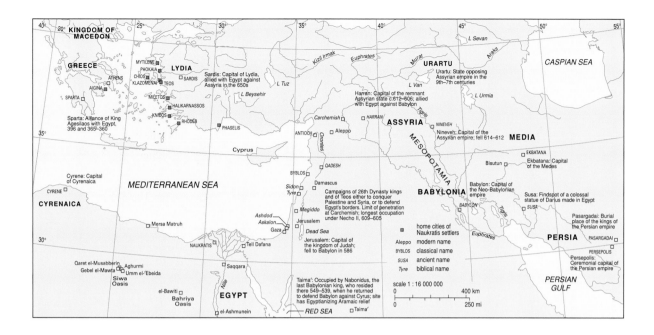

The following text labels appear on the map:

40° 20° 25° 30° 35° 40° 45° 50° 55°

KINGDOM OF MACEDON

GREECE

MYTILENE
PHOKAIA
CHIOS
KLAZOMENAI TEOS
ATHENS
AIGINA
SPARTA
MILETOS
KNIDOS
HALIKARNASSOS
RHODES
PHASELIS

LYDIA
Sardis: Capital of Lydia, allied with Egypt against Assyria in the 650s
SARDIS

L Tuz
L Beyshir

Sparta: Alliance of King Agesilaos with Egypt, 396 and 365–360

35°

Cyrene: Capital of Cyrenaica
CYRENE

CYRENAICA

MEDITERRANEAN SEA

Mersa Matruh

Qaret el-Musabberin
Gebel el-Mawta
Aghurmi
Umm el-'Ebeida
Siwa Oasis

30°

el-Bawiti
Bahriya Oasis

NAUKRATIS
Tell Dafana
Saqqara

EGYPT

el-Ashmunein
Nile
RED SEA

Cyprus

BYBLOS
Sidon
Tyre
Ashdod
Askalon
Gaza
Megiddo
Jerusalem
Dead Sea

Damascus
QADESH
Campaigns of 26th Dynasty kings and of Teos either to conquer Palestine and Syria, or to defend Egypt's borders. Limit of penetration at Carchemish; longest occupation under Necho II, 609–605

Jerusalem: Capital of the kingdom of Judah; fell to Babylon in 586

Orontes
ANTIOCH
Aleppo
Carchemish
HARRAN

Kizil Irmak
Euphrates

Harran: Capital of the remnant Assyrian state c.612–506; allied with Egypt against Babylon

ASSYRIA
NINEVEH
Nineveh: Capital of the Assyrian empire; fell 614–612

Murat
L Van
Tigris

URARTU
Urartu: State opposing Assyrian empire in the 9th–7th centuries

L Sevan
Araks
L Urmia

CASPIAN SEA

MEDIA

EKBATANA
Ekbatana: Capital of the Medes
Bisutun

MESOPOTAMIA

BABYLONIA
BABYLON
Babylon: Capital of the Neo-Babylonian empire

Euphrates
Tigris

SUSA
Susa: Findspot of a colossal statue of Darius made in Egypt

Pasargadai: Burial place of the kings of the Persian empire

PERSIA
PASARGADAI
PERSEPOLIS
Persepolis: Ceremonial capital of the Persian empire

PERSIAN GULF

home cities of Naukratis settlers

Aleppo   modern name
BYBLOS   classical name
SUSA   ancient name
Tyre   biblical name

Taima': Occupied by Nabonidus, the last Babylonian king, who resided there 549–539, when he returned to defend Babylon against Cyrus; site has Egyptianizing Aramaic relief

Taima'

scale 1 : 16 000 000
0   400 km
0   250 mi

▲ *A map showing Egypt, the Aegean, and the Near East in the Late Period. The map shows Egypt's neighbors in the region, from Cyrenaica and Greece in the east to Media and Persia in the west.*

Memphis their capital and residing in the country for some of the time. The half-century of Nubian rule produced as many monuments in Upper Egypt as the previous two centuries, and accelerated an existing artistic revival inspired by earlier periods.

Under Shebitku (c. 700–690) and Taharqa (c. 690–664), the economic improvement continued. In Thebes, Shebitku's sister Shepenwepet II was adopted by Amenirdis I, and members of the Nubian royal family held high religious offices. Under Taharqa, Shepenwepet II adopted Amenirdis II. Power in the area, however, lay with one or two local families. The most important person in Thebes was Montemhet, the fourth priest of Amun and "prince of the city," who was the effective ruler of much of Upper Egypt and survived well into the 26th Dynasty.

The unified Egyptian and Nubian state was a major power, whose only rival in the Near East was Assyria, which had been expanding since the 9th century. The Assyrian king Esarhaddon (681–669) attempted to conquer Egypt in 674, but was repulsed. A renewed attack in 671 was successful; Memphis was

taken and the country forced to pay tribute. Taharqa fled south but returned within two years to retake Memphis. Esarhaddon died on the way to Egypt for a counterattack, and the next campaign was sent by his son Assurbanipal (669–627) in about 667. Assurbanipal used the ruler of Sais, Necho I (before 672–664), and his son, the later King Psammetichus I, as his chief agents in re-establishing Assyrian rule. In 664, Tantamani (664–657 in Egypt, possibly later in Nubia) succeeded Taharqa and mounted a campaign as far as the delta. The local rulers accepted Tantamani fairly readily.

Sometime between 663 and 657, Assurbanipal led a campaign of reprisal, plundering as far south as Thebes, while Tantamani fled to Nubia. However, Assurbanipal had to turn his attention to a rebellion in Babylon. Consequently, Psammetichus I (664–610) was able to make himself completely independent before 653. Between 664 and 657, Psammetichus I eliminated all the local rulers in Lower Egypt, and in 656 he had his daughter Nitocris adopted by Shepenwepet II as the

future divine adoratrice in Thebes, bypassing Amenirdis II.

Psammetichus I's campaigns of unification were significant in another way. He was the first king to use Greek and Carian mercenaries, setting the pattern for more than 300 years. With the reunification of Egypt, and the imposition of a central administration in place of local rulers, prosperity resumed in the 25th and 26th Dynasties.

Policy of the 26th Dynasty toward West Asia aimed to maintain a balance of power by supporting the rivals of whichever major power was dominant. Thus Psammetichus I supported Lydia in Anatolia and later Babylon against Assyria until Assyria declined after 620, when he reversed his

◀ *Greco-Egyptian terracotta statuettes of the Egyptian protective dwarf god Bes (far left) holding a knife and Roman shield, and Horus the Child (Herakles-Harpokrates; left) seated on a goose.*

allegiance. In the 6th century, Egypt continued to support the enemies of Babylon until Persia had become the main power. Necho II (610–595), Psammetichus II (595–589), and Apries (589–570) moved over to attack. Necho II, probably continuing a campaign begun by Psammetichus prior to his death, campaigned in Syria from 610 to 605, but had to withdraw. In 601 he repulsed an attack by the Babylonian King Nebuchadnezzar II (604–562) on Egypt.

Psammetichus II made a single expedition to Asia, with no apparent long-term effects. His most significant political act, however, was a major campaign to Nubia in 592, which brought an end to 60 years of peaceful relations. The invading army reached Napata. On the return journey, the foreign soldiers left graffiti at Buhen and Abu Simbel in Lower Nubia; the course of the campaign has been reconstructed from these. After 592, the memory of the 25th-Dynasty kings was persecuted in Egypt.

In 595, the divine adoratrice of Amun, Nitocris, who must have been in her seventies, adopted Psammetichus II's daughter 'Ankhnesneferibre' as her successor. 'Ankhnesneferibre' took office in 586, and was still alive in 525. Thus for 130 years only two women represented the royal family in Thebes.

In 570, Apries sent an all-Egyptian army to support a local Libyan ruler in Cyrene in a struggle against Greek colonists. The army was defeated and then mutinied. Apries sent a general, Amasis, to quell the revolt, but he joined it, declared himself king (570–526), and drove Apries into exile. Around 567,

▲ Cleopatra on the Terraces of Philae (1896) by the American artist Frederick Arthur Bridgman. Cleopatra is shown preparing for her departure by boat from the idyllic island of Philae. The Kiosk of Trajan can be seen in the far left background. On display at the Dahesh Museum of Art, New York.

▶ Land reclamation in the Faiyam during the Greco-Roman Period made this one of the most prosperous area of Greek agricultural settlement.

Apries returned with a Babylonian army sent by Nebuchadnezzar II but was defeated and killed. Amasis buried him with royal honors.

Amasis' reign ended in the shadow of the growing power of Persia, but it was his short-lived successor Psammetichus III (526–525) who faced the successful Persian invasion. Cambyses (525–522), the first ruler of the 27th Dynasty, was also the first outsider whose main interest was not to become king. He undertook campaigns through Egypt to Nubia and to the western oasis of Siwa, but both failed. Darius I (521–486) followed a more conciliatory line, commissioning buildings and completing Necho II's Nile–Red Sea canal. Until it silted up, the canal provided a direct sea link between Persia and Egypt. Darius' reign was prosperous, but the Egyptians tolerated Persian rule only so long as there was no real chance of throwing it off. The Persian defeat at the battle of Marathon in Greece in 490

signaled the beginning of 80 years of resistance, in which Egyptian rebels traded grain with Greek states in return for military aid. The western delta was the center of revolts; Persian rule was more easily maintained in the Nile valley, which could be reached by the Red Sea or canal routes.

In 404, Amyrtaios of Sais (404–399) freed the delta from Persian rule, and by 400 the entire country was in his hands. Like some earlier rebels against the Persians, he styled himself king, but unlike them he became part of the official listing as the sole ruler of the 28th Dynasty. In 399, Nepherites I of Mendes (399–393) usurped the throne, founding the 29th Dynasty. He, Psammuthis (393), and Hakoris (393–380) built at many sites and with the help of Greek mercenaries warded off a Persian attack in 385–383.

Nectanebo I (380–362), a general from Sebennytos in the delta, usurped the throne from Nepherites II (380) and founded the

50

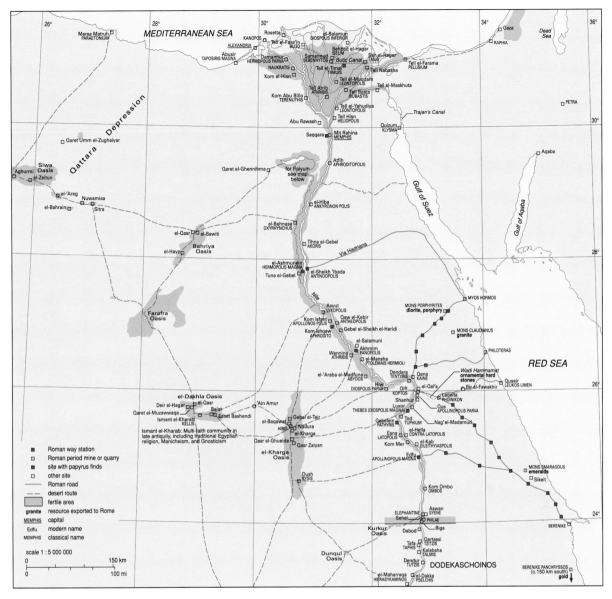

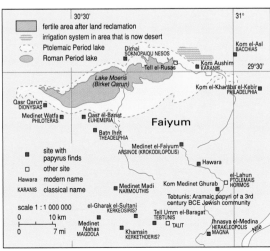

30th Dynasty. The dynasty was a time of prosperity, with widespread building. In 373, a Persian invasion was defeated, and in the 360s Nectanebo joined an alliance of Persian provinces. His successor, Teos (365–360), went on the offensive in Palestine but was betrayed by a rebellion in which his cousin, Nectanebo II, was placed on the throne, and by the defection of his Spartan ally to the new king.

▲ *A map showing Egypt during the Greco-Roman Period. The Roman way-stations were built along roads that led to the Red Sea ports, which were important trade links with East Africa and India.*

► *A map showing the maximum extent of Ptolemaic possessions in Egypt and the east Mediterranean during the reigns of Ptolemy III, Euergetes I, and IV Philopator. Almost all were lost before 30 BCE, by which time the entire area shown was taken into the Roman empire.*

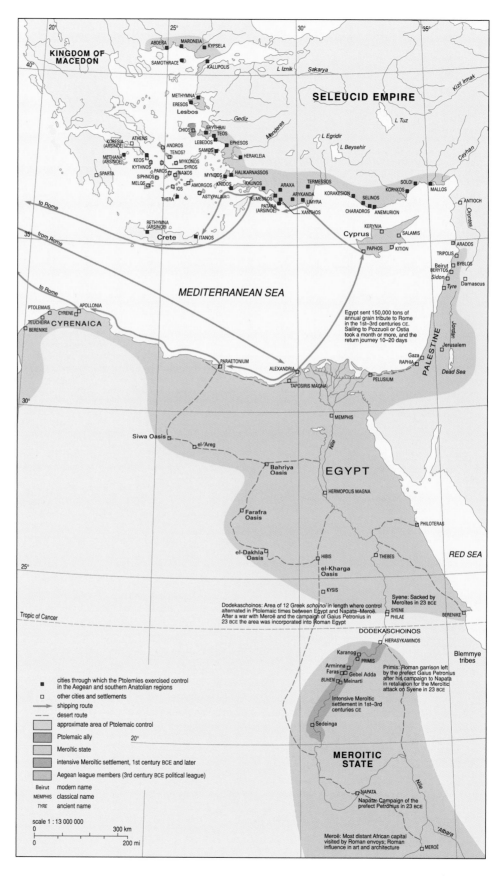

KINGDOM OF MACEDON

SELEUCID EMPIRE

ABDERA
MARONEIA
KYPSELA
SAMOTHRACE
KALLIPOLIS
L. Iznik
Sakarya
Kizil Irmak

METHYMNA
ERESOS
Lesbos
Gediz
L. Tuz
Menderes

CHIOS
ERYTHRAI
TEOS
L. Egridir
Ceyhan
ATHENS
LEBEDOS
EPHESOS
L. Beysehir
KORESIA (ARSINOE?)
ANDROS
SAMOS
HERAKLEIA
TENOS?
MYKONOS
METHANA (ARSINOE)
KEOS
SYROS
MYNDOS
HALIKARNASSOS
SPARTA
KYTHNOS
PAROS
NAXOS
SIPHNOS
MELOS
AMORGOS
KNIDOS
KAUNOS
ARAXA
TERMESSOS
KORAKESION
SOLOI
KORYKOS
MALLOS
IOS
ASTYPALAIA
TELMESSOS
ARYKANDA
SELINOS
ANTIOCH
THERA
PATARA (ARSINOE)
LIMYRA
CHARADROS
ANEMURION
Orontes
RETHYMNA (ARSINOE)
XANTHOS
KERYNIA
ARADOS
from Rome
Crete
ITANOS
Cyprus
SALAMIS
TRIPOLIS
to Rome
PAPHOS
KITION
Beirut
BYBLOS
BERYTOS
Sidon
Damascus
Tyre

MEDITERRANEAN SEA

Egypt sent 150,000 tons of annual grain tribute to Rome in the 1st–3rd centuries CE. Sailing to Pozzuoli or Ostia took a month or more, and the return journey 10–20 days

to Rome
PTOLEMAIS
APOLLONIA
CYRENE
TEUCHEIRA
CYRENAICA
BERENIKE
Jerusalem
Gaza
PALESTINE
RAPHIA
Jordan
PARAETONIUM
Dead Sea
ALEXANDRIA
PELUSIUM
TAPOSIRIS MAGNA

MEMPHIS

Siwa Oasis
el-'Areg
Nile
Bahriya Oasis
EGYPT
HERMOPOLIS MAGNA
Farafra Oasis
PHILOTERAS
RED SEA
el-Dakhla Oasis
HIBIS
THEBES
el-Kharga Oasis

Tropic of Cancer
KYSIS
Syene: Sacked by Meroïtes in 23 BCE
SYENE
BERENIKE
Dodekaschoinos: Area of 12 Greek *schoinoi* in length where control alternated in Ptolemaic times between Egypt and Napata–Meroë. After a war with Meroë and the campaign of Gaius Petronius in 23 BCE the area was incorporated into Roman Egypt
PHILAE
DODEKASCHOINOS
HIERASYKAMINOS
Blemmye tribes
Karanog
PRIMIS
Arminna
Primis: Roman garrison left by the prefect Gaius Petronius after his campaign to Napata in retaliation for the Meroïtic attack on Syene in 23 BCE
Faras
Gebel Adda
BUHEN
Meinarti
Intensive Meroïtic settlement in 1st–3rd centuries CE
Sedeinga
MEROITIC STATE
NAPATA
Napata: Campaign of the prefect Petronius in 23 BCE
'Atbara
Meroë: Most distant African capital visited by Roman envoys; Roman influence in art and architecture
MEROE

■ cities through which the Ptolemies exercised control in the Aegean and southern Anatolian regions
□ other cities and settlements
→ shipping route
--- desert route
　 approximate area of Ptolemaic control
　 Ptolemaic ally
　 Meroïtic state
　 intensive Meroïtic settlement, 1st century BCE and later
　 Aegean league members (3rd century BCE political league)

Beirut　modern name
MEMPHIS　classical name
TYRE　ancient name

scale 1 : 13 000 000
0　　　　　300 km
0　　　　200 mi

Nectanebo II withstood an invasion by the Persian Artaxerxes III Ochus in 350, but the attack of 343 was successful. The ten-year Second Persian Period (also called the 31st Dynasty) was oppressive and predisposed the country toward almost any alternative.

Greco-Roman Period

In 332 BCE, the Macedonian Greek Alexander the Great took control of Egypt, apparently without a struggle. At his death Ptolemy, son of Lagos, succeeded in acquiring Egypt as his satrapy. In 305–304, he followed the lead of other satraps and made himself the independent king of Egypt.

For the next 250 years, Egypt was ruled by Macedonian Greeks as a separate country with its own interests to pursue. The reigns of the first three Ptolemies were a period of development for Egypt, in which the country was brought into the Hellenistic world in terms of agriculture, commerce, and, for the Greek population, education.

The chief development was, however, foreign: the building of Alexandria, which became the leading city in the Greek world. In later parlance Alexandria was "adjoining," not "in," Egypt. By acting as a magnet for the country's wealth, and as the kings' chief concern, it restricted expansion in other areas, especially because of its location in the extreme northwest.

The 2nd century was a time of decline in the economy and of political strife. Within the ruling family there were conspiracies, while native revolts in Upper Egypt were common from the reign of Ptolemy IV Philopator (221–205 BCE) onward. Egypt lost most of its foreign dependencies, and was conquered by the Seleucid Antiochus IV Epiphanes, who was briefly proclaimed king in 168. In the 1st century the weakness of

government continued, working in some ways to the native population's advantage. But the overshadowing force of Rome doomed Ptolemaic and Egyptian independence.

During the first century or so of Roman rule (after 30 BCE), prosperity increased. Improved administration was aimed at securing wealth for Rome more than developing Egypt for its own sake, and excessive taxation and official coercion were serious. Some emperors, most notably Hadrian (117–138 CE), showed a special regard for Egypt, but new policies were not directed toward the benefit of the local Greek population, let alone the Egyptian (the two groups were kept more sharply separate than in Ptolemaic times). Unlike other provinces of the empire, Egypt was not granted significant local autonomy but was administered by a prefect under the emperor's direct jurisdiction.

Native Egyptian temples continued to be built in the Roman Period, with the long reign of the first emperor Augustus (30 BCE–14 CE) marking a peak of activity. Few new temples were constructed after the 1st century CE, perhaps in part because of economic difficulties, but the decoration of existing ones continued, even keeping up with the struggles for the imperial throne in the names used in cartouches. The latest inscription in hieroglyphs dates to 394 CE, while Egyptian demotic literary texts, as well as some documents, were common as late as the 3rd century.

The force that finally destroyed traditional Egyptian culture and led to the mutilation of traditional monuments was not Roman rule but Christianity. The notional end of ancient Egyptian history in 395 CE is the date of the final separation of the Roman Empire, by then strongly Christian, into east (Byzantine) and west; Egypt belonged with the east.

Art and Architecture

Egyptian representational art forms—sculpture in the round, relief, and painting—acquired a distinctive appearance by the beginning of the Dynastic Period. At the same time the level of work in decorative and functional art forms, such as painted patterning, stone vase manufacture, ivory carving, furniture making, and metalwork, was very high, while architecture evolved rapidly from then on, continuing to develop as new materials were mastered and new forms introduced. From the beginning, works of art in a wide range of genres are the most important single legacy from ancient Egypt.

Relief and painting

Relief achieves its effect through modeling, light and shade, while painting works with line and color. Relief can be raised or sunk, the latter being a characteristically Egyptian form. In raised relief the surface surrounding the figures is removed to the depth of a few millimeters, so that they stand out against it; in sunk relief the outlines of the figures are incised in the surface, which is then left, and the figures are modeled within it. Raised relief was generally used indoors, and sunk relief, which shows up better in the Sun, out of doors. Major religious buildings and the finer private tombs were decorated in relief. Although painting was second best, great works were created in the medium.

Egyptian writing and art are closely linked. Hieroglyphs are themselves pictures, whose conventions are not very different from those of representation. Most pictures contain hieroglyphic texts, which may comment on the scene or can dominate the visual component, as in some temple reliefs.

Methods of representation

Egyptian representation is not based on either of the two main principles of perspective: the use of foreshortening; and the adoption of a single, unified viewpoint for an entire picture. Instead, figures are rather like diagrams of what they show, whose aim is to convey information rather than a representational view.

When composing scenes and whole walls, the figures stand on horizontal lines, called base lines, which may represent the ground but more often do not and are spaced at intervals up the wall. Examples of the much less frequent "map" method of composition are plans of houses and areas of desert. The outline that defines the map may also serve as a base line for figures.

A vital characteristic of all Egyptian representation is the treatment of scale. Within a figure the parts are shown in their natural proportions, but compositions are organized by scale around main figures. The more important the figure, the larger it is.

Statuary

Almost all major statues show a figure that looks straight ahead in a line at right angles to the plane of the shoulders, with the limbs constrained within the same planes. Mostly it stands at rest or is seated. The chief exceptions to rigid geometry are heads that look up slightly, perhaps to see the Sun, or down, in scribe statues, to look at a papyrus unrolled across the lap. Kneeling figures sometimes have flexed calf muscles, presumably showing that their pose is a momentary gesture of deference. Details of this sort are restricted to the finest works.

Techniques in painting, relief, and statuary

In two and in three dimensions, the basis of the artist's work was the preparatory drawing and the laying out of compositions on large surfaces. Squared grids or sets of guidelines were used to ensure accurate representation. Preliminary drawings were then turned into the finished product over several stages of correction and elaboration.

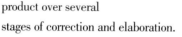

Statuary works started as squared blocks whose main sides served as surfaces for grids and preparatory drawings. The stone was then removed, with the drawing acting as a guide. As work progressed the drawings were renewed again and again. As in relief, the final stages involved smoothing the surface to remove tool marks and applying paint.

The difficulty of carving varied greatly with the material, but the Egyptians mastered most substances. For large works, technical problems turned into ones of engineering. The first stages had more in common with quarrying than with art. Such statues were probably roughed out before transport, to lighten the load, and completed at the destination. Moving them involved specially constructed roads and ships, and extensive earthworks for the final siting.

Architecture

Religious buildings form the vast majority of surviving works of architecture. Almost all were symbolic as well as narrowly functional. The symbolism in mortuary buildings—

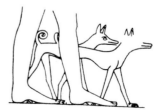

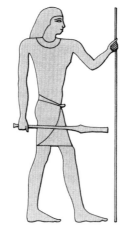

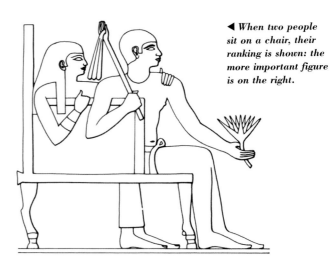

◀ *When two people sit on a chair, their ranking is shown: the more important figure is on the right.*

pyramids, mastabas, and rock-cut tombs—is probably similar to that of the temples: they recreate the cosmos or part of it. The aim is to make the inhabitant partake symbolically in the process of creation itself or in the cosmic cycles, in particular that of the Sun. This symbolism is expressed in the siting and design of temples and in the decoration of walls and ceilings. The structure is set apart from the outside world by a massive mud-brick enclosure wall built in undulating courses that may mimic the watery state of the cosmos at creation. Within this is the main pylon or entrance wall, which is the largest element in the temple. The theoretical orientation of most temples is east–west (this relates to the Nile, so there is considerable varation), so that the Sun "rises" in the pylon gateway, sending its rays into the sanctuary.

The most imposing part of the main temple is the hypostyle or columned hall, which conveniently summarizes the decorative scheme of the whole. The column capitals show aquatic plants, and the lowest register of the walls has similar plants in relief; symbolically the hall is the marsh of creation. The architraves and ceiling have reliefs of the sky, so that the decoration encompasses

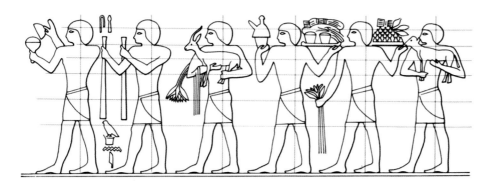

◀ *Egyptian artists used grids to plan reliefs and paintings; this early scheme uses six horizontal guidelines to define the proportions of the body.*

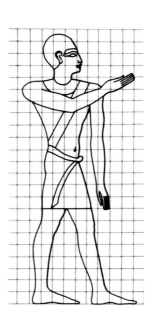

◀ *Over time, artists moved from a grid that measured 18 squares from the ground to the hairline (left) to one that measured 21 squares up to the eyes (right).*

▼ *A grid system was also used for drawing animals, such as this ox.*

the whole world. What is shown on the walls is the activity of this world. The lowest register may contain offering bearers who do duty for the king in bringing the produce of the land to provide for the temple. Neither is part of the more abstract main scheme, which consists of several registers of scenes, arranged like a checkerboard, showing the king, who faces in toward the sanctuary, making offerings to and performing rituals for the god. The god, who takes up residence in the temple, faces outward; the deities shown in the reliefs are a wider range than that worshiped in any one temple. Many scenes

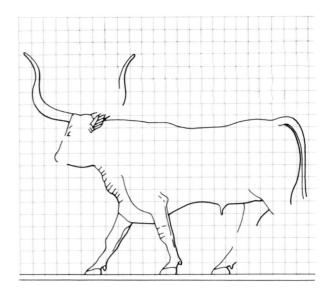

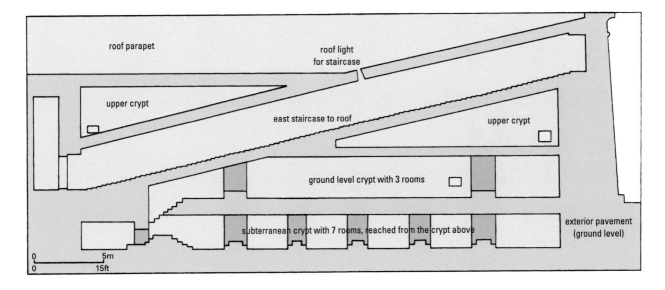

roof parapet

roof light
for staircase

upper crypt

upper crypt

east staircase to roof

ground level crypt with 3 rooms

subterranean crypt with 7 rooms, reached from the crypt above

exterior pavement
(ground level)

0   5m
0   15ft

*▲ A section of
the east wall of the
Temple of Dendara
(1st century BCE).
The temple's thick
wall encloses a suites
of rooms, or crypts,
and a staircase to
the roof. The squares
in the ground level
and upper crypts are
access holes from
within the temple.*

show rituals performed in the temple. In terms of the temple, the give and take between king and god is the focus of the world's activities. Most of the reliefs in the temple are of the same general character.

A number of smaller rooms surround the sanctuary, whose outside wall mimics the outside of a temple, forming a structure within a structure. The sanctuary represents the mound of creation, and relates to the marsh of the hypostyle hall; in passing toward the sanctuary a procession went through the stages of creation and renewal.

Techniques

Little is known of how the surveying of sites was done. The foundations of even sizable structures were often surprisingly meager, consisting of nothing more than a trench filled with sand and topped with a few courses of rough stonework. Only in the Greco-Roman Period were there regularly massive foundations of proper masonrys.

In masonry mortar was used very sparingly. The technique was to lay a course of blocks, level it along the top, coat the surface with a thin layer of mortar whose prime purpose was to act as a lubricant, and maneuver the next

course into position. Each block was fitted individually to the next, since the rising joints were not always vertical, or at right angles to the surface. A single block could even form an internal corner, and the levels of the horizontal courses might be maintained only for a short distance. Wooden cramps were often set into the horizontal joints behind the surface to provide extra rigidity or to prevent slippage while the mortar was setting. The main purpose of the complex jointing techniques was probably to minimize wasting stone and to use the largest size of block possible.

The Egyptians probably worked without mechanical lifting devices; the basic method of raising weights was to bury the wall that was being built behind a rubble ramp. This was added to continually until the walls reached their full height. The stones were then dressed smooth, either from the ramps as they were dismantled, or from wooden scaffolding, which was probably used later for carving the relief decoration. Several stages of work proceeded simultaneously, so that stonemasons, plasterers, draftsmen, relief carvers, and painters could all be employed together.

*▶ A gilt wood
statuette of the 18th
Dynasty king
Tut'ankhamun
(c. 1332–1322 BCE)
on a papyrus raft
with a harpoon.*

JOURNEY ON THE NILE

The land of Egypt has been likened to a lotus, with the flower of the delta in the north, the bud of the Faiyum nestling close by, and the long, thin stalk of the Nile valley running from south to north. The surrounding areas, with the exception of the chain of oases running parallel to the river on the west, were arid and unsuitable for settled habitation.

Two cities played very important roles in Egyptian history until the scene shifted north during the 19th Dynasty: Memphis, close to the apex of the delta, and Thebes, its counterbalance in the south. These provide two of the points at which we break our imaginary boat journey down the Nile through ancient Egypt—the first cataract in the south is our logical point of departure.

Nubia, the oases, and Sinai, though never fully recognized as parts of ancient Egypt, were colonized, in the case of the first two, and frequented, in the case of the third, to the extent that their inclusion is essential. Going upstream into Nubia is, however, a different proposition from sailing gently down the Nile, and a donkey must replace our boat for the journeys into the oases and Sinai.

◀ *Sailing boats like these near Aswan are still used for transportation on the Nile.*

Boats on the Nile

Before we begin our journey, it is worth becoming familiar with the most important means of transportation in ancient Egypt: the boat. Gographically, it is hard to imagine a more extreme form of land than that of Egypt: long and narrow, it is similar to a sprawling town bestriding a highway. The advantage of this distribution was ease of communication, because the Nile connected all important localities. The boat was the most important means of transportation. Northerly winds prevailed in the Nile valley which allowed boats to sail up the river; downstream traffic heading north, however, had to rely on oars.

The earliest craft were rafts, which were cheap and easily replaceable. As the next pages show, however, Egyptian boats soon evolved and became more complicated—and more efficient for their purpose.

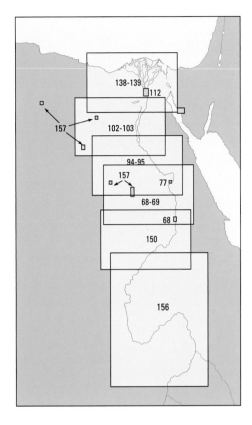

◀ Our journey begins in Southern Upper Egypt (page 68) and we travel north toward the Delta (page 138). The journey ends at Nubia (page 150) and the peripheral regions (page 156).

▼ Boats were so important to Egyptian life that the hieroglyph meaning "to travel north" showed oars, while that for traveling south showed a boat with its sail up.

▼ On this New Kingdom boat, a helmsman stands in front of two rudder oars used for steering; the boat has two covered watch posts, or castles, and a central deckhouse to protect passengers and crew from the hot sun.

◀ Sailing boats on the Nile at Beni Hasan, in Middle Egypt.

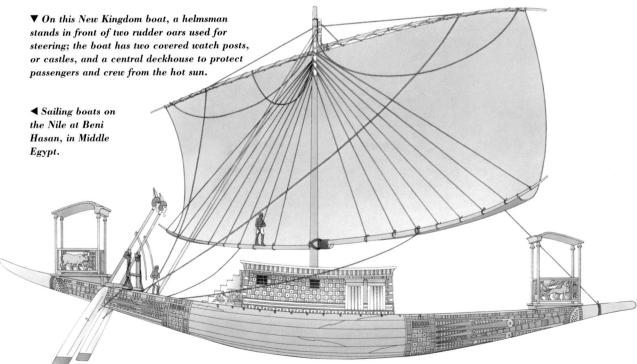

▶ *Rafts made of papyrus stalks lashed together with ropes were the earliest boats on the Nile.*

Our knowledge of ancient Egyptian shipping derives from representational evidence (reliefs and paintings), model boats found in tombs such as that of Tutankhamun, and isolated discoveries of buried funerary boats (at Giza and Dahshur). (Boats were considered important transportation for souls traveling in the Afterlife.) Textual sources are scarce and not every informative. Ancient Egyptian Nile boats varied greatly according to their purpose (traveling boats for passengers, cargo boats, ceremonial barks, and so on.), but a fairly reliable guide to their dating is provided by a combination of the appearance of the hull, the method of steering, the type of the mast and sail, the disposition of the deckhouses, and any unusual features, such as the inclusion of covered castles, or lookout posts. The drawings below, and on the previous page, provide a general guide to the evolution of these features from the Preynastic Period through the Old, Middle, and New Kingdoms to the Late Period.

▼ *This simple design allowed the mast to be raised and lowered for frequent changes from rowing to sailing.*

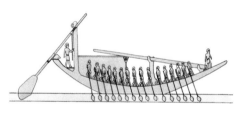

▲ *This Predynastic boat has a sharply upturned prow and stern, and even large Nile craft would have been made of papyrus or similar material. Predynastic vessels had at least one steering oar, a rectangular sail, deckhouse, and two banks of oars.*

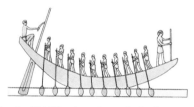

▲ *By the Old Kingdom, boats had taken on a "classical" Egyptian hull, made from wood. The sail was a trapezoid, and was usually taller than it was wide. From the 6th Dynasty, boats began to use specialized steering gear rather than plain steering oars.*

▼ *The main element of the steering gear was a massive rudder oar attached to a rudder post and the boat's stern. The boat was steered by moving the tiller sideways and thus rotating the stock of the rudder oar and its blade.*

tiller   rudder post

stock

blade of the
rudder oar

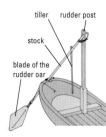

▲ *By the Middle Kingdom, a single helmsman steered the boat from a massive rudder post at the raised stern. In this illustration, the single mast is lowered and supported on a forked stanchion.*

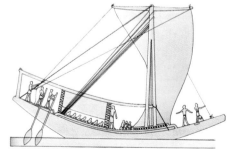

▲ *In the Late Period, the stern tended to grow even higher. By this time, shipbuilding had diverged into a wide range of more specialized vessels.*

The Nile was the lifeline of ancient Egypt. The river provided the means to transport goods from place to place. Settlements located along the waterway grew into centers of trade and finance.

Southern Upper Egypt

Because the Egyptians oriented toward the south, Aswan was the "first" town in the country north of the actual frontier at Biga Island.

The southernmost part of Egypt falls into the natural divisions of the 1st Upper Egyptian nome, from Biga to north of Gebel el-Silsila, and the 2nd–4th nomes as far as Thebes. The two are roughly equal in length along the river, but the former belongs to the sandstone belt of Nubia and is forbidding, infertile country, dominated by the desert and rich in minerals.

Kom el-Ahmar was one of the earliest urban centers, but declined in importance during the historical period. Probably became of the dominant position of Thebes, the districts to the south were included in the Viceroy of Nubia's territory during the New Kingdom. In this stretch of the river the valley is relatively narrow, and could not support as large an area as the Theban area. There are, however, desert routes for trade and mining expeditions to east and west that were significant at most periods.

As befits its early importance, Southern Upper Egypt has numerous Predynastic and Early Dynastic sites. The best-represented later periods are the late Old Kingdom and 1st Intermediate Period, early New Kingdom, and Greco-Roman Period. The most impressive monuments are now probably the chapels and shrines of Gebel el-Silsila and the major Greco-Roman temples, Philae, Kom Ombo, Edfu, and Esna.

Elephantine and Aswan

Elephantine was the capital of the 1st Upper Egyptian nome and a significant frontier post.

The site is strategically located at the north end of the first cataract near many mineral deposits. The area is barren and may have relied on supplies from the north, making its living as a garrison and by trade. The ancient word *swenet*, from which the name *Aswan* derives, means "trade."

Elephantine Island was inhabited at least from late Predynastic times. The core may have been an Early Dynastic fortress near a temple of the goddess Satis. The temple was replaced by larger buildings, culminating in one during the reign of Hatshepsut, which has been re-erected from discarded blocks. A small colonnaded temple of Amenhotep III of similar design was virtually intact around 1820, as was a building of Thutmose III; both have since disappeared. Only the main terrace of the 30th Dynasty temple of Khnum, together with a monumental granite gateway to its inner areas, remain in situ. Greco-Roman period burials of sacred rams of Khnum were excavated in the area of a temple of Alexander IV.

The best-known monument on Elephantine is the Nilometer, a staircase with cubit marks beside it for measuring the height of the inundation, on the east. The levels inscribed on it are of the Roman Period and later.

On the west bank, to the north at Qubbet el-Hawa, are rock-cut tombs of Old Kingdom notables and leaders of expeditions to Nubia, Middle Kingdom nomarchs, and some New Kingdom officials.

The granite rocks south of Aswan and some 3¾ miles (6 km) to the east bear marks of quarrying. Striking remains include an abandoned obelisk and a mummiform colossus. Rock outcrops in the river and

▶ *This map shows the main settlements of southern Upper Egypt, from Lake Nasser in the south to Luxor (Thebes) in the north.*

68

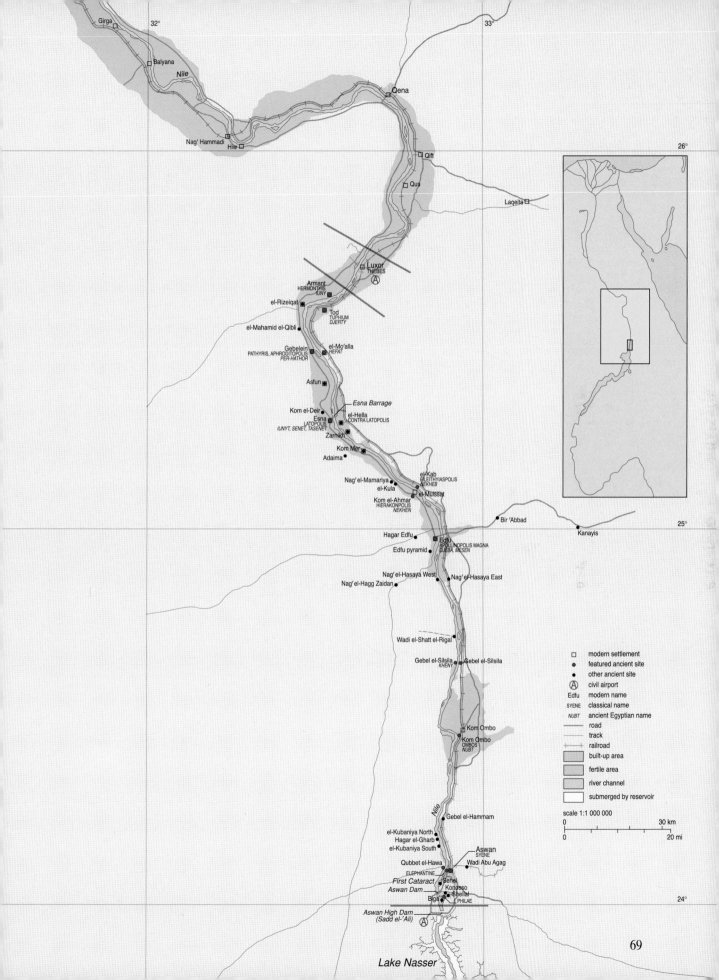

Girga

Balyana

Nile

Nag' Hammadi
Hiw

32°

33°

Qena

Qift

Qus

Laqeita

26°

25°

24°

Luxor
THEBES
Ⓐ

Armant
HERMONTHIS
IUNY

el-Rizeiqat

Tod
TUPHIUM
DJERTY

el-Mahamid el-Qibli

el-Mo'alla
HEFAT

Gebelein
PATHYRIS, APHRODITOPOLIS
PER-HATHOR

Asfun

Esna Barrage

Kom el-Deir
el-Hella
CONTRA LATOPOLIS
Esna
LATOPOLIS
IUNYT, SENET, TASENET
Zarnikh

Kom Mer

Adaima

el-Kab
ELEITHYIASPOLIS
NEKHEB
Nag' el-Mamariya
el-Kula
El-Muissat
Kom el-Ahmar
HIERAKONPOLIS
NEKHEN

Bir 'Abbad

Kanayis

Hagar Edfu
Edfu
APOLLINOPOLIS MAGNA
DJEBA, MESEN
Edfu pyramid

Nag' el-Hasaya West
Nag' el-Hasaya East
Nag' el-Hagg Zaidan

Wadi el-Shatt el-Rigal

Gebel el-Silsila
KHENY
Gebel el-Silsila

Kom Ombo
Kom Ombo
OMBOS
NUBT

Nile

Gebel el-Hammam

el-Kubaniya North
Hagar el-Gharb
el-Kubaniya South

Aswan
SYENE

Qubbet el-Hawa
Wadi Abu Agag
ELEPHANTINE
First Cataract
Sehel
Konosso
Aswan Dam
Shellal
Biga
PHILAE

Aswan High Dam
(Sadd el-'Ali)
Ⓐ

Lake Nasser

☐ modern settlement
● featured ancient site
• other ancient site
Ⓐ civil airport
Edfu modern name
SYENE classical name
NUBT ancient Egyptian name
――― road
――― track
+++++ railroad
▓▓ built-up area
▒▒ fertile area
░░ river channel
☐ submerged by reservoir

scale 1:1 000 000
0   30 km
0   20 mi

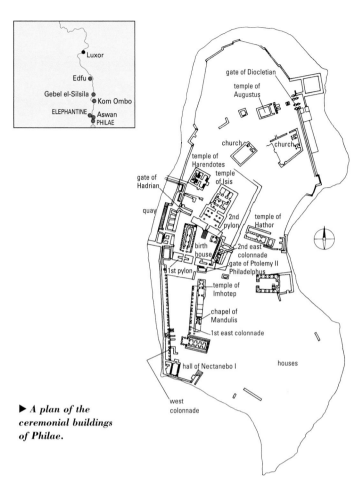

▶ *A plan of the ceremonial buildings of Philae.*

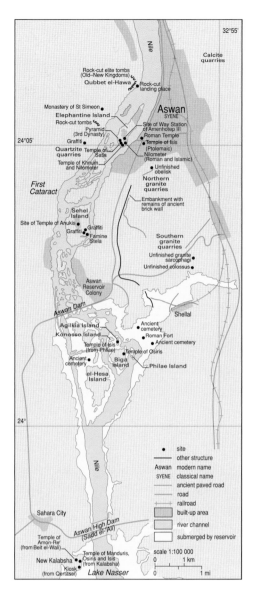

▲ *The original location of ancient sites on the island of Philae. Philae lies submerged for most of the year, so many important monuments have been relocated to nearby Agilkia.*

on land bear ancient graffiti. Few remains survive in Aswan itself. Two small Greco-Roman Period temples probably formed only a fraction of the original sacred area.

Philae

In its setting in the first cataract, the lush island of Philae was the most romantic tourist attraction in 19th century Egypt. The earliest monuments on the site are of the reign of Nectanebo I, but blocks discovered in foundations date back to the reign of Taharqa. On the east were temples dedicated to the Nubian gods Arensnuphis and Mandulis, and a temple of Imhotep, the deified official of the reign of Djoser.

The first part of the temple of Isis is composed of isolated elements. The decoration of is late Ptolemaic and early

Roman. The main temple is smaller than the other great temples of the period. On the roof are chapels dedicated to Osiris. The most notable of the remaining temples is that of Hathor, the mythical goddess who went south into Nubia spreading devastation and had to be pacified by Thoth.

In the 1970s, after the building of the High Dam, the temples on Philae were dismantled and re-erected on the nearby Agilkia.

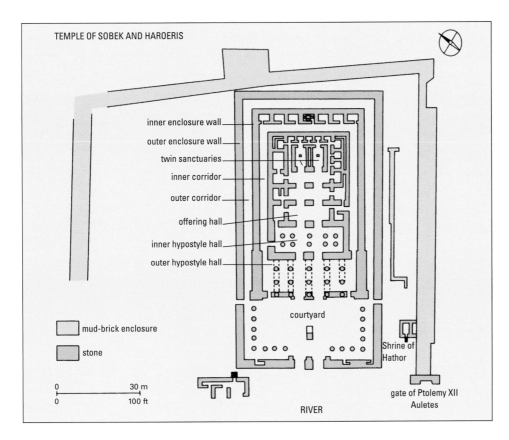

TEMPLE OF SOBEK AND HAROERIS

inner enclosure wall

outer enclosure wall

twin sanctuaries

inner corridor

outer corridor

offering hall

inner hypostyle hall

outer hypostyle hall

courtyard

mud-brick enclosure

stone

Shrine of Hathor

0   30 m

0   100 ft

gate of Ptolemy XII Auletes

RIVER

◄ *A plan of the Temple of Sobek and Haroeris at Kom Ombo. Although the temple dates from the Ptolemaic Period, a mound behind the enclosure contains sherds from the First Intermediate Period, showing that the site is far more ancient than the temple itself.*

Kom Ombo

Kom Ombo stands on a promontory at a bend in the Nile, at the northern end of the largest area of agricultural land south of Gebel el-Silsila. It was prominent in Ptolemaic times, to which almost all the monuments date. The earliest king named in the temple is Ptolemy VI Philometor; most of the decoration was completed by Ptolemy XII Auletes. The temple is dedicated to two triads of deities: Sobek, Hathor, and Khons; and Haroeris (Horus the Elder), Tasenetnofret (the Perfect Companion), and Panebtawy (the Lord of the Two Lands).

Numerous reliefs in the temple's inner corridor and small rooms are unfinished, giving an insight into artists' methods in the Greco-Roman period. Scenes in the outer corridor include a representation of instruments that have generally been assumed to be those of a surgeon.

Gebel el-Silsila

Some 40 miles (65 km) north of Aswan, at Gebel el-Silsila, steep sandstone cliffs narrow the stream and present a natural barrier to river traffic. The rock faces on both sides of the river abound in rock stelae and graffiti. On the west bank is the Great Speos (rock-cut chapel) of Haremhab. The seven deities to whom the chapel was dedicated were represented as seated statues in the niche at the back of the sanctuary, with the local crocodile god Sobek and King Harembab himself among them.

Edfu

The Ptolemaic temple of Horus at Edfu is the most completely preserved in Egypt and a perfect example of Egyptian temple design, although the unusual orientation toward the south may be due to constraints of the site. The building inscriptions, written in

horizontal bands in the outer areas, give numerous details of construction. Building began in 237 BCE (Ptolemy III Euergetes I). The inner part was finished in 212 BCE (Ptolemy IV Philopator) and decorated by 142 BCE (Ptolemy VIII Euergetes II). The outer hypostyle was built separately, being completed, still under Ptolemy VIII, in 124 BCE. Decoration of this and the other outer parts was finished in 57 BCE.

A striking feature of the inner parts is the subtle exploitation of scarce light. Some rooms are completely dark, while elsewhere the light comes from the openings between the columns of the hypostyle hall and from apertures in the roof or at the angle between roof and wall. The general progress is from light to dark, with the sanctuary receiving illumination only from the axis. The effect of all this must have been incomparably richer when the reliefs retained their original colors.

Like other late temples, Edfu was emptied of furniture and equipment when it fell out of use. A fortunate survival is the pair of colossal statues of hawks flanking the entrance and a single one by the door into the hypostyle hall. A group of over-lifesize hardstone statues of nude boys—probably the young gods Ihy or Harsomtus—that lay in the courtyard must also have formed part of the temple's decoration

Kom el-Ahmar

Kom el-Ahmar ("The Red Mound")—ancient *Nekhen;* Greek Hierakonpolis—lies a little over ⅔ mile (1 km) southwest of the village of el-Muissat, on the west bank of the Nile.

Extensive remains of Predynastic settlements and cemeteries are discernible for some 2 miles (3 km) along the edge of the desert to the south and southwest of el-Muissat, and are particularly dense east of

the wadi opposite which Kom el-Ahmar is situated. A mud-brick structure known as "The Fort" stands some 545 yards (500 m) into the wadi. Fragments of a granite doorway of Kha'sekhem of the 2nd Dynasty come from here, suggesting that it was constructed for his funerary cult.

The famous "Decorated Tomb 100" (now lost) was found in the easternmost part of the settlement/cemetery area at the end of the 19th century. It probably belonged to a local chief of the Predynastic Naqada II Period, and is important as an indicator of the growing social stratification, as well as displaying the conventions and motifs of Egyptian art in process of formation.

At the beginning of the 1st Dynasty, the irregularly shaped town enclosure Kom el-Ahmar replaced the earlier settlement. J. E. Quibell and F. W. Green uncovered the temple complex in 1897–1899. The main benefactor was King 'Na'rmer, together with Kha'sekhem/Kha'sekhemwy. At an unknown date, many votive objects that had been presented to the temple were brought together and deposited in a cache (the "Main Deposit"). Many objects in the Main Deposit, which included palettes, mace heads, stone vessels, and ivory figures, date between the Naqada III period and the 1st Dynasty. Monuments of later periods include two large copper statues of Pepy I and perhaps his

◀ *The inner hypostyle hall of the Temple of Horus in Edfu. The height and close spacing of the huge columns restrict the feeling of space.*

▼ *A plan of the site of Kom el-Ahmar, early center of the 3rd Upper Egyptian nome, including the site of the remains of Predynastic settlements and cemeteries.*

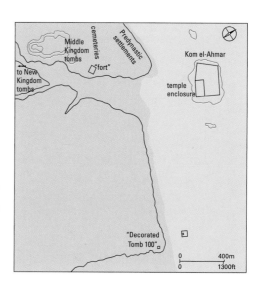

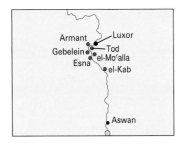

son Merenre', a granite stela showing a king Pepy in the company of Horus and Hathor, and a statue base of Pepy II.

Excavations in the Hierakonpolis area, directed by M. A. Hoffman, R. Friedman, and B. Adams since the late 1960s, have revealed a host of Predynastic remains, including very large, perhaps royal, tombs of the Naqada III period and one of the oldest ever mass brewing installations.

Decorated and inscribed rock-cut tombs ranging from the 6th to the 18th Dynasties have been found in the wadi of the "Fort" and its subsidiary branches.

el-Kab

The earliest traces of human activities in the area of el-Kab go back to about 6000 BCE: the "Kabian" is a microlithic industry that predates the known Neolithic cultures of Upper Egypt. The town enclosure of el-Kab measures 600 × 600 yards (550 × 550 m) and is surrounded by massive mud-brick

walls. It contains the main temple of Nekhbet with several subsidiary structures, including a birth house, smaller temples, a sacred lake, and an extensive Predynastic cemetery.

Temple structures were erected at el-Kab from an early date, but major building activities in the temple of Nekhbet started in the 18th Dynasty. Almost all the kings of the period contributed in smaller or larger measure, but Thutmose III and Amenhotep II seem to have been the most prominent.

Esna

The temple of Esna is about 220 yards (200 m) from the river in the middle of the modern town. Because of the accumulation of debris and silt, it is now about 29½ feet (9 m) below street level. Texts in the temple relate it to four others in the area, three to the north and one on the east bank, all of which have now disappeared completely, although

▼ *The location of the main features of el-Ka (below) and the floorplan of the Temple of Nekhbet (right).*

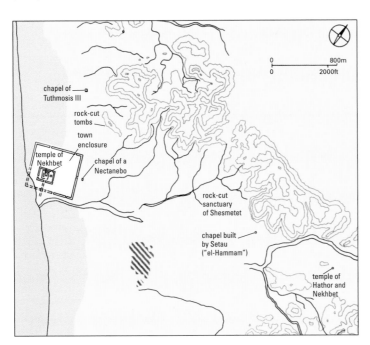

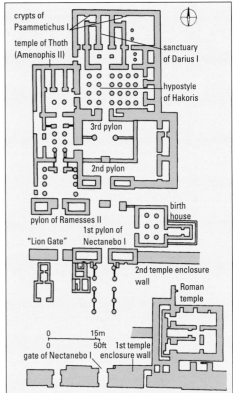

parts were visible in the 19th century. Another temple of the same period has been identified at Kom Mer, 7½ miles (12 km) to the south, but cannot be excavated because a modern village is built over it. The temple is dedicated to Khnum with several other deities, of whom the most prominent are Neith and Heka, who is here a child deity.

el-Mo'alla

Two decorated rock-cut tombs of the early 1st Intermediate Period, belonging to 'Ankhtifi and Sebekhotep, are the most important monuments at el-Mo'alla (probably ancient Egyptian *Hefat*). Apart from its lively and unconventional paintings, the tomb of 'Ankhtifi contains extensive biographical texts of its period, exalting his status and describing the situation in the southern nomes at the end of the Old Kingdom.

Gebelein

The name of this place means "The Two Hills," which derives from the most conspicuous landmark visible on the west bank of the Nile at the point where the 3rd and 4th Upper Egyptian nomes meet.

Gebelein has produced Predynastic finds, notably fragments of linen with the oldest known large painting. Tombs, mainly of the 1st Intermediate Period, were found on the west hill, while on the east hill stood a temple of Hathor, which existed as early as the 3rd Dynasty. Reliefs, stelae, or inscriptions of Nebhepetre' Mentuhotep, and several kings of the 13th and 15th Dynasties, have also been discovered. The temple continued to function in the Greco-Roman Period, and demotic and Greek papyri have been found in the area.

Tod

During the reign of Userkaf of the 5th Dynasty, there apparently already stood a mud-brick chapel at ancient Egyptian *Djerty* (Tuphium of the Greco-Roman Period) on the east bank of the Nile. Major construction started in the Middle Kingdom, during the

▲ *The Avenue of the Sphinxes at Luxor linked the temple with Karnak, nearly 2 miles (3 km) away; the lions have the head of Nectanebo I.*

reigns of Nebhepetre' Mentuhotep, S'ankhkare' Mentuhotep, and Senwosret I, and the base of the latter's temple wall was incorporated into the Ptolemaic structure. In the New Kingdom, Thutmose III erected a shrine to the war god Montu. Amenhotep II, Sety I, Amenmesse, and Ramesses III and IV carried out restoration work. Ptolemy VIII Euergetes II added his temple with a sacred lake in front of the temple of Senwosret I.

Armant

Ancient Iuny, on the west bank of the Nile in the 4th Upper Egyptian nome, was one of the most important places of worship of Montu. A temple to Montu existed at Armant as early

as the 11th Dynasty, which perhaps began there, and Nebhepetre' Mentuhotep is the earliest builder known with certainty. Important additions were made during the 12th Dynasty and the New Kingdom; only the remains of the pylon of Thutmose III are still visible. The temple was destroyed during the Late Period. A new temple was probably started under Nectanebo II and continued by the Ptolemies. An important contribution to the appearance of the site was made by Cleopatra VII Philopator and Ptolemy XV Caesarion, who built a birth house with a sacred lake. The building is now destroyed. Two gates, one of them erected by Antoninus Pius, have also been found.

Thebes

Ancient Egyptian *Waset* was called Thebai by the Greeks, but the reason is unclear. *Waset* was in the 4th Upper Egyptian nome, deep in the south. Its geographical position contributed greatly to the town's importance: it was close to Nubia and the eastern desert with their valuable mineral resources and trade routes, and distant from the restricting power centers in the north. Theban local rulers of the earlier part of Egyptian history pursued active expansionist policies, particularly during the 1st and 2nd Intermediate Periods; in the latter this was disguised as an Egyptian reaction against foreign invaders (the Hyksos). Monuments earlier than the end of the Old Kingdom are scarce, and *Waset* was little more than a provincial town.

Its rise to prominence occurred during the 11th Dynasty; although the capital was moved to Itjtawy at the beginning of the 12th Dynasty. Thebes, with its god Amun, was established as the administrative center of southern Upper Egypt and the foundations were laid for its role as Egypt's religious capital. The peak came during the 18th Dynasty, when Thebes was the administrative capital of the country. The temples at Thebes were the most important and the wealthiest in the land, and the tombs prepared were the most luxurious Egypt ever saw. Even when the center of royal activities moved north (el-'Amarna, Memphis, and Pi-Ri'amsese), the Theban temples continued to flourish, monarchs were still buried in the Valley of the Kings, and Thebes retained importance as an administrative center. During the 3rd Intermediate Period, Thebes, with the High Priest of Amun at its head, formed a counterbalance to the realm of the 21st- and 22nd-Dynasty kings, who ruled from the delta. Theban political influence receded only in the Late Period.

The main part of the town and the principal temples were on the east bank. Across the river, on the west bank, was the necropolis with tombs and mortuary temples.

Luxor

A sanctuary stood on the site of the Luxor temple since the beginning of the 18th Dynasty, or even earlier, but the temple we see today was built under the instruction of two kings, Amenhotep III (the inner part) and Ramesses II (the outer part). Several other rulers contributed to its relief decoration and inscriptions, added minor structures, or made alterations, chiefly Tut'ankhamun, Haremhab, and Alexander the Great.

The temple was dedicated to Amun (Amenemope) and linked to the royal *ka* (the generative principle that carried down the generations) and the annual renewal of the king's divine powers. Every year, during the second and third months of the inundation season, a long religious festival was held at Luxor during which the image of Amun of Karnak visited his *Ipet-resyt*, "Southern Ipet," as the temple was called.

At the end of the reign of the Roman Emperor Diocletian, just after 300 CE, the first antechamber in the inner part of the temple was converted into a sanctuary and decorated with exquisite paintings that are now almost completely lost. A small mosque of Abu el-Haggag was built in the court of

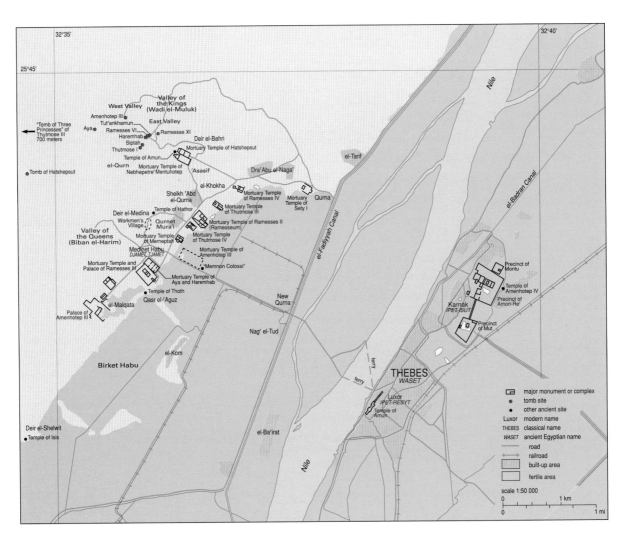

▲ *Map showing the main sites around Thebes and Karnak, the temples of the West Bank, and the royal tombs of el-Tarif, Dra' Abu el-Naga', and the Valley of the Kings.*

Ramesses II in the Fatimid Period (11th century CE).

An alley of human-headed sphinxes of Nectanebo I linked Karnak, 2 miles (3 km) to the north, with Luxor, and brought the visitor to a mud-brick enclosure wall. Several later structures stood in the forecourt in front of the temple itself, including a

colonnade of Shabaka (later dismantled) and chapels of Hathor, built by Taharqa, and of Sarapis, built by Hadrian.

The temple is fronted by a pylon of Ramesses II, with reliefs and texts on its outside relating the story of the famous battle against the Hittites at Qadesh in Syria in c. 1274 BCE. Two red granite obelisks once stood in front of the pylon but only one now remains: the other was removed to Place de la Concorde in Paris in 1835–1836. Several colossal statues of Ramesses II, two of them seated, flank the entrance.

The peristyle court of Ramesses II, which opens behind the pylon, has 74 papyrus columns with scenes of the king before various deities. The columns are arranged in a double row around its sides and are interrupted by a shrine consisting of three chapels of Amun (center), Mut (left), and Khons (right), built by Hatshepsut and Thutmose III and restored by Ramesses II.

The entrance to the processional colonnade of Amenhotep III has two seated colossi of Ramesses II, with Queen Nefertari by his right leg on the north side, while there are two seated double statues of Amun and Mut on the south side. The walls behind the large columns were decorated under Haremhab and Tut'ankhamun, with reliefs depicting the Festival of Opet. Those on the west wall show a procession of barks from Karnak to Luxor; the east wall shows their homeward journey.

A peristyle forecourt of Amenhotep III is fused with the hypostyle hall, which is the first room in the inner, originally roofed, part of the temple. This leads to a series of four antechambers. The "Birth Room," east of the second antechamber is decorated with reliefs that depict the "divine birth" of Amenhotep III. Alexander the Great built a bark shrine in the third antechamber. The sanctuary of Amenhotep III is the final room.

In 1988, a cache of 21 royal and divine statues was found in the court of Amenhotep III, left during a renovation of the temple.

Karnak

The name *Karnak* describes a vast complex of temples, chapels, and other buildings of various dates. This was ancient Egyptian *Ipet-isut*, perhaps "The Most Select of Places," the main place of worship of the Theban triad, with the god Amun (often, especially during the New Kingdom, called Amon-Re') at its head. No site in Egypt makes a more overwhelming and

◄ *A plan of the temple at Luxor, built mainly by Amenhotep III and Ramesses II. The overall length of the temple between the pylon and the rear wall is 850 feet (260 meters).*

▶ *One of the granite colossi, representing Ramesses II seated at his throne, at the entrance of the Temple of Luxor.*

lasting impression than this apparent chaos of walls, obelisks, columns, statues, stelae, and decorated blocks. Theban kings and the god Amun came to prominence at the beginning of the Middle Kingdom. From that time, the temples of Karnak were built, enlarged, torn down, added to, and restored for more than 2,000 years. The temple of Amun was the most important temple establishment in the whole of Egypt.

The site is divided into three groups. The largest and most important is the well-preserved central enclosure, the temple of Amun. The northern enclosure is dedicated to Montu, the original god of the Theban area. The enclosure of Mut lies to the south. An avenue bordered by sphinxes linked Karnak with the Luxor temple. Canals connected the temples of Amun and Montu with the Nile.

Amenhotep IV (Akhenaten) erected several temples for his new state deity, the Aten, to the east of the central enclosure of Amun. The temples were dismantled after his reign and the stone blocks reused.

The precinct of Amon-Re'

The central enclosure contains the Great Temple of Amon-Re', built along two axes (east–west and north–south), a number of smaller temples and chapels, and a sacred lake. The layout consists of a series of pylons, with courts or halls between them, leading to the main sanctuary. The earliest are Pylons IV and V, by Thutmose I.

Pylon I is preceded by a quay and an avenue of ram-headed sphinxes protecting the king,. South of the avenue are several smaller structures, such as a bark shrine of Psammuthis and Hakoris. A court opens behind the pylon and contains a triple bark shrine of Sety II, consisting of three chapels

dedicated to Amun, Mut, and Khons. In the center of the forecourt there are remains of a colonnaded entrance of Taharqa. A small temple (bark station) of Ramesses III faces into the forecourt from the south.

Pylon II, probably a work of Haremhab, is preceded by colossal statues of Ramesses II, including one (on the north) showing him with Princess Bent'anta. Behind the pylon, the now lost roof of the hypostyle hall was borne by 134 papyrus columns. The relief decoration of the hypostyle hall is the work of Sety I and Ramesses II and depict military various military campaigns of these kings.

Pylon III was built by Amenhotep III, but the porch in front of it was decorated by Sety I and Ramesses II. Four obelisks stood behind Pylon III and were erected by Thutmose I and III to mark the entrance to the original temple; only one is still standing.

Between Pylons IV and V, both of Thutmose I, is the earliest part of the temple still standing, with 14 papyrus columns and two obelisks of Hatshepsut (one standing, one fallen). Pylon VI and the court which precedes it were built by Thutmose III.

Another four pylons were added along a new axis, which extended the Great Temple of Amon-Re' to the south. North of Pylon VII is the "Cachette Court." Thousands of statues, which once stood in the temple, were found here early in the 20th century. Pylons VII and VIII were built under Hatshepsut and Thutmose III; the court between them contains the latter's bark station.

Pylons IX and X were decorated under Haremhab; Pylon X may have been built, at least in part, by Amenhotep III. A *sed*-festival temple of Amenhotep II stands in the court between them.

The temple of Khons stands in the southwestern corner of the precinct. Its

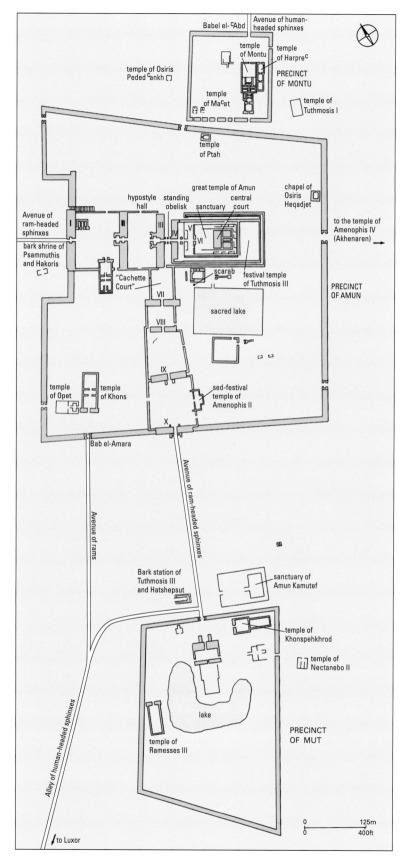

propylon in the main enclosure wall, built by Ptolemy III Euergetes I, is approached from the south by an avenue of ram-sphinxes protecting Amenhotep III. The temple of Opet, close to that of Khons, was built by Ptolemy VIII Euergetes II. Nearly 20 other small chapels and temples are within the precinct of Amon-Re'.

The precinct of Montu

The square northern enclosure is the smallest of the three precincts, and its monuments are poorly preserved. It contains the main temple of Montu, several smaller structures (such as the temples of Harpre' and Ma'at), and a sacred lake. In 1970, a structure that is interpreted as a temple treasury, built by Thutmose I, was discovered outside the east enclosure wall.

The temple of Montu is fronted by an avenue of human-headed sphinxes, which approaches from the north. The propylon was built by Ptolemy III Euergetes I and IV Philopator, and the temple by Amenhotep III.

The precinct of Mut

The southern enclosure contains the temple of Mut, which is surrounded by a crescent-shaped lake, and subsidiary structures, such as the temple of Khonspekhrod of the 18th Dynasty, and the temple of Ramesses III.

The temple of Mut was built under Amenhotep III, but again the propylon in the enclosure wall is Ptolemaic (Ptolemy II Philadelphus and III Euergetes I). There are later additions to the temple by Taharqa and Nectanebo I, among others.

The West Bank—The Temples

Across the Nile from the temples of Karnak and Luxor, the remains of temples occupy a stretch of some 4½ miles (7·5 km). Most were royal mortuary temples of the New Kingdom. The most important are those of Deir el-Bahri, the Ramesseum, and Medinet Habu. The mortuary temple of Sety I stands at Qurna, while only huge seated statues, the "Memnon Colossi," mark the site of the temple of Amenhotep III. Several temples on the West Bank were not mortuary, such as those of Hathor (Deir el-Medina), Thoth (Qasr el-'Aguz), and Isis (Deir el-Shelwit).

Deir el-Bahri

Deir el-Bahri was traditionally connected with the goddess Hathor, the chief deity of the Theban necropolis. It was chosen by Nebhepetre' Mentuhotep of the 11th Dynasty and Queen Hatshepsut of the 18th Dynasty for the site of their mortuary temples. Thutmose III built a temple complex for the god Amun (*Djeser-akhet*) and a chapel for Hathor between the two earlier structures, and a kiosk (*Djeser-menu*) in the court of Mentuhotep's temple.

The mortuary temple of Nebhepetre' Mentuhotep *(Akh-isut)* The upper part of the temple is approached by a causeway, originally lined with statues, which started at the now lost valley temple. The free-standing front part of the upper temple consists of a forecourt, enclosed by walls on its three sides, and a terrace with a now ruined mastaba-shaped structure. In the east part of the forecourt is the opening known as "Bab el-Hosan," which is connected by a long underground passage with a symbolic royal tomb, left unfinished. Behind the colonnades at the west end of the forecourt and on the terrace were reliefs showing scenes such as boat processions and foreign campaigns. The mastaba-shaped structure, which was the main feature of the temple, is surrounded by a pillared roofed ambulatory on all sides. In its west wall are six statue-shrines of royal ladies of the reign of Nebhepetre' (from the north: Myt, 'Ashayt, Zadeh, Kawit, Kemsyt, and Henhenet).

The inner part of the temple, cut into the cliff, consists of peristyle and hypostyle courts located east and west of the entrance to an underground passage, which after some 490 feet (150 m) leads to the tomb proper. The rock-cut shrine at the back of the inner part of the building was the main cult place of the deceased king in the temple.

The mortuary temple of Hatshepsut *(Djeser-djeseru)* The temple is a part rock-cut and part free-standing terraced structure. In its incompletely preserved state, the temple conveys a unique harmony between human creation and the natural environment. The effect of its original appearance, with trees, flowerbeds, and numerous sphinxes and statues, must have been overwhelming.

The valley temple of the complex is attested by its foundation deposits, but the building itself has now disappeared. The monumental causeway, lined by sphinxes and provided with a bark chapel, led to a series of three courts at different levels, approached by ramps and separated by colonnades (porticoes) protecting the now famous reliefs. Vaulted rooms on the north and south sides of the upper court were dedicated to Hatshepsut and her father Thutmose I, and the gods Re'-Harakhty and Amun. Theirs were the main cults maintained in the temple. A series of niches at the back (the west side) of the hall contained statues of the

◀ *A plan of the precincts of Amon-Re', Mut, and Montu at Karnak. The Karnak temple complex covers an area of about half a square mile (1.3 km²) and is the largest ancient religious site in the world.*

▶ *(overleaf) A line of ram-headed sphinxes outside Pylon I in the Precinct of Amun at Karnak. The ram was the sacred animal of Amun. The motif of an animal protecting a king was common in Egyptian sculpture.*

queen. An entrance in the same wall led to the sanctuary proper. The innermost room of the present sanctuary was cut by Ptolemy VIII Euergetes II; otherwise, the temple's architecture is remarkably free from later interference. Shrines of Anubis and Hathor were approached from the second court.

The mortuary temple of Ramesses II (Khnemt-waset) The mortuary complex of Ramesses II, today called the Ramesseum, consists of the temple proper and the surrounding mud-brick magazines and other buildings (Ramesses II's tomb is KV 7 in the Valley of the Kings).

The interior disposition of the stone temple is fairly orthodox, although somewhat more elaborate than usual: two courts, a hypostyle hall, a series of antechambers and subsidiary rooms, the bark hall, and the sanctuary. The overall plan of the temple is a parallelogram rather than a rectangle. This is probably a result of the orientation of an earlier small temple to the north of the Ramesseum's hypostyle hall, dedicated to Tuya, the mother of Ramesses II, while making the pylons face the Luxor Temple on the east bank.

The 1st and 2nd pylons of the Ramesseum are decorated with reliefs. Two granite colossi of Ramesses II originally stood before a platform preceding the hypostyle hall: the upper part of the southern statue is now in the British Museum, but the head of the companion piece can still be seen in the Ramesseum. The bases of the rear walls of the hypostyle hall are decorated with long processions showing sons of Ramesses II (their tomb is KV 5 in the Valley of the Kings). The first room behind the hypostyle hall has an astronomical ceiling and might have served as a library. The usual temple palace stood south of the first court.

Medinet Habu

Situated opposite Luxor, ancient Egyptian *Tjamet/Djamet* (Coptic *Djeme/Djemi*) was one of the earliest Theban sites to be associated with Amun as a creator god. Hatshepsut and Thutmose III built a temple for him there on the site of an 11th dynasty precursor. Next to it, Ramesses III erected his mortuary temple, enclosing both structures within a large mud-brick enclosure alongside administrative buildings, workshops, and dwellings of priests and officials. Medinet Habu became the focus of economic and administrative life in Thebes, a role it continued to play for the next several hundred years.

The temple of Amun (Djeser-iset) The temple, built by

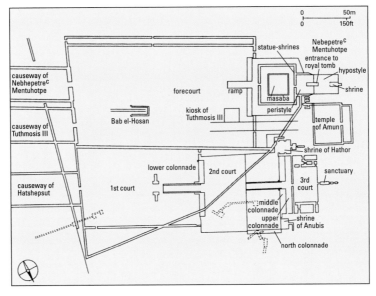

► *A plan of the mortuary temples of the 11th Dynasty king Nebhepetre' Mentuhotep and the 18th Dynasty queen Hatshepsut. The site at Deir el-Bahri is situated almost directly opposite the Karnak temple complex on the West Bank of the Nile.*

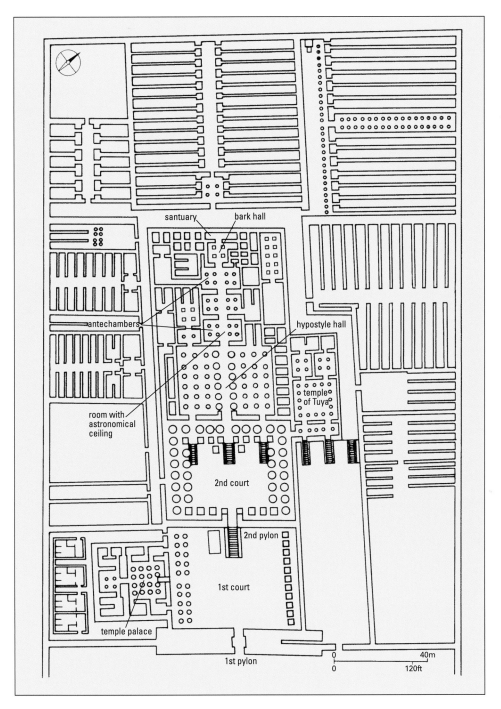

santuary

bark hall

antechambers

hypostyle hall

room with
astronomical
ceiling

temple
of Tuya

2nd court

2nd pylon

1st court

temple palace

| 0 | | 40m |
| 0 | | 120ft |

1st pylon

◀ *A plan of the
mortuary temple
of Ramesses II.
The design of the
Ramesseum, as it is
commonly called, is
fairly typical of New
Kingdom temple
architecture.*

Hatshepsut and Thutmose III, underwent many alterations over the following 1,500 years—during Dynasties 20 (Ramesses III), 25 (Shabaka and Taharqa), 26, 29 (Hakoris), 30 (Nectanebo I), and the Greco-Roman Period (Ptolemy VIII Euergetes II, X Alexander I, and Antoninus Pius)—which extended its plan by adding a columned hall, two pylons, and a forecourt.

The mortuary temple of Ramesses III (Khnemt-neheh) The temple is of orthodox design and resembles closely the mortuary temple of Ramesses II (the Ramesseum).

South of the first court stood the mud-brick palace, now badly damaged, which was used by the king during religious festivals held at Medinet Habu.

Some of the reliefs at Medinet Habu are not only artistically but also historically important, recording events of the reign of Ramesses III:

1st pylon: The king is shown smiting foreign captives before Amun and Re‘-Harakhty in symbolic scenes of triumph. The subjugated foreign lands and towns are represented by their names inscribed in rings surmounted by human heads.

2nd pylon: On the outside (east face) of the south massif, the king presents captives to Amun and Mut. On the inside, and also on the south and north walls of the 2nd court, are representations of the festivals of Sokar and Min.

Temple exterior: Campaigns against the Libyans, Asiatics, and "Sea Peoples" are shown on the north wall. Scenes of the king offering to deities are on other parts of the exterior wall and the inner part of the temple.

West Bank—Royal tombs

el-Tarif The ambitious rulers of the early Theban 11th Dynasty, who vied with the northern Herakleopolitan (9th/10th) Dynasty for supremacy over Egypt, built their tombs at el-Tarif. The truly monumental size of

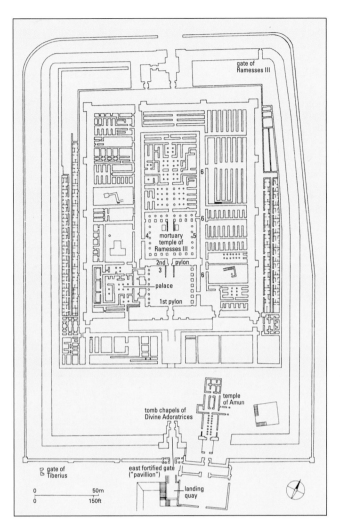

◄ *Plan of the mortuary temple complex of Ramesses III and temple of Amun at Medinet Habu. The key shows the location of the main cycles of reliefs.*

1 Ramesses III smiling captives

2 Ramesses III hunting

3 Ramesses III presents captives to Amun and Mut

4 festival of Sokar and Libyan war

5 festivals of Min and Amun

6 campaigns against the Libyans, Asiatics and the "sea people"

the tombs connect them with the mortuary temple and tomb of the king who finally gained control over the whole of Egypt, Nebhepetre‘ Mentuhotep, at Deir el-Bahri.

The tombs consist of an open excavation into the rock that forms a huge court. At the back a series of doorlike openings creates the impression of a pillared facade. This gave the tombs the name *saff-tombs* (from *saff*, meaning "row" in Arabic). Three are known:

Inyotef I (Horus Sehertawy): Saff el-Dawaba

Inyotef II (Horus Wah‘ankh): Saff el-Kisasiya

Inyotef III (Horus Nakhtnebtepnufer): Saff el-Baqar.

◄ *The focal point of the Deir el-Bahri temple complex is the Djeser-Djeseru, meaning "the Holy of Holies," the mortuary temple of Hatshepsut.*

Dra' Abu el-Naga' Theban rulers of the 17th Dynasty and their families were buried in modest tombs at Dra' Abu el-Naga', between el-Tarif and Deir el-Bahri. The position of these tombs and their ownership are known from a papyrus recording an inspection of them around 1080 bce (the Abbott Papyrus). A number of inscribed objects, decorated weapons, and jewelry, were found during excavations conducted by A. Mariette before 1860. The architecture of the tombs, which may have had small mud-brick pyramids, is little known.

The Valley of the Kings ("Wadi el-Muluk") After the defeat of the Hyksos, the Theban rulers of the 18th Dynasty began to build themselves tombs in a style befitting kings of all Egypt. The tomb of Amenhotep I was probably at Dra' Abu el-Naga', probably the earliest tomb of the new type. Thutmose I was the first to have his tomb cut in the cliffs of a desolate wadi behind Deir el-Bahri, now the Valley of the Kings. The total number of tombs is 62 (tomb KV 62 is that of Tut'ankhamun, found last). Some are not royal tombs, while the ownership of others is still disputed.

The plan of the royal tombs of the 18th to 20th Dynasties (the last is the tomb of Ramesses XI) in the Valley of the Kings consists of a long inclined rock-cut corridor with one or more halls (sometimes pillared), terminating in the burial chamber itself. The decoration within the tombs is almost exclusively religious. There are numerous scenes of the king in the presence of gods, but the most striking elements of the decoration are the texts and accompanying illustrations of various religious compositions ("books"). From the end of the 18th Dynasty, the tomb decoration was carved in relief.

It is not easy to imagine the original wealth and beauty of the contents of these royal sepulchers. The only one which has been found largely intact, and which provides a tantalizing glimpse of what is lost, that of Tut'ankhamun, may well not be typical.

The Valley of the Kings may still have some surprises left. In 1989, a remarkable discovery was made when the entrance to the long-lost tomb KV 5 was rediscovered by an American expedition led by Kent Weeks. The tomb, which had been plundered in antiquity, proved to be an huge communal family burial of the sons of Ramesses II.

The workmen's village at Deir el-Medina The everyday life of the workmen ("Servants in the Place of Truth") who constructed the royal tombs in the Valley of the Kings can be reconstructed in considerable detail from ostraca, papyri, and other evidence. The ruins of the walled settlement (around 70 houses), in which workmen and their families lived from the reign of Thutmose I, can be seen in a small wadi behind a hill at Deir el-Medina.

The workmen, numbering 60 men or

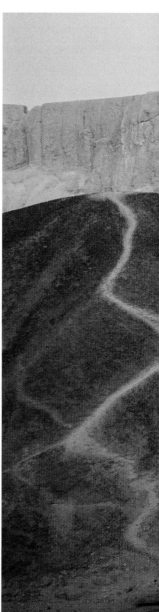

more, were divided into two "sides," or teams, each of which had a foreman, his deputy, and one or more scribes. Their superior, the vizier, sometimes either came himself or sent one of the royal "butlers" to visit the site and inspect the progress of work. The workmen stayed at the site of the tomb in the Valley of the Kings during the working "week" of 10 days, returning to the village for rest days or for religious festivals, which were also holidays. They were paid in goods, mainly grain, at the end of each month. Other commodities, such as fish and vegetables, and occasionally meat, wine, and salt were also supplied.

West Bank—Nonroyal tombs

The larger Theban tombs are concentrated in several areas of the west bank. Starting from the river north, these are: Dra' Abu el-Naga', Deir el-Bahri, el-Khokha, 'Asasif, Sheikh 'Abd el-Qurna, Deir el-Medina, and Qurnet Mura'i. The list was revised in 1960 to include 409 tombs, but others have since been added, and close to fifty tombs were seen in the past but have now been lost or

▼ *The tomb of Horemheb, last of the 18th-Dynasty kings, lies in the Valley of the Kings at Thebes. A tomb he had built earlier at Saqqara was used to bury his queen.*

destroyed. For each decorated tomb there were hundreds, if not thousands, of simple graves. The large tombs range from the Early Dynastic Period to the Greco-Roman Period, but most are of the New Kingdom. There are further tombs in the Valley of the Queens, south of Deir el-Medina, which have their own numbering, and in smaller valleys nearby, including the "Tomb of Three Princesses" of the reign of Thutmose III in Wadi Qubbanet el-Qirud ("Valley of the Tombs of the Monkeys") with a treasure of gold and silver vessels, now in the Metropolitan Museum in New York.

Many of the lesser tombs at el-Tarif and Dra' Abu el-Naga' are contemporary with royal tombs of the 11th and 17th Dynasties, but Dra' Abu el-Naga' in particular continued to be used well into the Late Period. An important discovery of a cemetery of small New-Kingdom tombs with free-standing chapels was made there in 1991 by a German team led by D. Polz.

In an excavation of 1891, E. Grébaut and G. Daressy found a large cache of coffins of priests of Amun from the 3rd Intermediate Period at Deir el-Bahri. It was the second find of this type—in 1858, Mariette had found a cache of coffins of priests of Montu. The most spectacular of these secret hideaways was found in tomb TT 320, in the first of the wadis south of Deir el-Bahri, in 1881. It contained the coffins and mummies of renowned Egyptian kings of the 17th to 20th Dynasties, assembled there for security during the 21st Dynasty.

As the name suggests, the Valley of the Queens ("Biban el-Harim") contains tombs of queens and other members of the royal family, particularly Ramessid princes. Although the design of the tombs is on a much smaller scale, it is reminiscent of that

of royal tombs because it consists of a complex burial chamber without a chapel.

Most of the larger Theban tombs were rock-cut, and relatively few had any free-standing superstructure. The plans of these tombs vary greatly; the following are only very general characteristics.

Late Old Kingdom One or two rooms of irregular shapes, sometimes with pillars. Sloping shafts lead to one or more burial chambers.

Middle Kingdom The rear wall of an open forecourt forms the facade. A long corridor is followed by a chapel connected with the burial chamber by a sloping passage.

New Kingdom An open forecourt, often with stelae, precedes the facade, which has a row of pottery "funerary cones" above the doorway. A transverse ("broad") hall, sometimes with stelae on its end walls, is followed by a "long" hall on the central axis. The sanctuary has a statue niche or a false door. All inner rooms can have pillars. The shaft of the burial chamber is usually cut in the forecourt.

Ramessid tombs at Deir el-Medina combine a completely, or partly, free-standing superstructure (pylon, open court, portico, and vaulted chapel with statue niche and mud-brick pyramid above) with rock-cut chambers approached by a shaft.

Late Period Some of these tombs are enormous and their plans complex. Mud-brick pylons and open sunk courts precede a series of underground rooms, usually with pillars, leading to the burial chamber.

Painting is the usual method of decoration of Theban tombs, but relief is not uncommon. The subject matter includes both scenes of everyday life and religious themes, which predominate from the Ramessid Period on.

◀ This bust of the young king Tut'ankhamun, made from stuccoed and painted wood, was probably used as a mannequin for the king's clothes or jewelry.

Northern Upper Egypt

▶ *The ancient sites of Northern Upper Egypt include the imposing Temple of Hathor at Dendara and the town and temple of Osiris at Abydos.*

Northern Upper Egypt extends between Thebes and Asyut. It was the heart of ancient Egypt, the hinterland which remained Egyptian in times of crisis and from which, with Thebes at the head, movements for new political unity were launched. Control of access to the gold and minerals of the eastern desert was always of paramount importance, while politically Thebes in the south dictated the course of events from the 11th Dynasty.

Naqada, Qift, and Abydos dominated the scene in the Predynastic and Early Dynastic Periods, with Dendara gaining in importance during the Old Kingdom. Abydos became a religious center in the Middle Kingdom. The rise of Thebes stifled its northerly neighbors in the New Kingdom, though Abydos held its position, and Qift continued to be favored by royal building activities. The temple of Dendara is easily the most impressive structure of late antiquity in the area.

Nag' el-Madamud

Ancient Egyptian *Madu* was an important place of worship of the falcon-headed god Montu. The early temple, now destroyed, dated to the Middle Kingdom (Senwosret III), but stood on the site of a shrine of the Old Kingdom or the 1st Intermediate Period. Kings of the late Middle Kingdom and the 2nd Intermediate Period continued to build there, and there are also scattered monuments of the New Kingdom and the Late Period.

The temple of Montu, Ra'ttawy, and Harpokrates, which is still partly standing, is of the Greco-Roman Period. Immediately behind is a second temple, dedicated to the sacred bull of Montu. The exterior walls of the temples were decorated by Domitian and

Trajan. An early Ptolemaic temple (Ptolemy II Philadelphus, III Euergetes I, and IV Philopator) once stood in the southwest corner of the enclosure.

Shanhur

Shanhur is the site of a temple of Isis and Mut built during the Greco-Roman Period. It contains scenes showing Emperors Augustus and Tiberius before various Egyptian deities and a remarkable astronomical ceiling.

Naqada and Tukh

Naqada I–III are Predynastic cultures named for cemeteries excavated by W. M. Flinders Petrie in 1895. Naqada is the largest modern settlement in the area, but the cemeteries are about 4⅓ miles (7 km) north of it, between Tukh and el-Ballas.

About 1⅘ miles (3 km) northwest of the village of Naqada, an Early Dynastic mastaba tomb was found by J. de Morgan in 1897. The tomb contained ivory tablets, vase fragments, and clay sealings bearing the names of King 'Aha and Neithotep—perhaps his wife and queen regnant. The nearby cemeteries have also produced stelae of the end of the Old Kingdom and the 1st Intermediate Period.

The size of the cemeteries and settlement sites excavated by Petrie ("Naqada") shows that ancient *Nubt* (Greek Ombos) must have been important in the later Predynastic Period. The name probably derives from ancient Egyptian *nub*, meaning "gold," on account of the nearby gold mines in the eastern desert. A New Kingdom temple dedicated to the local god Seth (*Nubty*, "The Ombite") has been located to which various

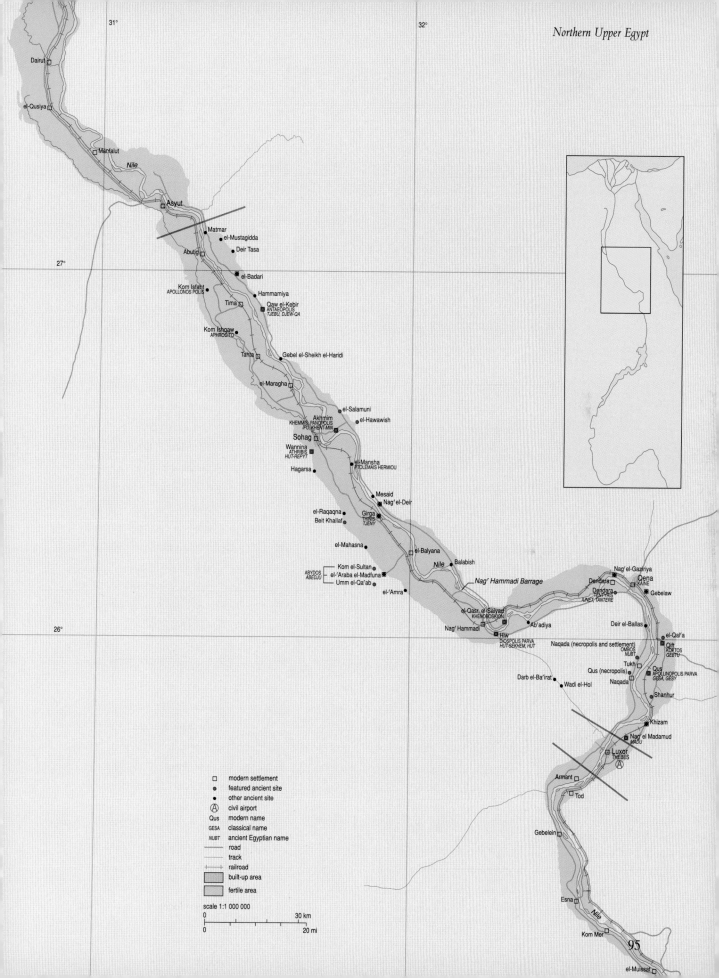

Dairut

el-Qusiya

Mantalut

Nile

Asyut

Matmar
el-Mustagidda
Deir Tasa

Abutig

el-Badari

Kom Isfaht
APOLLONOS POLIS
Hammamiya

Tima

Qaw el-Kebir
ANTAEOPOLIS
TJEBU, DJEW-QA

Kom Ishgaw
APHRODITO

Tahta

Gebel el-Sheikh el-Haridi

el-Maragha

el-Salamuni

Akhmim
KHEMMIS, PANOPOLIS
IPU, KHENT-MIN

el-Hawawish

Sohag

Wannina
ATHRIBIS
HUT-REPYT

el-Mansha
PTOLEMAIS HERMIOU

Hagarsa

Mesaid
Nag' el-Deir

el-Raqaqna
Beit Khallaf

Girga
THINIS
TJENY

el-Mahasna

el-Balyana

Nile
Balabish

Kom el-Sultan
ABYDOS   el-'Araba el-Madfuna
ABEDJU   Umm el-Qa'ab

el-'Amra

Nag' Hammadi Barrage

Nag' el-Gaziriya

Dendara

Qena
KAINE

Dendara
TENTYRIS
IUNET, TANTERE

Gebelaw

el-Qasr, el-Saiyad
KHENOBOSKION

Deir el-Ballas

Nag' Hammadi

Hiw
DIOSPOLIS PARVA
HUT-SEKHEM, HUT

Ab'adiya

el-Qal'a

Qilt
KORTOS
GEBTU

Naqada (necropolis and settlement)
OMBOS
NUBT

Tukh

Qus
APOLLINOPOLIS PARVA
GESA, GESY

Qus (necropolis)

Darb el-Ba'irat

Wadi el-Hol

Naqada

Shanhur

Khizam

Nag' el Madamud
MADU

Luxor
THEBES

Armant

Tod

Gebelein

Esna

Nile

Kom Mer

el-Muissat

Legend

□ modern settlement
● featured ancient site
• other ancient site
Ⓐ civil airport
Qus modern name
GESA classical name
NUBT ancient Egyptian name
——— road
——— track
+++ railroad
▨ built-up area
▨ fertile area

scale 1:1 000 000

0   30 km
0   20 mi

31°   32°

27°

26°

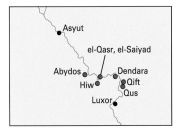

kings of the 18th Dynasty (Thutmose I and III, Amenhotep II) and several Ramessids contributed.

The small step pyramid of Ombos (or Tukh or Naqada) probably dates to the end of the 3rd Dynasty. It is one of a series of such monuments which provided focus points for the cult of the king in the provinces.

Qus

Qus, northwest of Naqada, on the opposite bank of the Nile, was an important town in the early part of Egyptian history. This was probably because at that time it served as the point of departure for expeditions to Wadi Hammamat quarries and the Red Sea. Today, only two pylons of the Ptolemaic temple of Haroeris and Heqet remain.

Qift

The town of *Gebtu* (Coptic *Kebto* or *Keft;* Greek Koptos), modern Qift, was the capital of the 5th Upper Egyptian nome. The town's prominence was due to its position: it was here (or at Qus) that trading expeditions left the Nile valley, heading for the Red Sea, and mining expeditions into the eastern desert. *Gebtu* soon became the most important religious center of the area. The local god, Min, was also god of the desert region to the east. Isis and Horus were connected with Qift during the Greco-Roman Period; one of the reasons for this was a reinterpretation of the two falcons of the nome standard as Horus and Min. As one would expect, monuments discovered at Qift span Egyptian history. Only temple structures of the Late and Greco-Roman Periods were found *in situ.*

Remains of three temple groups were uncovered during the excavations of W. M.

Flinders Petrie (1893–1894) and Raymond Weill and Adolphe Joseph Reinach (1910–1911). The Northern Temple of Min and Isis, which still stands, was the work of an official called Sennuu on behalf of Ptolemy II Philadelphus, with some additions of Ptolemy IV Philopator, Caligula, and Nero (particularly the three pylons). The site of the Middle Temple has a long history, but the temple itself was built by Ptolemy II Philadelphus, with additions by Caligula, Claudius, and Trajan. Gates of Nectanebo II, Caligula, and Claudius, and a chapel of Cleopatra VII Philopator and Ptolemy XV Caesarion, were found at the site of the Southern Temple. Claudius also built a small temple dedicated to Min, Isis, and Horus at el-Qal'a northeast of Qift,

Dendara

Dendara—ancient Egyptian *Iunet/Tantere,* Greek Tentyris—was the capital of the 6th nome of Upper Egypt and an important town. The temple complex stands isolated on the desert edge. It is oriented, as usual, toward the Nile, which here flows east–west, so that the temple faces north, although this was symbolically "east."

The main temple of Hathor is the most elaborately decorated of its period and follows the classic plan. Within the temple the most distinctive parts are the decorated "crypts." These are suites of rooms on three stories, set in the thickness of the outside wall; unlike other crypts, those at Dendara are decorated in relief. Their main use was for keeping cult equipment, archives, and magical emblems for the temple's protection. On the roof is a kiosk, in which the ritual of the goddess's union with the Sun disk was performed. There is also a pair of shrines of Osiris, from one of which came the famous

Dendara zodiac. Dendara was one of Osiris' many tombs, and the shrines, which have no link with Hathor, were used to celebrate his resurrection. South of the temple of Hathor is the temple of Isis. To the east lay part of the town, which the temple texts mention as having a temple of Horus of Edfu in its midst. The triads of deities worshiped at Edfu and at Dendara were similar, consisting of Horus, Hathor (or Isis), and Ihy or Harsomtus. Hathor of Dendara and Horus of Edfu met at a sacred "marriage" ceremony, when she made a progress to the south.

el-Qasr and el-Saiyad

The rock-cut tombs at Gebel el-Tarif, near the villages of el-Qasr, el-Saiyad, and Hamra Dom, northeast of Hiw, on the right bank of the Nile in the 7th Upper Egyptian nome, date to the end of the Old Kingdom. Two of them, of the "Great Overlords of the Nome" Idu Seneni and Tjauti, from the reign of Pepy II, deserve attention because of their preserved relief decoration.

Hiw

Hiw was a major settlement in Predynastic times. During the reign of Senwosret I, a royal estate "Kheperkare' (Senwosret I) the Justified is Mighty" was founded on the west bank of the Nile in the 7th Upper Egyptian nome. It became more important than the original nome capital, and its long-winded name started being abbreviated to *Hut-sekhem* or *Hut*. The Coptic version of the name, *Ho/Hou*, led to its present name.

Temples of the Dynastic Period at Hiw are mentioned in such documents as Papyrus Harris I, but none has been identified on site. The two principal surviving structures date to the Greco-Roman Period.

Abydos

Ancient *Abedju* (Greek Abydos; Coptic *Ebot/Abot*) was the most important burial ground in Egypt at the start of the Dynastic Period, and its cemeteries contain graves dating back to Predynastic Naqada I times.

The early funerary areas From the late Naqada I period, a cemetery developed about 1¼ miles (2 km) from the cultivation, running toward a prominent cleft in the desert escarpment. This developed into Cemetery U, a large elite burial ground of late Naqada II–III, and thence into Cemetery B and Umm el-Qa'ab, the royal cemeteries of Dynasty 0 and the 1st Dynasty. Tomb U-j is the oldest known royal tomb, dating to perhaps 3200 BCE and containing the earliest writing so far found in Egypt.

The town and temple of Osiris The ancient walled town is in the area called Kom el-Sultan, enclosed by massive mud-brick walls of the 30th Dynasty. The most important feature must have been the temple, at first of Khentamentiu and from the 12th Dynasty of Osiris. The temple is almost completely destroyed. Early objects from the 1st Dynasty include a vase fragment of King 'Aha and small stone and faience figures of men and animals. Starting with Khufu of the 4th Dynasty (ivory statuette, the only preserved likeness of him), most kings of the Old Kingdom down

▼ *A plan showing the central area of the main enclosure of the temple at Dendara. The temple stands within a massive mud-brick enclosure wall and is accessed through the giant gateway of Domitian and Trajan.*

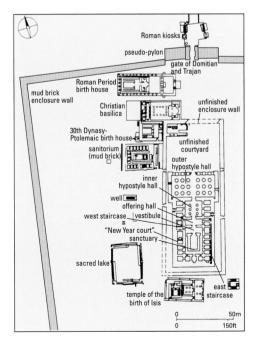

to Pepy II are attested in the find. In the Middle Kingdom, Nebhepetre' Mentuhotep probably added a small shrine to the existing temple. From then on, many kings down to the 17th Dynasty dedicated objects. In the 18th Dynasty, Amenhotep I, Thutmose III, and Amenhotep III did rebuilding work. All the major Ramessids are represented— Ramesses II by a complete temple that was built over the Middle Kingdom cenotaphs, while for the Late Period Apries, Amasis, and Nectanebo I are prominent. The temple probably continued to function in the Greco-Roman Period.

Royal cenotaphs and temples The oldest known monument at Abydos South is the small 3rd Dynasty pyramid of Sinki, which may have been a focus for a royal cult. Some Middle and early New Kingdom kings built cenotaphs—secondary mortuary complexes—a little farther north; the earliest identifiable one is of Senwosret III. Other excavated buildings in the area are connected with 'Ahmose, including one he built for his grandmother Tetisheri. His own temple had many reliefs, including battle scenes with the earliest representations of the horse in Egypt.

The large temple of Sety I has an unusual L-shaped plan, but its internal arrangements are a variation of the norm. It has two largely destroyed pylons with courts and pillared porticoes, followed by two hypostyle halls and seven chapels side by side. From the south, the chapels were dedicated to: Sety I, Ptah, Re'-Harakhty, Amon-Re', Osiris, Isis, and Horus. The Osiris chapel leads into a transverse area devoted to the Osiris cult that includes two halls and two sets of three chapels for Osiris, Isis, and Horus; adjacent is a room with two pillars that was designed to be inaccessible. The temple's southern

extension contains rooms for the cult of the Memphite gods Nefertem and Ptah-Sokar and a gallery with one of Egypt's few king lists, here serving the cult of the royal ancestors.

The reliefs of the reign of Sety I in the inner parts of the temple are exceptional. The outer areas, including the first hypostyle hall, were completed by Ramesses II, often overlaying work of his father.

Behind the temple and on the same axis is the cenotaph of Sety I. Both in its plan, and in decoration (mainly executed by Merneptah), it resembles a royal tomb.

Ramesses II built himself a smaller temple northwest of his father's. This is noteworthy for the excellent color preservation on its reliefs, which may be seen in full sunlight; only the lower parts of the walls survive.

Beit Khallaf

Five large mud-brick mastabas with clay sealings bearing the names of the 3rd Dynasty kings Netjerykhet (Djoser) and Zanakht were found near Beit Khallaf, 12½ miles (20 km) northwest of Abydos. The tombs were probably made for administrators of the Thinite area of the early 3rd Dynasty.

Akhmim

Akhmim (ancient Egyptian *Ipu/Khent-min;* Coptic *Khmin/Shmin;* Greek Khemmis and hence the modern name) was once the center of the important 9th Upper Egyptian nome. Little of its past glory remains: nothing is left of the town, the temples were almost completely dismantled and their material reused in the later Middle Ages, and the extensive cemeteries of ancient Akhmim have not yet been fully explored.

Northeast of Akhmim, at el-Salamuni, is a rock chapel dedicated to the local god Min.

◄ *The temple of Sety I is the largest temple at the ancient site of Abydos and includes numerous temples dedicated to the gods.*

▼ *A relief in the temple of Ramesses II shows the king in full war dress. The bright colors of the relief are well preserved.*

The chapel was created during the reign of Aya by the "First Priest of Min," Nakhtmin. The two temples, which once stood west of the modern town of Akhmim, were built for Min (Pan) and the goddess Triphis (Repyt), who was regarded as his companion.

Three groups of cemeteries and rock-cut tombs of various dates are known in the area. The tombs at el-Hawawish (Beit el-Medina) were made for officials of the Panopolite nome during the late Old Kingdom and the 1st Intermediate Period and were thoroughly

explored in the 1980s by an expedition of Macquarie University led by N. Kanawati.

Wannina

Wannina, some 6⅛ miles (10 km) southwest of Akhmim, is the site of a temple (ancient *Hut-Repyt;* Greek Athribis) built for the goddess Triphis (Repyt) by Ptolemy XV Caesarion and several Roman Emperors. South of it was an earlier temple of Ptolemy IX Soter II. One of the tombs nearby, belonging to the brothers Ibpemeny "the younger" and Pemehyt of the late 2nd century CE, has two zodiacs on its ceiling.

Qaw el-Kebir

Several large terraced funerary complexes built by officials of the 10th Upper Egyptian nome near the modern village of Qaw el-Kebir during the 12th and 13th Dynasties represent the peak of nonroyal funerary

architecture of the Middle Kingdom. Cemeteries of other dates have been found nearby. A Ptolemaic temple (probably of Ptolemy IV Philopator, enlarged and restored under Ptolemy VI Philometor and Marcus Aurelius), was destroyed in the first half of the 19th century.

▼ *The ruins of Abydos. The city may have extended onto the floodplain and was concentrated at the northern end of the site. The royal and private funerary monuments lie toward the south.*

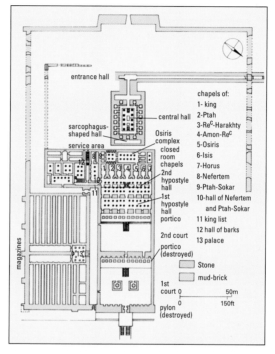

entrance hall

sarcophagus-shaped hall

central hall

service area

Osiris complex

closed room chapels

2nd hypostyle hall

1st hypostyle hall portico

2nd court portico (destroyed)

1st court

pylon (destroyed)

magazines

chapels of:
1- king
2-Ptah
3-Re^c-Harakhty
4-Amon-Re^c
5-Osiris
6-Isis
7-Horus
8-Nefertem
9-Ptah-Sokar
10-hall of Nefertem and Ptah-Sokar
11 king list
12 hall of barks
13 palace

Stone
mud-brick

0   50m
0   150ft

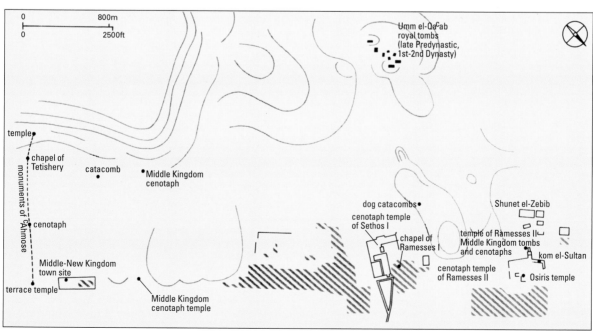

0   800m
0   2500ft

Umm el-Qa^cab royal tombs (late Predynastic, 1st-2nd Dynasty)

temple

chapel of Tetishery

catacomb

Middle Kingdom cenotaph

monuments of Ahmose

cenotaph

Middle-New Kingdom town site

terrace temple

Middle Kingdom cenotaph temple

dog catacombs

cenotaph temple of Sethos I

chapel of Ramesses I

Shunet el-Zebib

temple of Ramesses II
Middle Kingdom tombs and cenotaphs

kom el-Sultan

cenotaph temple of Ramesses II

Osiris temple

Middle Egypt

Middle Egypt describes the area between Asyut and Memphis or, in traditional terminology, the northern part of Upper Egypt. Asyut became the southernmost area of the Herakleopolitan kingdom in the 1st Intermediate Period. The boundary between southern and northern administrative regions remained in its vicinity until the end of the New Kingdom.

The area is characterized by the provincial tombs of the late Old Kingdom and 1st Intermediate Period cut in the desert escarpment. Ihnasya el-Medina was the residence of the Herakleopolitans; in the 12th Dynasty, the royal residence was farther north, at Itjtawy, near el-Lisht. During the Middle Kingdom, the Faiyum gained importance. El-'Amarna became the royal residence for a few years in the 18th Dynasty. Middle Egypt during the 3rd Intermediate and Late Periods was the meeting ground of the delta and the south. In late antiquity, it prospered and traded extensively with the oases: although smaller and less spectacular than their southern contemporaries, many temples testify to the renewed vitality of Middle Egyptian towns in those times.

Asyut

Asyut (ancient Egyptian *Zawty*) was the capital of the 13th nome of Upper Egypt. Its place in Egyptian history was ensured by its strategic position at a point where the Libyan desert encroaches on the cultivated land and narrows the Nile valley, and where the Darb el-Arba'in caravan route departs for el-Kharga oasis and farther south.

Asyut and its shrines (especially the temple of the local jackal god Wepwawet) are often mentioned in Egyptian texts, but the remains so far discovered are almost exclusively connected with the Asyut necropolis, west of the modern town. The most important tombs date to Dynasties 9/10 and 12, but the Ramessid tombs of Siese and Amenhotep have also been found.

During the 1st Intermediate Period, the "Great Overlords of the Lycopolite Nome," Khety I, Itefibi, and Khety II, were staunch supporters of the Herakleopolitan kings, of whose domain the nome formed the southern limit. The city was a main center of artistic production of the period. Inscriptions at Asyut provide valuable information about the Herakleopolitan conflict with "the southern nomes" in the 11th Dynasty).

Deir el-Gabrawi

During the 6th Dynasty, the powerful nomarchs of the 12th Upper Egyptian nome were buried in two groups of rock-cut tombs near the modern village of Deir el-Gabrawi. Some of these local rulers also held the title of the "Great Overlord of the Abydene Nomr" and so controlled a large area extending from the 8th nome (Abydos) in the south as far north as the 12th (or 13th) nome.

It is remarkable that some scenes in the tomb of one of them, Ibi, occur again in the Theban tomb (TT 36) of a man of the same name from the reign of Psammetichus I, about 1,600 years later.

Meir

The village of Meir is about 4⅓ miles (7 km) west of el-Qusiya, the site of ancient Qis (Kusai), once the center of the 14th Upper Egyptian nome. Meir gave its name to several

▶ *A map showing the main settlements of Middle Egypt, from Asyut in the south to the Faiyum and el-Lisht in the north.*

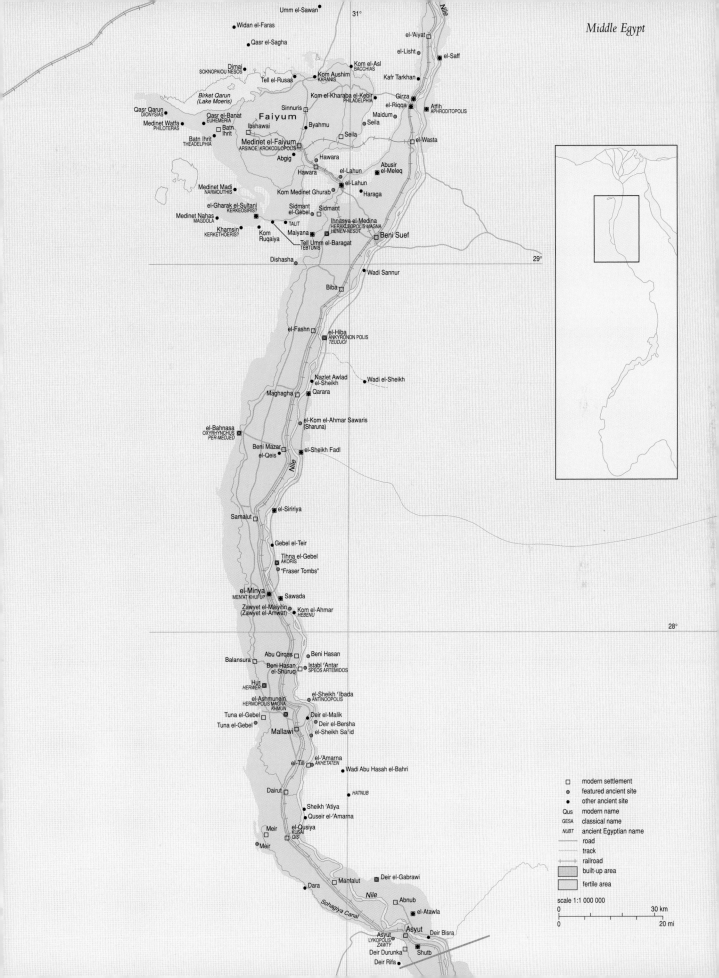

groups of rock-cut tombs farther west, in a low slope leading on to the desert plateau.

The most important of these tombs belong to the men who were in charge of the nome during the 6th and 12th Dynasties. Most were decorated in relief, with lively scenes were created by the craftsmen of the 12th Dynasty. In the past, Meir suffered much from illicit digging. The most prominent among the archaeologists who worked there in the first half of the 20th century was Aylward M. Blackman.

el-'Amarna

El-'Amarna, ancient Egyptian *Akhetaten* ("The Horizon of the Sun Disk"), was the short-lived capital of Egypt during much of the reign of King Akhenaten, and the center of the new state religion he introduced. It is one of the few Egyptian cities that has been excavated to significant extent. Akhenaten built it on virgin soil, not sullied by an earlier presence of people or gods. The boundaries of Akhetaten were marked by a chain of stelae surrounding the area on both banks of the river. On the west bank, the northernmost of these (Stela A) is at Tuna el-Gebel, while on the east bank Akhetaten extended close to the tombs of el-Sheikh Sa'id (Stela X).

The most important central part of the town contained the *Per-Aten-em-Akhetaten* ("The Temple of the Aten in Akhetaten"), or "The Great Temple," several other temples of the Aten, and the official state building, "The Great Palace." Akhenaten's private residence was across the road from "The Great Palace" and was connected with it by a bridge and surrounded by private houses, workshops, sculptors' studios, and official buildings.

Near the southern extremity of 'Amarna bay was the Maru-Aten, a group of buildings that also included an artificial lake, a kiosk

on an island, and flower beds. The north part of Akhetaten contained the "North Palace." 'Amarna officials had their tombs in the escarpment encircling the plain. How many of these tombs were put to use is not clear; some owners had other tombs made elsewhere, either before the move to el-'Amarna or afterward. Tomb No. 25 of the south group was prepared for Aya, who later became the penultimate king of the 18th Dynasty and was buried in a tomb in the Valley of the Kings at Thebes (KV 23). For his own family tomb, Akhenaten chose a ravine 3¾ miles (6 km) from the mouth of the large Wadi Abu Hasah el-Bahri.

el-Sheikh Sa'id

The tombs of the men governing the Hare nome (15th Upper Egyptian nome) during the 6th Dynasty were cut in steep cliffs later named for a Muslim saint buried in the area. Their importance is greatly enhanced by the absence of contemporary evidence from el-Ashmunein, the capital of the nome.

Deir el-Bersha

Almost opposite the town of Mallawi, on the east bank of the Nile, a desert valley called the Wadi el-Nakhla breaks southeast through the cliffs. It contains a number of rock-cut tombs, some of which belong to the nomarchs of the 15th Upper Egyptian nome and date to the 11th and 12th Dynasties. The most spectacular tomb was made for the "Great Overlord of the Hare nome," Djehutihotep, who lived during the reigns of Amenemhet II, Senwosret II, and Senwosret III.

el-Ashmunein

El-Ashmunein, ancient Egyptian *Khmun* ("8-town"), named for the group of eight deities (ogdoad) who represented the world before creation, was the capital of the 15th Upper Egyptian nome and the main cult center of Thoth, the god of healing and of wisdom, and the patron of scribes. The site is now badly ruined, with small parts of temples standing above the general rubble. No early remains have been found there, probably because they now lie beneath the water table.

The central sacred area of the town was surrounded by massive mud-brick enclosure walls of the Ramessid period and the 30th Dynasty. The temple of Thoth was rebuilt on many occasions. Only traces remain of the late extension that was standing until 1826. About 985 feet (300 m) to the south is the

pylon of Ramesses II in whose foundations more than 1,500 decorated blocks from dismantled temples of Akhenaten at el-'Amarna were found in the 1930s.

Several colossal statues of baboons were erected by Amenhotep III. A small temple of Ramesses II re-built by Nero is in the southern area. Roads laid out in the Greco-Roman Period were adorned with monumental objects then up to 1,500 years old, including an altar of Amenhotep III.

Tuna el-Gebel

The monuments of Tuna el-Gebel are scattered for about 1⅞ miles (3 km) along

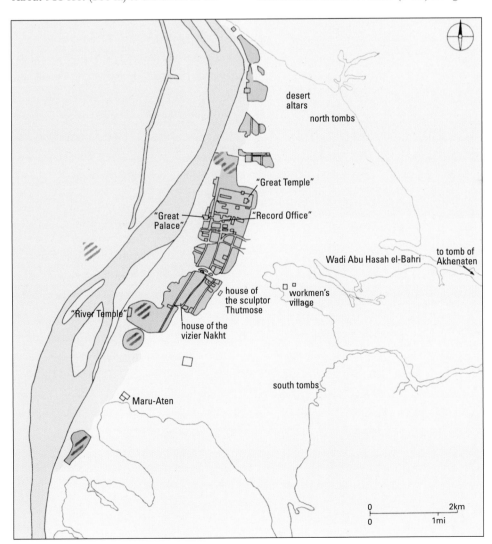

desert altars

north tombs

"Great Temple"

"Great Palace"

"Record Office"

Wadi Abu Hasah el-Bahri

to tomb of Akhenaten

house of the sculptor Thutmose

workmen's village

"River Temple"

house of the vizier Nakht

south tombs

Maru-Aten

0   2km
0   1mi

◀ *A map showing the site el-'Amarna— the ancient capital of Egypt during the reign of the 18th Dynasty king Akhenaten. The site is home to "The Great Temple," dedicated to the sun disk Aten.*

▲ *The painted limestone bust of Queen Nefertiti is attributed to the sculptor Thutmose. It and was found with many other pieces in the ruins of his studio at el-'Amarna. On display at the Altes in Berlin, Germany.*

the desert 4⅓ miles (7 km) west of el-Ashmunein. A boundary stela of Akhenaten, the earliest monument, consists of a rock-cut "shrine" a little way up the escarpment.

To the south is the late necropolis of el-Ashmunein. The earliest objects found here are Aramaic administrative papyri of the 5th century Persian occupation discovered in a jar in the catacombs of ibis and baboon burials, which are the largest feature of the site and include a baboon sarcophagus dated to Darius I. Ibis and baboon are the sacred animals of Thoth, the god of el-Ashmunein.

The site also contains the tomb of the family of Petosiris, which probably dates to the early Greco-Roman period. It is in the form of a temple, with an entrance portico and a cult chapel behind; the burials are in underground chambers.

el-Sheikh 'Ibada

This is the site of the ancient Antinoopolis, founded by Emperor Hadrian in 130 CE to commemorate his favorite Antinous who had drowned here. Among the earlier monuments, the largest is the temple of Ramesses II, which is dedicated to the gods of el-Ashmunein and Heliopolis.

Beni Hasan with Speos Artemidos

Beni Hasan, some 14⅓ miles (23 km) south of el-Minya, on the east bank of the Nile, is the most important Middle Kingdom provincial necropolis between Asyut and Memphis. It contains 39 large rock-cut tombs, of which at least eight belong to the "Great Overlords of the Oryx nome" (the 16th nome of Upper Egypt) of the end of the 11th and the early 12th Dynasties.

South of Beni Hasan is Speos Artemidos (locally known as Istabl 'Antar), a rock temple dedicated to the local lioness goddess Pakhet, built by Queen Hatshepsut. The architrave bears a long dedicatory text with her famous denunciation of the Hyksos.

Zawyet el-Maiyitin

This site (also known as Zawyet el-Amwat) contains a step pyramid of the late 3rd Dynasty, and a necropolis of rock-cut tombs, mainly of the end of the Old Kingdom, which belonged to ancient Hebenu, the early capital of the 16th Upper Egyptian nome.

Tihna el-Gebel

The rock-cut tombs ("Fraser Tombs") at Tihna date to the Old Kingdom. About 1¼ miles (2 km) north of them, near the modern village, are remains of the ancient town of Akoris, as well as three small temples and a necropolis of the Greco-Roman Period.

Oxyrhynchus

Little is known about *Per-medjed* (Coptic *Pemdje*), the capital of the 19th Upper Egyptian nome, from the Dynastic Period. Its pharaonic remains are unknown. The modern name of the locality is el-Bahnasa.

The town came to prominence during the Greco-Roman Period, when it was called Oxyrhynchus, after the local cult of the *Mormyrus* fish. Its rubbish heaps have produced tens of thousands of Greek papyri, the first discovered around 1900; the papyri are approached in numbers only by those found in the towns of the Faiyum.

el-Hiba

This is a town site (ancient Egyptian *Teudjoi*) with a much-destroyed originally temple built by Shoshenq I. The town marked the northern limit of the Thebaid during the 21st–25th Dynasties.

Dishasha

Dishasha is known for its late Old Kingdom tombs, including some belonging to the chief officials of the 20th Upper Egyptian nome. The rock-cut tomb of Inti contains a rare scene of the siege of a fortified town.

Ihnasya el-Medina

About 9⅓ miles (15 km) west of Beni Suef is the modern village of Ihnasya el-Medina, site of the capital of the 20th Upper Egyptian nome. The remains of the temple of local god Harsaphes lie southwest of the village. The earliest monuments date to the 12th Dynasty. During the 18th Dynasty, the temple was enlarged; major rebuilding was due to Ramesses II. The temple was used during the 3rd Intermediate and Late Periods.

During the 1st Intermediate Period, Ihnasya el-Medina (Greek Herakleopolis) was the seat of the rulers of the 9th/10th (Herakleopolitan) Dynasty, but no temples of this, or earlier, periods have been located.

Southeast of the temple of Harsaphes, at Kom el-ʿAqarib, was another temple built by Ramesses II. Sidmant el-Gebel, about 4⅓

▼ *This scene from the tomb of Djehutihotep at Deir el-Bersha was copied by John Gardner Wilkinson before 1856.*

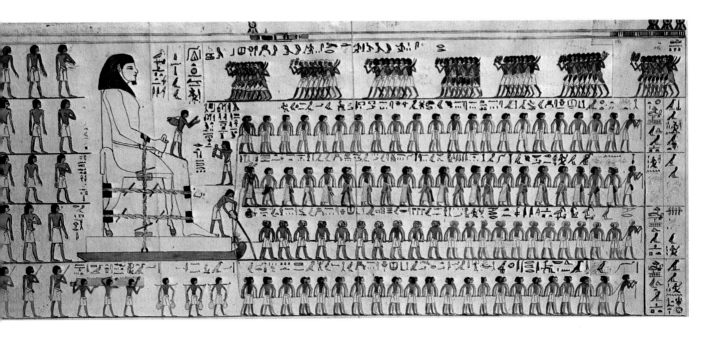

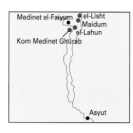

miles (7 km) to the west, was probably the main necropolis for the town, with graves and rock-cut tombs ranging from the 1st Intermediate to the Greco-Roman Periods.

Kom Medinet Ghurab

At the south side of the entrance to the Faiyum, some 1⅘ miles (3 km) southwest of el-Lahun on the edge of the desert, are scant remains of one or two temples and adjacent palace and town quarters and cemeteries. The larger temple was built by Thutmose III, and the settlement thrived during the second half of the 18th and the 19th Dynasty. Many objects found are connected with Amenhotep III and Queen Teye, and one of the buildings is often described as a palace of his reign.

el-Lahun

The pyramid of el-Lahun, some 1⅘ miles (3 km) north of the modern town of the same name, was built by Senwosret II. It is on the right side of the opening through which the Bahr Yusuf enters the Faiyum, opposite Kom Medinet Ghurab, and overlooks the lakeside region to which the kings of the 12th Dynasty devoted much attention. The pyramid builders used a natural knoll of rock to site the monument and employed the well-established Middle Kingdom method of core construction. This was based on stone retaining walls radiating from the center, and the filling of chambers formed between them with mud bricks. The entrance to the interior was through two shafts near the south face; this is unusual (normally the entrance is in the north face). Beautiful Middle Kingdom jewelry was found south of the pyramid in the shaft tomb of Princess Sithathoriunet.

There are mastabas and graves dating from the Middle Kingdom to Roman times in the neighborhood of the pyramid. The valley temple lies about ⅔ mile (1 km) to the east, near the line of cultivation. Close to it is the walled settlement of el-Lahun (also known as Kahun), which housed priests and officials connected with the pyramid. The town is known for the hundreds of Middle Kingdom hieratic papyri ("Kahun Papyri") found there.

The Faiyum

Usually described as an oasis, the Faiyum is actually connected to the Nile by a river arm known as the Bahr Yusuf (Arabic: "The River of Joseph"). The Faiyum (ancient Egyptian *She-resy,* "The Southern Lake," later divided into *She-resy* and *Mer-wer,* "The Great Lake," Greek Moeris) is a large, extremely fertile depression some 40 miles (65 km) from east to west, with a lake (Birket Qarun, Lake Moeris of Classical writers) in the northwest. The lake now occupies only about one fifth of the Faiyum and is 145 feet (44 m) below sea level, but in the past it was much larger.

The majority of temples and settlements uncovered in the Faiyum so far date to the Greco-Roman Period. Thousands of Egyptian (demotic) and Greek papyri have been found in Faiyum town sites of this period.

Maidum

A huge tower-shaped structure appearing above a hill formed by stone debris marks the remains of one of the earliest true pyramids ever attempted in Egypt. Along with the "Bent Pyramid" at Dahshur, the Maidum pyramid is one of the oldest pyramid complexes.

▼ *A map showing some of the most important sites of interest in the Faiyum—a fertile oasis west of the Nile valley and south of Memphis.*

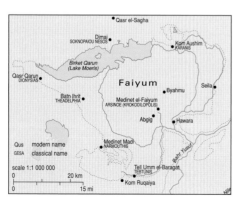

The monument started as a seven-stepped pyramid but was altered to have eight steps; the steps were filled and an outer casing was applied to transform it into the smooth pyramidal form. New Kingdom graffiti tell us that the Egyptians connected it with Snofru, the first king of the 4th Dynasty, and current opinion favours him, not Huni, the last ruler of the 3rd Dynasty, as the original builder.

The smooth dressing of the walls, which had originally been intended to be exposed as outer faces of the step pyramid (some can still be seen on the pyramid), did not provide sufficient bonding to the fill leaning against them. Furthermore, the outer casing did not rest on sound foundations, and the method employed in laying its blocks was not well chosen. As a result of these constructional deficiencies, the bases of the four outer buttress walls gave way. The walls slid down and collapsed, creating the tower we can see today. The date of the collapse is still disputed; attempts have been made to connect the disaster with the change of the angle of the "Bent Pyramid" at Dahshur. However, the presence of a contemporary necropolis speaks against such an early date. It is possible that the quarrying activities of later stone-robbers looking for building material were what mainly created the pyramid's present appearance.

el-Lisht

Amenemhet I, the first king of the 12th Dynasty, moved the administrative capital of Egypt, and the royal residence from Thebes, to Itjtawy, a newly founded walled town between the Faiyum and Memphis. The town has not been located, but the pyramid field of el-Lisht was its main necropolis and Itjtawy probably in the cultivated area to the east of it. The town retained its importance

for at least 300 years, only to relinquish it to the Hyksos center Avaris in the northeastern delta and to Thebes during the 2nd Intermediate Period.

The main features of el-Lisht are the two dilapidated pyramids of Amenemhet I and his son Senwosret I, some 1 mile (1·5 km) apart, surrounded by smaller pyramids and mastabas of members of the royal family and officials, as well as cemeteries of ordinary graves.

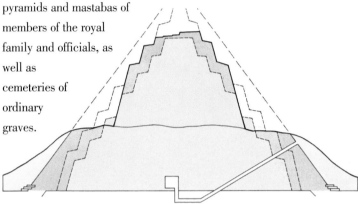

▼ *A cross section of the Maidum pyramid looking west. The vast amount of debris surrounding the remains of pyramid core resulted from a partial collapse of the structure at some unknown date.*

The nearby Memphite necropolis provided Amenemhet I with a source of conveniently prepared building material, and many decorated blocks originating in earlier pyramids and temples have been recovered from the core of the pyramid. These can be traced to Saqqara, Abusir, and Giza.

The most interesting among the 12th-Dynasty mastabas near the north pyramid of Amenemhet I belong to the Vizier Inyotefoqer, the Chief Steward Nakht, the Overseer of Sealers Rehuerdjersen, and the Mistress of the House Senebtisy. Close to the south pyramid of Senwosret I are the tombs of the Vizier Mentuhotep, the High Priest of Heliopolis Imhotep, with its walls covered with Pyramid Texts, the Steward Sehetepibre-'ankh, the High Priest of Memphis Senwosret-'ankh, again with Pyramid Texts, among others. The monuments of el-Lisht have been explored by the expeditions of the Institut Français d'Archéologie Orientale and more recently the Metropolitan Museum of Art in New York.

▶ *(Overleaf) The outer sarcophagus of the mummy of Zed-Khons-uef-ankh in a tomb at El Bawiti in the Bahariya Oasis.*

Memphis

▶ *A map showing the most important sites of Memphis—capital during the Early Dynastic Period and Old Kingdom.*

▼ *Children play in a stream in the city of Memphis—one of the most important sites in ancient Egyptian history. The site is home to some of the most familiar monuments in Egypt, including the Great Pyramids and Sphinx at Giza.*

The city of Memphis was the capital of Egypt and the royal residence during the Early Dynastic Period and the Old Kingdom. It always remained one of the most populous and renowned places of Egypt and, indeed, of the whole ancient world.

A reflection of the size and importance of Memphis is the area covered by its vast cemeteries, which stretch more than 18⅔ miles (30 km) along the edge of the desert on the west bank of the Nile, together with Helwan on the east. The cemeteries form the Memphite necropolis but all retain their own separate names: (1) Dahshur, (2) Saqqara, (3) Abusir, (4) Zawyet el-'Aryan, (5) Giza, (6) Abu Rawash.

The names by which the various parts of the Memphite necropolis are now known derive from the names of modern villages nearby. Egyptians themselves had no special term for the whole necropolis, but its most conspicuous features, the royal pyramids, sometimes lent their names to the adjacent quarters of the city that had grown out of the original "pyramid towns" of priests and pyramid officials. One of these terms, the name of the pyramid of Pepy I at Saqqara, *Mennufer* (Memphis in its Classical form; Coptic *Menfe*), was adopted as early as the 18th Dynasty to describe the whole city.

The city itself lies in the cultivated area to the east of the necropolis, buried under the

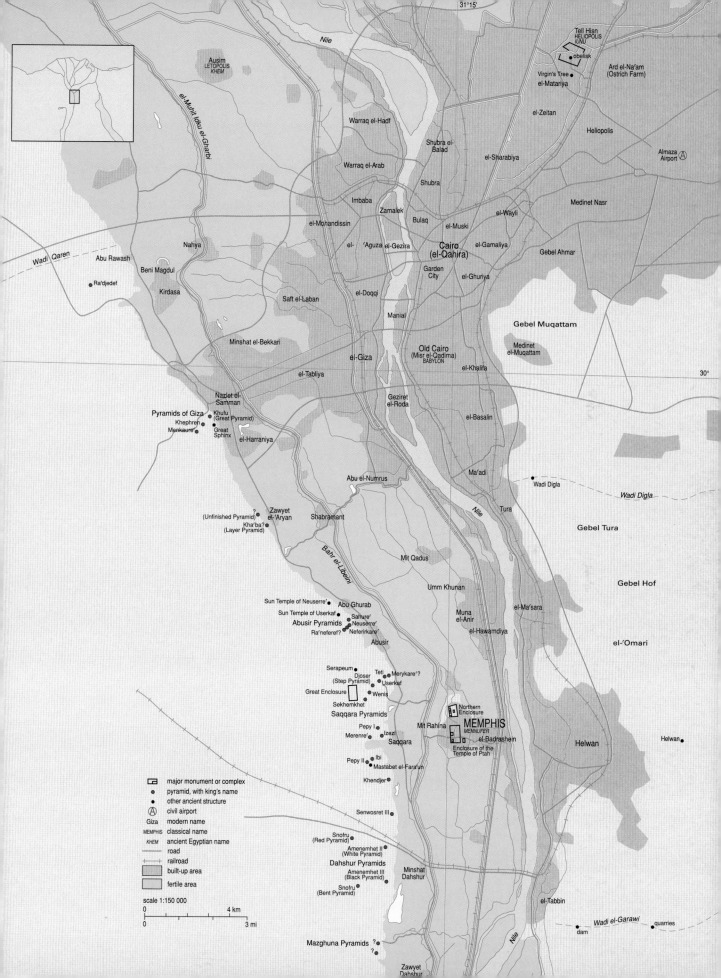

▶ *(opposite) The imposing figure of the Great Sphinx lies due east of the pyramid of Khephren and is perhaps the most iconic figure of ancient Egypt.*

deposits of silt left behind by the floodwaters and covered by modern settlements, fields, and vegetation. Only small parts have been revealed at Mit Rahina and at Saqqara (east of the pyramid of Teti). From the beginning, the religious center of Memphis with the temple of the god Ptah was in the area of the modern village of Mit Rahina. The extent of the city did not remain stable throughout Egyptian history. So our modern concept of the city and the necropolis is therefore artificial; neither was ever active over its entire extent at any one time.

Classical sources, as well as archaeological evidence, show that Memphis became one of the most important administrative centers of the country at the very beginning of Egyptian history, after 2950 BCE. Concerns about the environmental setting played a decisive role in the city's development, especially the need to protect it from the Nile floodwaters and the effects of the gradual eastward movement of the river.

Only Thebes was comparable in religious, political, and economic importance to the city of Memphis, yet our knowledge of the remains of this truly national shrine of Egypt is altogether smaller. To foreigners, Memphis represented Egypt. The name of one of its temples, *Hikuptah* ("The Temple of the *ka* of Ptah"), gave rise to the name of the whole country, Greek Aigyptos, our "Egypt." This is also the etymology of the word "Coptic."

Memphis did not survive the gradual eclipse of ancient Egypt in the early centuries of the Common Era. Economically, it suffered even earlier from the growth of Alexandria. The religious importance was lost when Theodosius I (379–95 CE) decreed that Christianity should be the religion of the whole of the Roman Empire. The final *coup de grâce* came in 641 CE, when the Muslim conqueror 'Amr ibn el-'As founded a new capital of Egypt, el-Fustat, on the east bank of the Nile at the south end of modern Cairo.

Mit Rahina

Extensive remains of ancient Memphis can be seen in a picturesque setting of palm groves close to the modern village of Mit Rahina. The most obvious remaining monument is the Ramessid enclosure with the temple of Ptah. It was built to mark one of the early *sed*-festivals celebrated by Ramesses II, perhaps that of his year 30 (c. 1250 BCE). The Apis Bull probably was the original deity of the area, but Ptah had become the chief Memphite god by the very beginning of the Dynastic Period, if not earlier, and in Classical antiquity was identified with Hephaistos and Vulcan.

▶ *A map showing the layout of the ancient remains at the village of Mit Rahina. The Ramessid enclosure of the temple of Ptah is perhaps the most conspicuous feature of the site.*

palace of Apries

northern enclosure

Kom el-Nawa

village of Mit Rahina

enclosure of the temple of Ptah

hypostyle hall

Kom el-Fakhry

Kom el-Arba⊂in

west pylon

embalming house of Apis bulls

colossus of Ramesses II

to Saqqara

alabaster sphinx

palace of Merneptah

tombs of the 1st Intermediate Period

Kom el-Rabi⊂a

chapel of Sethos I

temple of Ptah

Kom el-Qal⊂a

tombs of the 22nd Dynasty

0   300m
0   1000ft

THE PYRAMIDS: TYPES

Between c. 2650 and 1630 BCE, Egyptian kings built for themselves tombs in the form of pyramids. There are two basic types: the step pyramid and the true pyramid.

The step pyramid

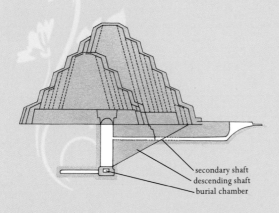

secondary shaft
descending shaft
burial chamber

The pyramid and subsidiary buildings are surrounded by an enclosure wall. The main axis of the enclosure points to the north.

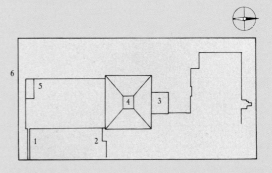

Step pyramid enclosure of Djoser (Dynasty 3) at Saqqara

The earliest pyramids, dating to the 3rd Dynasty, consist of several "steps." The burial chamber is situated below ground level, and is approached by a descending shaft from the north. Underground galleries *(magazines) surround the pyramid on the east, north, and west sides. The first step pyramid, and probably the only one which was completed, is at Saqqara and belonged to King Djoser.*

The subsidiary buildings, in particular the south tomb and the mortuary temple, ensured the deceased king's well-being in his *new existence, and served to maintain his cult. Djoser's sed-festival complex is a special feature not attested elsewhere.*

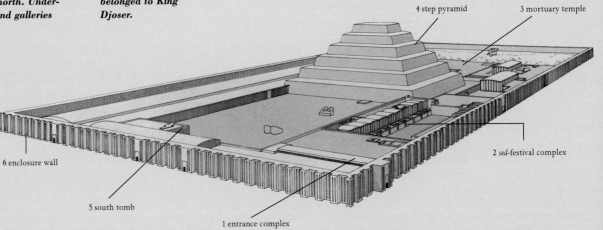

4 step pyramid

3 mortuary temple

2 *sed*-festival complex

6 enclosure wall

5 south tomb

1 entrance complex

The true pyramid

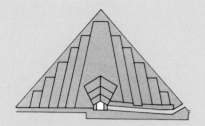

The true pyramid was introduced at the beginning of the 4th Dynasty. It was a natural development of the earlier step pyramid.

The main new elements of the developed pyramid complex are the valley temple and the causeway. The mortuary temple is normally against the east face of the pyramid, and a subsidiary pyramid is often near its southeast corner. The longer axis of the complex points to the west.

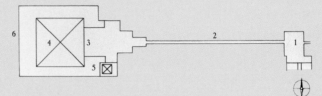

Pyramid complex of Sahure' (Dynasty 5) at Abusir

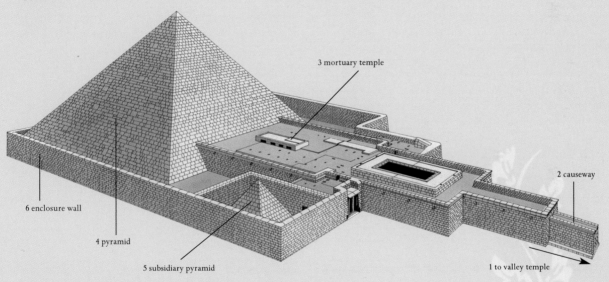

3 mortuary temple

2 causeway

6 enclosure wall

4 pyramid

5 subsidiary pyramid

1 to valley temple

The funerary monument of Sahure' at Abusir is a good example of the pyramid complex. The landing stages of the valley temple show that it could be approached by boat. The ascending causeway connects it with the mortuary temple. This consists of the outer part, with an entrance passage and a columned court, and the inner part, with five niches for statues, magazines to the north and south, and a sanctuary. In most pyramids the interior is reached by a descending passage starting in the north face. The roof of the burial chamber is formed by the largest and heaviest blocks in the whole structure.

THE PYRAMIDS: CONSTRUCTION

Architectural, as well as religious, considerations played a part in the pyramid's introduction and development; although united by their purpose, pyramids differ in their form, size, interior design, construction, and other details.

INTERNAL CONSTRUCTION
In most true pyramids, the structure consists of a series of buttress walls (coatings of masonry) surrounding the central core. The buttress walls decrease in height from the center outward; in other words, there is a step pyramid within most true pyramids. This clever internal arrangement added stability to the structure but evolved historically, together with the pyramid itself. Packing blocks were used to fill the "steps" formed by the faces of the outermost buttress walls, and casing blocks (often of better-quality Tura limestone) completed the transformation into a true pyramid. A different method of construction was employed in the pyramids of the 12th and 13th Dynasties. The main reason for its introduction was economy: it was suitable for relatively modest structures in inferior materials. Solid stone walls ran from the center of the pyramid, while shorter cross walls created a series of internal chambers filled with stone blocks, rubble or mud bricks. The whole structure then received the usual outer casing. Although quite effective in the short term, this could not compare with the earlier constructional methods, and all pyramids built in this way are now very dilapidated.

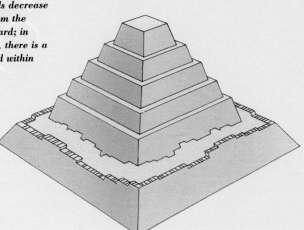

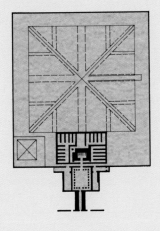

OTHER METHODS OF LIFTING
The size of the ramps and the volume of material required to build them have prompted alternative suggestions as to how the problem of raising the building blocks was solved. One, proposed by L. Croon, uses the principle of the shaduf. The Egyptians of the New Kingdom knew the shaduf for raising water, but there is no evidence that they used a similar device for lifting weights. This is the main objection to this and similar ideas. Models of "rockers," wooden cradle-like appliances, are known, and it has been thought that these were used to lift stone blocks. The rocker, with the stone placed on it, would have been raised by positioning wedges below its sides and rocking it up onto them. Stones might have been handled this way at some stage, but as a main lifting method this does not seem adequate.

THE PYRAMIDS: CHECKLIST

This list contains all the known royal pyramids in Egypt to date, including provincial step pyramids for the maintenance of the royal cult. The pyramids tend to form pyramid fields, which are called by the names of the modern villages situated nearby. There are many reasons for these groupings.

Broadly speaking, Old Kingdom pyramids were concentrated near Memphis; those of the Middle Kingdom were built close to Itjtawy (near modern el-Lisht), the capital of the land at that time. At the beginning of the 4th Dynasty the pyramids, together with their associated buildings, were given names.

Each entry in the table lists the following information (if available): king's name and dynasty; ancient name of pyramid in English; modern name; dimensions; associated pyramids (△).

Abu Rawash	'Re'djedef/Dyn 4. 343 ft sq/104.5 m sq. Planned ht 302 ft/92m. Subsidiary △ unfinished.
Giza	Khufu/Dyn 4. "The Pyramid which is the Place of Sunrise and Sunset" Modern name: "The Great Pyramid" or "The First Pyramid of Giza." 755 ft sq/230 m sq. Original ht 480 ft/146 m. Subsidiary △△△.
	Khephren/Dyn 4. "The Second Pyramid of Giza." 704 ft sq/214.5 m sq. Height 471 ft/143·5 m. Subsidiary △.
	Menkaure'/Dyn 4. "Third Pyramid of Giza." 345 ft sq/105 m sq. Original ht 215 ft/65·5 m. Subsidiary △△△
Zawyet el-'Aryan	Owner unknown (probably the successor of Khephren). "The Unfinished Pyramid." 685 ft sq/209 m sq. Only underground part begun.
	Probably Kha'ba/Dyn 3. "The Layer Pyramid" or "el-Medowwara." 258 ft sq/78.5 m sq. Unfinished.
Abusir	Sahure'/Dyn 5. "The Pyramid where the Ba-spirit rises." 258 ft sq/78·5 m sq. Original ht 154 ft/47 m Subsidiary △.
	Neferirkare'/Dyn 5. "The Pyramid of the Ba-spirit" 345 ft sq/105 m sq. Original ht 230 ft/70 m.
	Re'neferef/Dyn 5. "The Pyramid which is Divine of the Ba-spirits" 231 ft sq/65 m sq. Hardly begun.
Saqqara	Teti/Dyn 6. "The Pyramid which is Enduring of Places." 258 ft sq/78·5 m sq. Original ht 172 ft/52·5 m.
	Probably Merykare'/Dyn 9 or 10. "The Pyramid which is Flourishing of Places." 164 ft sq/50 m sq.
	Userkaf/Dyn 5. "El-Haram el-Makharbish" 241 ft sq/73·5 m sq. Original ht 161 ft/49 m. Subsidiary △
	Netjerykhet (Djoser)/Dyn 3. "The Step Pyramid." 460 x 387 ft/140 x 118 m. Ht 197 ft/60 m. The
earliest	first pyramid built in Egypt.
	Wenis/Dyn 5. "The Pyramid which is Beautiful of Places" 189 ft sq/57·5m sq. Original ht 141 ft/ 43 m. Subsidiary △
	Sekhemkhet/Dyn 3. "The Buried Pyramid." 394 ft sq/120 m sq. Unfinished.
	Pepy I/Dyn 6. "The Established and Beautiful Pyramid." 258 ft sq/78·5 m sq. Original ht 172 ft/ 52·5 m. Subsidiary △△△△△
	Izezi/Dyn 5. "El-Shawwaf." 258 ft sq/78·5 m sq. Original ht 172 ft/52·5 m. Subsidiary △
	Merenre'/Dyn 6. "The Shining and Beautiful Pyramid." 258 ft sq/78·5 m sq. Original ht 172 ft/52·5 m.
	Ibi/Dyn 8. Name unknown. Too damaged to provide accurate measurements
	Pepy II/Dyn 6. "The Established and Living Pyramid." 258 ft sq/78·5 m sq. Original ht 172 ft/52·5 m. Subsidiary △△△

Shepseskaf/Dyn 4. "The Purified Pyramid." 326 x 244 ft/99·5 x 74·5 m.

Khendjer/Dyn 13. Name unknown. 172 ft sq/52·5 m sq. Original 121 ft/ht 37 m.

Owner unknown/Dyn 13. Name unknown. Too damaged to provide accurate measurements

Dahshur

Senwosret III/Dyn 12. Name not certain. 345 ft sq/105 m sq. Original ht 258 ft/78·5 m.

Snofru/Dyn 4. "The Red Pyramid" etc. 722 ft sq/220 m sq. Original ht 345 ft/105 m.

Snofru (another pyramid)/Dyn 4. "The Bent Pyramid" etc. 617 ft sq/188 m sq. Original ht 345 ft/ 105 m.

Amenemhet II/Dyn 12. "The White Pyramid." Too damaged to provide accurate measurements.

Amenyqemau/Dyn 13. Name unknown. 148 ft sq/45 m sq. Unfinished.

Owner unknown, probably Dyn 13.

Amenemhet III/Dyn 12. "The Black Pyramid." 345 ft sq/105 m sq. Original ht 267 ft/81.5 m.

Amenyqemau/Dyn 13. Name unknown. 148 ft sq/45 m sq. Unfinished.

Mazghuna

Owner unknown. Name unknown. No structure remains.

Owner unknown. Name unknown. 172 ft sq/52·5m sq.

el-Lisht

Amenemhet I/Dyn 12. "The Pyramid of the Places of Arising." 276 ft sq/84 m sq. Original ht 180 ft/55 m.

Senwosret I/Dyn 12. "The Pyramid which Overlooks the Two Lands." 344 ft sq/105 m sq. Original ht 200 ft/61 m.

Maidum Probably Huni/Dyn 3 or Snofru/Dyn 4. 472 ft sq/144 m sq. Original ht 302 ft/92 m. Subsidiary △

Seila Royal cult pyramid, late Dyn 3. 85 ft sq/26 m sq.

Hawara Amenemhet III/Dyn 12. Name unknown. 344 ft sq/105 m sq. Original ht 190 ft/58 m.

el-Lahun Senwosret II/Dyn 12. Name not certain. 346 ft sq/106 m sq. Original ht 157 ft/48 m. Subsidiary △

Zawyet el-Maiyitin Royal cult pyramid, late Dyn 3. 59 ft sq/18 m sq.

Dara Probably Khui/Dyn 7–10. Name unknown. 426 ft sq/130 m sq.

Abydos (Sinki) Royal cult pyramid, late Dyn 3. 59 ft sq/18 m sq.

Tukh (Nubt, Ombos) Owner unknown, poss Dyn 3. 59ft sq/18 m sq.

el-Kula (Hierakonpolis) Royal cult pyramid, late Dyn 3. 59 ft/18 m sq

Location unknown

Menkauhor/Dyn 5. Undoubtedly at Saqqara. "The Pyramid which is Divine of Places."

NeferkareA/Dyn 7 or 8. Almost certainly at Saqqara. "The Enduring and Living Pyramid."

Ity/Dyns 7–10. "The Pyramid of the Ba-spirits"

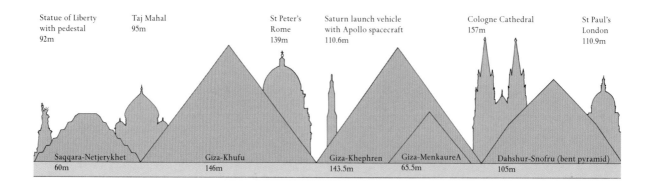

Statue of Liberty with pedestal 92m

Taj Mahal 95m

St Peter's Rome 139m

Saturn launch vehicle with Apollo spacecraft 110.6m

Cologne Cathedral 157m

St Paul's London 110.9m

Saqqara-Netjerykhet 60m

Giza-Khufu 146m

Giza-Khephren 143.5m

Giza-MenkaureA 65.5m

Dahshur-Snofru (bent pyramid) 105m

One of the colossal statues near the enclosure's south gate is known as Abu 'l-Hol and is housed recumbent in a small museum on the site. A large calcite sphinx, as well as another two colossi of Ramesses II (probably usurped from earlier kings), have been re-erected in the museum's gardens. Smaller sanctuaries and shrines were along the southern approach and in its vicinity, including those dedicated to Ptah, Hathor, and the deified Ramesses II himself. Later kings continued to build in the enclosure, especially Shoshenq I, who added an embalming house for Apis Bulls.

Foundation deposits discovered west of the Ptah enclosure indicate the existence of a temple built by Thutmose IV. But the earliest temple of Ptah, of the Early Dynastic Period or Old Kingdom, is almost certainly still hidden under the mound of Kom el-Fakhry, farther west of the enclosure of Ramesses II.

A number of mounds formed by continuous habitation are located around the Ramessid Ptah enclosure. One of these is Kom el-Qal'a, to the east, with a smaller temple dedicated to Ptah and a palace of Merneptah. A temple of Aten, built during the reign of Akhenaten, was probably in the same area.

There are few tombs at Mit Rahina. The most important date to the 1st Intermediate Period or early Middle Kingdom, at Kom el-Fakhry, and to the 22nd Dynasty (tombs of the High Priests of Memphis: Shoshenq, Tjekerti, Peteese, and Harsiese),

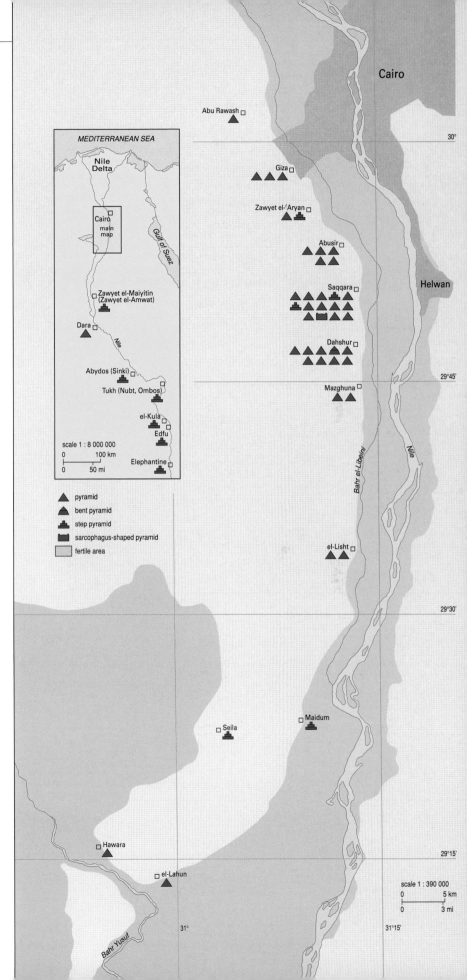

*◀ (previous page)
This map shows
the main sites of
pyramids in Egypt
(inset) and the dense
concentration of
pyramids from Cairo,
the modern capital,
south to el-Lahun.*

*▶ The Step Pyramid
of Djoser at Saqqara
was originally built
as a large mastaba
tomb but ended up
as a pyramid with
six steep steps.*

close to the southwestern corner of the Ptah enclosure.

Dahshur

The pyramid field of Dahshur forms the southernmost extension of the Memphite necropolis. The site is 2¼ miles (3.5 km) long, and the pyramid variously called "Bent," "Blunted," "Rhomboidal," or "False," the only one of its shape in Egypt, is the most conspicuous landmark.

For royal tombs, the change from the 3rd to the 4th Dynasty is evident from the transition from step pyramid to true pyramid, and the pyramids in which the process can be observed are at Maidum and Dahshur. The southern pyramid at Dahshur, of Snofru, was the earliest planned as a true pyramid from its inception. When it reached more than half of its intended height, however, the slope of the pyramid's outer faces was sharply reduced, probably to compensate for constructional flaws. The Bent Pyramid is unique because it has two separate entrances—one in its north face and another in its west face. Large areas of the pyramid have retained their original smooth exterior casing. South of the pyramid is the usual subsidiary ritual pyramid.

Later in his reign, Snofru had the "Red" or "Pink Pyramid" (from the color of its reddish limestone) erected 1⅓ miles (2 km) to the north. From the beginning, the slope of the faces of this pyramid was similar to the upper part of the Bent Pyramid. The dimensions of its base are surpassed only by those of the Great Pyramid of Khufu at Giza.

Three of the remaining pyramids at Dahshur, at some distance from each other and not forming any group, belong to the kings of the 12th Dynasty, Amenemhet II (the "White Pyramid"), Senwosret III, and

Amenemhet III (the "Black Pyramid"). The remarkable discovery of at least six wooden boats was made near the pyramid of Senwosret III, comparable to the find of a dismantled boat of Khufu at Giza. Near the pyramid of Amenemhet III is the tomb of the ephemeral king Awibreʻ Hor, and a small pyramidal structure of Amenyqemau, both of the 13th Dynasty. Three other pyramids at Dahshur are probably of the same date, although one of them, northeast of the Red Pyramid, may date from the Old Kingdom.

There are two groups of Old-Kingdom nonroyal tombs at Dahshur. Near the pyramids of Amenemhet II and Senwosret III, but still within the pyramid enclosure walls, are the mastabas of princesses (Iti, Khnemt, Itiwert, and Sitmerhut, all daughters of Amenemhet II, as well as Ment and Sentsenebtisi, daughters of Senwosret III) and queens. These tombs contained some superb examples of jewelry now in the Egyptian Museum in Cairo.

Saqqara

Saqqara is the most important link in the chain of cemeteries belonging to the ancient city of Memphis.

Nonroyal tombs of Dynasties 1 and 2
The earliest royal name found at Saqqara is that of the late Predynastic ruler Naʻrmer, engraved on a porphyry bowl, which was found in one of the subterranean magazines under the Step Pyramid of Djoser, along with thousands of other complete and fragmentary vessels. The first mastaba tomb at Saqqara is only a little later, dating to the reign of King ʻAha who was perhaps the same as Menes, the legendary founder of Memphis.

Mastabas of the 1st Dynasty form an almost continuous line along the eastern edge

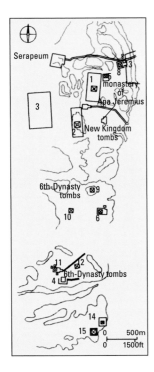

of the desert plateau (gebel) north of the Step Pyramid of Djoser, above the modern village of Abusir. These tombs belonged to high officials and members of the royal family. Chambers for funerary equipment were situated in the core of the brick mastaba, while the substructure cut into the rock consisted of a centrally placed burial chamber and subsidiary rooms.

Royal tombs of the 2nd Dynasty

A large complex of underground rock-cut galleries is concealed under the east side of the pyramid of Wenis, and another about 460 feet (140 m) east of it. Nothing has survived of the mud-brick superstructures, but the names on clay sealings suggest that these galleries are substructures of the tombs of Re'neb and Ninetjer, two kings of the early 2nd Dynasty.

The huge enclosed area west of the pyramid of Sekhemkhet, known as *Qisr el-Mudir* ("Great Enclosure" on early maps), may represent the remains of a royal tomb complex of one of Djoser's predecessors.

The pyramids of Dynasties 3–13

At least 14 royal pyramids are known from Saqqara, treated here in chronological order. Most have now lost their original, geometrical forms and appear as artificial hills. Amazing though it may seem, other pyramids almost certainly await discovery.

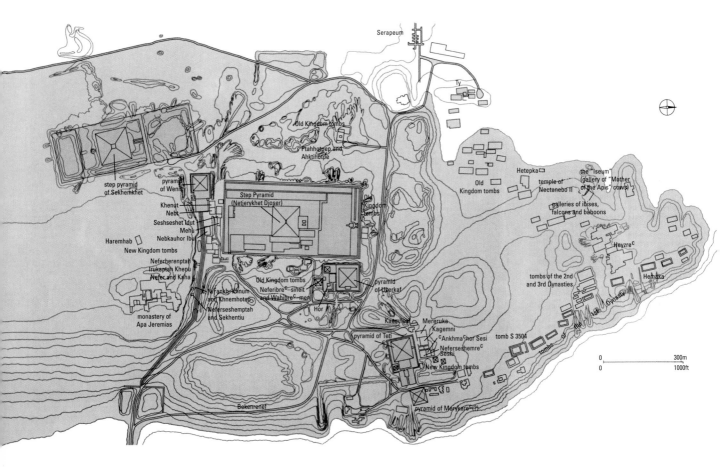

1. The Step Pyramid of Djoser was built some time after 2650 BCE. It was the first pyramid in Egyptian history, and the earliest stone structure of its size in the world. The design of the Step Pyramid was credited to Imuthes (Imhotep). During an excavation of the entrance complex of the Step Pyramid in 1925–1926, the name of Imhotep was found inscribed on the pedestal of a statue of Djoser, providing evidence for the correctness of Manetho's statement.

2. King Sekhemkhet intended to build an even larger step structure southwest of his predecessor's, but the pyramid remained unfinished and disappeared under the sand. In 1950, it was found by the Egyptian M. Zakaria Goneim, who called it "The Buried Pyramid." The sealed calcite sarcophagus in the burial chamber was, however, empty.

3. The burial complex at South Saqqara of Shepseskaf, one of the last kings of the 4th Dynasty, is not a pyramid but an enormous sarcophagus. Known as *Mastabet el-FaraAun* ("The Mastaba of the Pharaoh"), the only parallel is the Giza tomb of Khentkaus, the mother of two early kings of the 5th Dynasty.

3. Userkaf, first king of the 5th Dynasty, built his pyramid near the northeast corner of Djoser's enclosure, but his successors abandoned Saqqara for Abusir, farther north.

5. The pyramid of Izezi, the penultimate king of the 5th Dynasty, is at South Saqqara.

6. The pyramid of Wenis, the last king of the 5th Dynasty, stands at the southwestern corner of the enclosure of the Step Pyramid of Djoser. The interior walls of this pyramid are inscribed with the so-called Pyramid Text—spells that were designed to help the deceased king in the netherworld. The pyramid of Wenis was the first to contain such texts, which are found in all later Old Kingdom pyramids.

7. The pyramid of Teti, the first king of the 6th Dynasty, is the northernmost royal pyramid of Saqqara. The other rulers of the dynasty, Pepy I (8), Merenre' (9), and Pepy II (10), followed Izezi's example and moved to South Saqqara. The name of the pyramid of Pepy I, and the settlement near its valley temple, *Pepy-mennufer,* eventually became adopted for the ancient Egyptian capital, Mennufer (Memphis). Since 1965, the pyramids of the 6th Dynasty at South Saqqara have been systematically explored, and the Pyramid Texts inscribed on their walls copied and studied by French scholars of the *Mission archéologique française de Saqqara*. A spectacular result of their work has been the identification and excavation of five small pyramids of queens of Pepy I.

11. The small brick pyramid of King Ibi of the 8th Dynasty is in the same area.

12. The unexcavated remains of a pyramid to the east of the pyramid of Teti, at North Saqqara, might belong to King Merykare', of the Herakleopolitan Period (9th/10th Dynasty). Other possible owners of this structure have been proposed, especially Menkauhor of the 5th Dynasty.

13 & 14. The two southernmost Saqqara pyramids belong to kings of the 13th Dynasty and, characteristically for the period, are built of sun-dried bricks. One of these pyramids belonged to Khendjer, while the owner of the other remains unknown.

Nonroyal tombs of Old and Middle Kingdoms

The largest conglomeration of nonroyal tombs of the Old Kingdom occupies the area north of the Step Pyramid of Djoser. Many were excavated during the mid-19th century under French archaeologist Auguste Mariette.

From the beginning of the 4th Dynasty,

◀ A map showing the site of tombs at the pyramid complex of Saqqara, south of the present-day capital of Cairo. The site covers an area more than 3½ miles (6 km) long and 1 mile (1.6 km) across at its widest point.

Key to top map
1 Netjerykhet Djoser
2 Sekhemkhet
3 "Great Enclosure"
4 Shepseskaf
5 Userkaf
6 Izezi
7 Wenis
8 Teti
9 Pepy I
10 Mernere'
11 Pepy II
12 Ibi
13 Merykare' (?)
14 Khendjey
15 Unknown king of 13th Dynasty

▲ *The entrance to the Step Pyramid of Djoser near the southeastern corner of the recessed enclosure wall.*

pyramids were surrounded by cemeteries of nonroyal tombs. During this period, however, only Userkaf, first king of the 5th Dynasty, and Wenis, the last, were buried at North Saqqara. The tombs south of the pyramid of Userkaf obstructed the construction of the pyramid of Wenis and some were simply covered by Wenis' causeway, avoiding the destruction and plundering of later times. Late 5th and 6th Dynasty tombs occupy the space between Wenis' causeway and the south wall of the enclosure of Djoser.

The few tombs of the Middle Kingdom at Saqqara are in areas popular during the late Old Kingdom and 1st Intermediate Period, especially around the pyramid of Teti (the large tombs of Hetep and Ihy), north of the causeway of Wenis, and at South Saqqara.

Nonroyal tombs of the New Kingdom
Tombs of the New Kingdom are concentrated in two parts of Saqqara. The first is a wadi running in a westerly direction some 980 feet

(300 m) southeast of the pyramid of Teti. The steep northern face of the wadi is honeycombed with rock-cut tombs dating from the mid-18th Dynasty to the Ramessid Period. The most spectacular tomb belongs to Vizier 'Aperia ('Aper-El), who probably lived late in the reign of Amenhotep III. The tomb was excavated, in difficult working conditions, by the French Egyptologist Alain-Pierre Zivie. Somewhat later free-standing tombs were built on the plateau between the wadi and the pyramid of Teti.

The second area with New Kingdom tombs lies south of the causeway of Wenis. They are free-standing tomb chapels. The two main groups consist of Ramessid tombs, such as that of Neferronpet, the vizier of Ramesses II, close to the causeway of Wenis, and tombs in the vicinity of the tomb of Haremhab in the southern section of the plateau.

Large, free-standing tombs of the New Kingdom appeared at Saqqara during the reign of Amenhotep III, but most excavated thus far are later. When Tut'ankhamun abandoned el-'Amarna, and the royal residence moved to Memphis, the Saqqara cemetery experienced a period of remarkable activity. The best craftsmen accompanied the court and worked on the royal and nonroyal tombs. They retained elements of 'Amarna art during this period. Saqqara remained important—even when royal attention began to focus on the northeast delta during the reign of Ramesses II.

The standard features of the New-Kingdom free-standing tomb chapel at Saqqara were an open court, often with round columns or square pillars on one or more of its sides, and the cult room situated at the back of the mastaba. The main element of the cult room was a stela on the central east–west axis of the tomb, while there were often further stelae and statues in other parts of the chapel. A small pyramid was usually built above or behind the cult room. The mouth of the shaft leading to the underground burial chamber opened into the court.

New Kingdom tombs of Apis bulls

The cult of the Apis bull was connected with that of the chief Memphite god, Ptah. From the reign of Amenhotep III onward, the tombs of the mummified Apis bulls are known from the Serapeum at Saqqara.

Nonroyal tombs of the Late and Greco-Roman Periods

During the 26th Dynasty, the designers of Egyptian tombs apparently achieved what their predecessors had vainly attempted for the previous two millennia—they designed an almost completely robber-proof tomb. In many Saqqara tombs of this period, a vaulted burial chamber was built at the bottom of a large, deep shaft, which was subsequently

filled with sand. The other type of tomb known from this period is the more conventional rock-cut tomb.

The majority of the tombs of the Late and Greco-Roman Periods are found near the Step Pyramid enclosure:

1. to the north, along the avenue of sphinxes that link the temples on the eastern edge of the plateau with the Serapeum (mainly 30th Dynasty and later);

2. to the east, particularly shaft tombs in the area of the pyramid of Userkaf, with rock-cut tombs farther east, in the escarpment (mainly 26th Dynasty);

3. to the west, and continuing northward toward Abusir (mainly Greco-Roman);

4. to the south, and close to the pyramid of Wenis (mainly 26th and 27th Dynasties, but also a large Ptolemaic tomb).

The Serapeum and the sacred animal necropolis

The Apis bulls were the most important cult animals buried at Saqqara. Ramesses II abandoned the earlier individual tombs and started an underground gallery (the "Lesser Vaults") in which the mummified bodies of Apis bulls were deposited in large niches on either side. Since there was only one of these animals at a time, an Apis bull burial occurred about once every 14 years. The gallery of Ramesses II ultimately reached a length of 220 feet (68 m). A second gallery (the "Greater Vaults"), cut at right angles to the earlier one, was inaugurated during the 26th Dynasty, and the first Apis bull laid to rest there died in year 52 of Psammetichus I.

A complex of chapels and small temples grew up near the catacombs of Apis bulls, together forming the Serapeum. Nectanebo I and II of the 30th Dynasty were the two most distinguished contributors; the former may also have set up the alley of human-headed sphinxes that approached the Serapeum from the city of Memphis, in the east, below the Saqqara plateau. At the east end of the alley of sphinxes there were temples, among them the Anubieion and the Asklepieion, most of which were built by the Ptolemies. These temples were associated with animal cults and in their vicinity are communal burials of mummified jackals and cats.

Abusir

The solar temple

The northernmost monument at Abusir, midway between Abu Ghurab and the Abusir pyramids, is the solar temple built by King Userkaf at the beginning of the 5th Dynasty.

This is the earliest preserved solar temple in Egypt, so its simplicity and lack of relief decoration come as no surprise; but Userkaf's short reign did not allow him to complete the temple. Some Egyptian texts write its name with a hieroglyphic sign of an obelisk base surrounded by an enclosure wall, which indicates that the obelisk was a later feature.

The pyramids

Userkaf built his pyramid at Saqqara, but the next five kings of the 5th Dynasty (and possibly also Menkauhor) moved to Abusir.

The pyramid complex of Sahure' was

▼ *Reconstruction of the solar temple complex of the 5th Dynasty king Neuserre' at Abu Ghurab.*

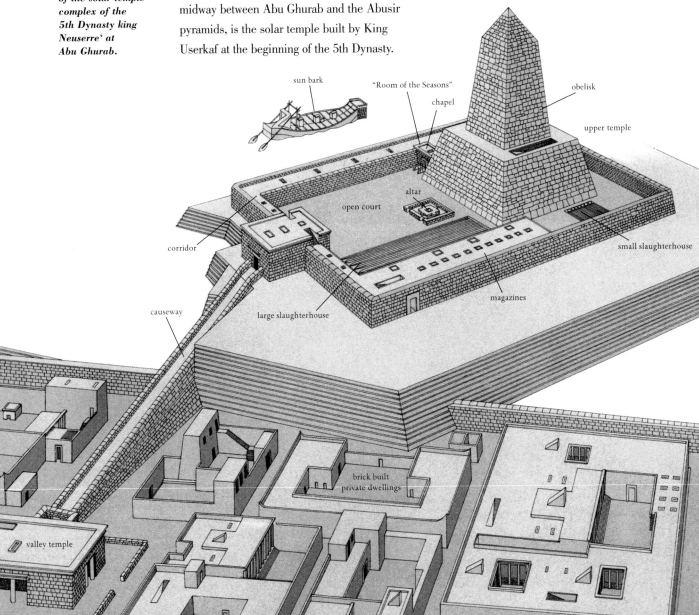

sun bark

"Room of the Seasons"

chapel

obelisk

upper temple

corridor

open court

altar

small slaughterhouse

causeway

large slaughterhouse

magazines

brick built private dwellings

valley temple

a magnificent structure, both in size and decoration. The plan is typical of Egyptian royal funerary architecture of the 5th Dynasty. Fragments of the reliefs that decorated the causeway linking the king's valley and pyramid temples were discovered in the early 1990s. They show the transport of Sahure''s pyramid capstone, men at military training, dancers, rows of officials, emaciated desert tribesmen, and other topics.

The pyramid complexes of Neferirkare' and Neuserre' have suffered even more than that of their predecessor. Neferirkare' designed his funerary complex on a larger scale than Sahure' but did not complete it; its un-finished lower part was appropriated by Neuserre', who diverted the causeway to his own pyramid temple. The southernmost pyramid at Abusir, which was hardly begun, belonged to Re'neferef;. The early stage of the building of yet another pyramid, perhaps of the shadowy king Shepseskare', is at north Abusir.

The nonroyal tombs

Among the nonroyal tombs at Abusir, the most important is the family mastaba of Ptahshepses, the vizier and son-in-law of Neuserre'. It is northeast of the pyramid of Neuserre' and was restored in the 1970s and 1980s. It is one of the largest nonroyal tombs of the Old Kingdom. Other mastabas are to the southeast of Neuserre''s pyramid and in the south part of Abusir.

Abu Ghurab

The rulers of the 5th Dynasty, with the exception of Shepseskare', Izezi, and Wenis, hoped to ensure the continuation of their relationship with the Heliopolitan Sun god Re' in the afterlife by building special temples for this purpose. Each king built only one such structure. Unlike temples of other deities, they were situated on the desert margin, not far from the royal pyramids. The names of six of these solar temples are known from Egyptian texts but only two have so far been located by archaeologists.

The solar temple built by King Neuserre' at Abu Ghurab is the finest example and is unlikely to be surpassed even if the four as yet undiscovered are found in the future. In its general features it owes much to the typical pyramid complex of the same period. Its main axis is east–west and it consists of:

1. the valley temple (close to a canal, so that it could be approached by boat);

2. the causeway (linking the valley temple with the upper part of the complex);

3. the upper temple.

The dominant feature of the upper temple was a large open court with an altar and a masonry-built obelisk, the symbol of the Sun god. Highly unusual were scenes in the "Chamber of the Seasons." The creative influence which the Sun god exerted on nature was expressed there by scenes characteristic of the Egyptian countryside in the *akhet* season (the inundation) and the *shemu* season (the harvest). Depictions of animals and plants dominate these reliefs; human beings play only a limited role.

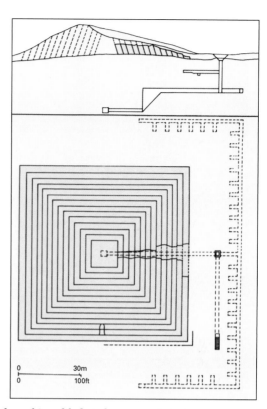

▲ *A plan and cross section of the 3rd Dynasty "Layer Pyramid" at Zawyet el-'Aryan.*

The three pyramids at Giza rise behind the queens' pyramids associated with the pyramid of Menkaure (left). The pyramids are the best-known symbol of ancient Egypt—and possibly of the whole ancient world.

Zawyet el-'Aryan

Neither of the two pyramids at Zawyet el-'Aryan was ever completed. The earlier "Layer Pyramid" started construction as a step pyramid but is tentatively attributed to King Kha'ba of the 3rd Dynasty, while the other, the "Unfinished Pyramid," is dated to the 4th Dynasty by its more advanced architectural features and the method of recording its owner's name in builders' graffiti. One of the tombs near the pyramid of Kha'ba contained clay sealings and a pottery fragment with the name of the Dynasty 0 ruler Na'rmer.

Giza

The three Giza pyramids of the 4th Dynasty start looming on the horizon as soon as you pass through the Cairo suburb that lent them its name and proceed in a southwesterly direction along Sharia' al-Ahram (Avenue of the Pyramids). The history of the site goes back much further, at least to the reign of King Ninetjer of the 2nd Dynasty, whose name occurs on some jar sealings found in a tomb in the south part of the site. An even earlier tomb of the reign of King Wadj of the 1st Dynasty was located to the south of the area, described as the Giza necropolis.

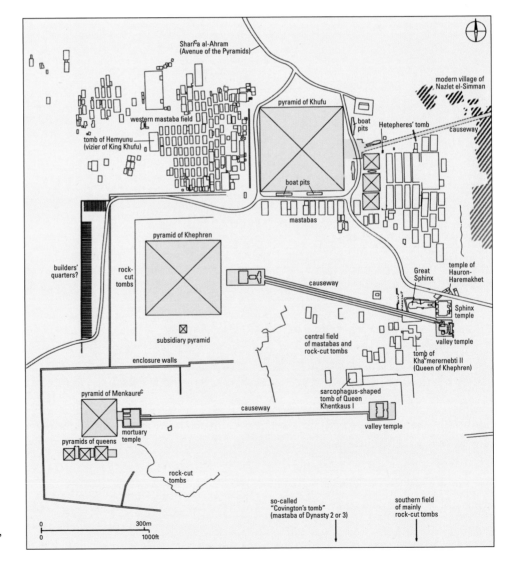

▶ *A plan of the pyramid complex at Giza. The accompanying cross sections show the hidden chambers and passageways inside the pyramids of Khufu, Khephren, and Menkaure'.*

The site falls naturally into two well-defined groups situated on higher ground. The first unit, which is much the larger and more important, consists of the pyramids and the surrounding fields of nonroyal mastabas. The valley temples of the pyramids, and the Great Sphinx with the adjacent temples, are situated below this elevated plateau. There is little doubt that the Giza pyramids are mutually related on the ground, but this is probably due to the techniques used when the sites for each of them were surveyed. The smaller and less important south group, containing only nonroyal tombs, is on a ridge to the southeast.

The systematic study of Giza started in the first half of the 19th century. Although probably more systematically excavated than any other Egyptian site, recent discoveries by the Egyptian Supreme Council of Antiquities and others show that exploration of the site cannot be regarded as complete.

The pyramid complex of Khufu

Khufu's pyramid, the "Great Pyramid," is one of the most famous monuments in the world. Its size and perfection of construction have made it the focus of attention of visitors to the Memphite area since time immemorial. The Great Pyramid was almost certainly robbed of its original contents during the period of political instability and unrest that followed the collapse of the central royal power after the end of the Old Kingdom. Modern explorers found it empty, with only the massive granite sarcophagus in the burial chamber indicating its original purpose.

The question of whether the interior of the Great Pyramid underwent alterations in the process of the construction, or whether its final form was planned from the beginning, has not yet been fully answered. The modern visitor enters the pyramid by an opening forced by Caliph Ma'mun's men in the 9th century CE, which is situated below and somewhat west of the original entrance. The descending passage leads to a chamber below ground level. Another chamber (called the "Queen's Chamber" in modern terms, although there is no evidence that it would have been used for the burial of a queen), possibly the burial chamber of the 2nd plan, is in the mass of the pyramid and can be approached by ascending and level passages. The ascending passage is extended by the great gallery to reach the burial chamber proper (the "King's Chamber"). The great gallery, with its high corbeled ceiling, is easily the most impressive part of the whole interior. One of its purposes was probably to provide space for storing the granite blocks that were slid down the ascending passage after the funeral to seal it.

Narrow shafts run between the "Queen's Chamber" and the "King's Chamber" in what appears to be the shortest route toward the outside of the pyramid. Their description as "air shafts" is probably incorrect but their purpose is not yet known. If they are aligned astronomically, as has been suggested, they may be important for dating of the pyramid. In 1993, Rudolf Gantenbrink explored the south shaft in the "Queen's Chamber" using a robot equipped with a video camera. He found a limestone slab with copper fittings some 210 feet (65 m) into the shaft. The idea that there is a hidden chamber behind this slab is unlikely. It may just mark the point reached when the design of the pyramid was changed during its construction.

Even today, building the Great Pyramid would present technological and managerial problems. The project must have been more or less completed by the end of Khufu's

▲ *The Triad of
Menkaure' shows king
Menkaure' holding
the hand of the
goddess Hathor, with
the deity of the 7th
Egyptian nome on his
left. The sculpture
was discovered at the
mortuary temple of
Menkaure' at Giza.
On display at the
Egyptian Museum
in Cairo.*

had not yet been invented, so the problems connected with moving and lifting heavy stone blocks must have been enormous. At least as many people as those dealing with the stone blocks must have been engaged in auxiliary works such as construction of inclined ramps along which the blocks were dragged, maintenance of tools, and the provision of food and water. Because of the uncertainty about the methods the Egyptians actually used, any estimate of the size of the labor force must remain a mere guess.

A remarkable discovery was made in the early 1950s. A rectangular pit close to the south face of the pyramid of Khufu contained parts of a dismantled wooden boat. In the airtight surroundings, they remained almost perfectly preserved. The vessel is more than 130 feet (40 m) long, with a displacement of 40 tons (tonnes). The location of another pit, also containing a boat, is known, but the pit is still to be opened. The boats were perhaps used to convey the body of the deceased king to the place of purification and embalming and finally to the valley temple.

The pyramid complex of Khephren

Khufu's son and successor Re'djedef started to build his pyramid at Abu Rawash, north of Giza, but the next king, Khephren, another son of Khufu, built his funerary complex beside his father's. Although it was designed on a more modest scale, a slight increase in the incline of the pyramid's faces made it seem comparable in size to the Great Pyramid. The so-called "Second Pyramid" retains some of its original smooth outer casing near its apex, which may be due to a new method of positioning the blocks.

The valley temple of Khephren's pyramid complex, next to the Great Sphinx, is a soberly designed building which, in the

23-year reign, which meant that every year 100,000 large blocks (about 285 every day), each weighing about 2½ tons (tonnes), were quarried, dressed, brought to the site, and set in place. As building progressed, the height to which it was necessary to lift the blocks increased, while at the same time the working platform at the top of the pyramid decreased rapidly in size. Once "off the ground," transport of the blocks was almost certainly by human force, because restricted space prevented the use of draft animals. Even simple devices such as as the pulley absence of almost any decoration, relies on the effect produced by the polished granite casing of the walls of its rooms and its calcite floors. A pit in one of the rooms was found to contain a set of diorite-gneiss and graywacke sculptures of Khephren, deposited there in a later period, among them probably one of the most famous Egyptian statues, which shows the king seated with a hawk perched on the back slab of the statue.

The pyramid complex of Menkaure'

The pyramid complex of Menkaure', king of the 4th Dynasty, is somewhat dwarfed by its two Giza companions. Although hastily finished in mud brick, its valley temple produced a superb collection of royal statues. Some of these were triads (groups of three figures) and showed the king accompanied by the Memphite goddess Hathor and personifications of nomes (provinces) of Egypt. There was also a standing double statue of the king and one of his wives, the earliest of this type in Egyptian statuary.

This so-called "Third Pyramid" was refurbished, probably during the 26th Dynasty, when the cult of the kings buried at Giza was revived. The basalt sarcophagus found in the burial chamber was lost at sea while being shipped to England, but the remains of a wooden coffin, purporting to be that of Menkaure', were certainly put in the pyramid some 1,900 years later. In 1968, an inscription discovered in the remains of the casing near the entrance of the pyramid probably refers to this remarkable ancient effort of restoration.

Nonroyal tombs

Close to each pyramid complex are the tombs of officials and priests. Many of these tombs were built by royal craftsmen and presented to their eventual occupants by the king himself. A large number of people buried in these tombs had held priestly positions connected with the Giza necropolis during their lifetimes.

The most extensive mastaba fields are to the west, south, and east of the pyramid of Khufu. These cemeteries continued to be used through the rest of the Old Kingdom, with smaller tombs often being added in between the larger mastabas. The quarries to the southeast of the pyramids of Khephren and Menkaure', with their artificially created rock faces, provided ideal conditions for decorated rock-cut tombs, the earliest of this type in Egypt.

A typical mastaba, such as was built at Giza in the reign of Khufu, had a stone-built superstructure with a rectangular plan and slightly sloping faces. A shaft sunk through this superstructure and cut in the rock substratum terminated in a simple burial chamber. This shaft was permanently sealed after the burial had been deposited in the chamber. The original cult chapel consisted of one or two mud-brick rooms against the east face of the mastaba. The main element of this chapel was an inscribed slab stela with a representation of the deceased seated at a table along with a list of offerings. Offerings were brought for the *ka* (spirit) of the deceased before this stela on prescribed days. There were no other decorated elements in the tomb.

The mastabas at Giza were among the earliest nonroyal stone-built tombs anywhere in Egypt, and their original simple design underwent a rapid development. The greatest changes occurred in the chapel. An interior chapel was introduced in some of the tombs in which the offering chamber and subsidiary rooms were contained in the core

▲ *The Great Sphinx
at Giza is the largest
monolith statute in
the world. Partially
buried beneath the
desert for thousands
of years, the Sphinx
has been regularly
cleared of sand to
prevent any damage
to the structure.*

of the mastaba itself, while other tombs
continued to be built with an exterior chapel.
The customary slab stela was replaced by
a false door, and the walls of the chapel
began to be lined with fine limestone and
decorated with reliefs.

The chief royal wives were the only people
apart from the king himself who could be
buried in pyramids. A shaft with a chamber
that contained furniture as well as funerary

items of Queen Hetepheres, the wife of
Snofru and the mother of Khufu, was found
to the east of the Great Pyramid in 1925.
It lacked a superstructure of any kind, and
the queen's mummy was not present.

The Great Sphinx
The concept of the sphinx, a creature with a
human head and a lion's body, is of uncertain
origin or age, but it is not known from Egypt

before the reign of Re'djedef, Khephren's immediate predecessor. The most famous sphinx, the Great Sphinx at Giza, is almost as universally recognizable as the Great Pyramid itself. The Great Sphinx is probably associated with the pyramid complex of Khephren, however, rather than with that of Khufu, as was once traditionally suggested. Another suggestion—that the Great Sphinx predates other monuments at Giza—by several thousand years carries little conviction. The temple in front of the statue bears some similarity to the later solar temples built by the kings of the 5th Dynasty at Abu Ghurab and Abusir, but it was only some 1,000 years later that the colossal statue started being identified with the god Harmakhis ("Horus on the Horizon"), the local form of the god Horus.

The desert sand that builds up to cover the body of the Sphinx has had to be cleared several times. The earliest recorded clearance was undertaken by King Thutmose IV, who left a record of the task on the so-called "Dream Stela" erected between its forepaws. In the eyes of many, the Great Sphinx at Giza is a symbol of Egypt, and anything connected with it arouses much scholarly as well as public interest. Its restoration is an ongoing project.

Giza after the end of the Old Kingdom
With the end of the Old Kingdom, Giza's ceremonial heyday was over. For the next 600 years, little if anything of any significance took place at the site. In the New Kingdom, however, Giza profited from the renewed importance of Memphis (Mit Rahina). King Amenhotep II of the 18th Dynasty built a small brick temple for Harmakhis northeast of the Great Sphinx, and Sety I later enlarged it.

Abu Rawash

The site of Abu Rawash took its name from the village situated to the east and served as the necropolis for an administrative center at the very beginning of Egyptian history. Excavations have revealed objects inscribed with the names of two kings of the 1st Dynasty, 'Aha and Den.

King Re'djedef chose the commanding plateau of Abu Rawash for the site of his pyramid complex and therefore did not move onto virgin ground. The pyramid itself is the northernmost in the Memphite necropolis. Remains of building material visible at the site indicate that it was planned to be at least partly cased with red granite. The causeway, about 1 mile (1.5 km) long, approaches the pyramid and its temple from the northeast instead of from the customary east, but this was determined by the character of the terrain rather than religious considerations. Because Re'djedef reigned for only eight years, his funerary monument hardly got beyond the initial stages of its construction.

The pyramid complex produced some excellent examples of royal statuary, though even these are sadly fragmentary. The statues are made of the hard red quartzite of Gebel Ahmar (east of modern Cairo). Apart from providing the somewhat idealized features of the king, one of them is an attractive seated statue with a small figure of Re'djedef's queen Khentetka, kneeling and holding the leg of her husband. Although eagerly taken up by makers of nonroyal statues, this type was not repeated in royal sculpture.

Abu Rawash never regained its shortlived importance under Re'djedef. However, one of the late structures at Wadi Qaren, north of the pyramid, yielded the upper part of a beautiful statuette of Queen Arsinoe II, the sister and wife of Ptolemy II Philadelphus.

The Delta

▶ *A map showing the main sites around the Delta region of Lower Egypt, north of the present-day capital of Cairo.*

Much of the delta's prehistory and most ancient history are buried under silt. Only now is the area beginning to receive the attention it deserves.

The eastern delta was the meeting point of Egypt and Asia. In the later Middle Kingdom, it was settled by Asiatics and became the center from which they ruled; subsequently it was the Egyptian base for campaigns to Asia.

When the royal residence was moved to Pi-Ri'amsese in the 19th Dynasty, the delta took over leadership of Egypt. Several of its cities saw their rulers lead Egypt during the 3rd Intermediate and Late Periods. The delta's proximity to the main centers of the ancient world favored its development under the Ptolemies and Romans.

Ausim

Ancient Egyptian *Khem* (Greek Letopolis), some 8 miles (13 km) northwest of Cairo, was the capital of the 2nd Lower Egyptian nome. The nome and its falcon god Khenty-irty (a form of Horus) are mentioned in texts from the 4th Dynasty, but only a few late monuments, bearing the names Necho II, Psammetichus II, Hakoris, and Nectanebo I, have been found at the site.

Kom Abu Billo

At the point where the route leading from Wadi el-Natrun approaches the Rosetta branch of the Nile, there lies the town of Tarrana (Coptic *Terenouti*; classical Terenuthis). The name derives from that of the serpent goddess Renenutet (Termuthis). The remains of the temple and the

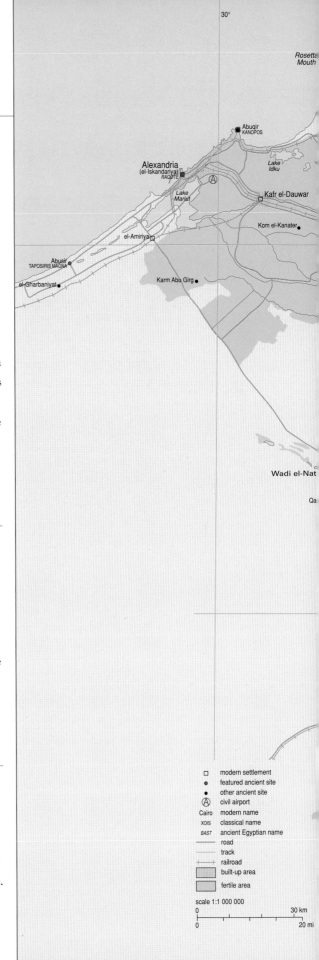

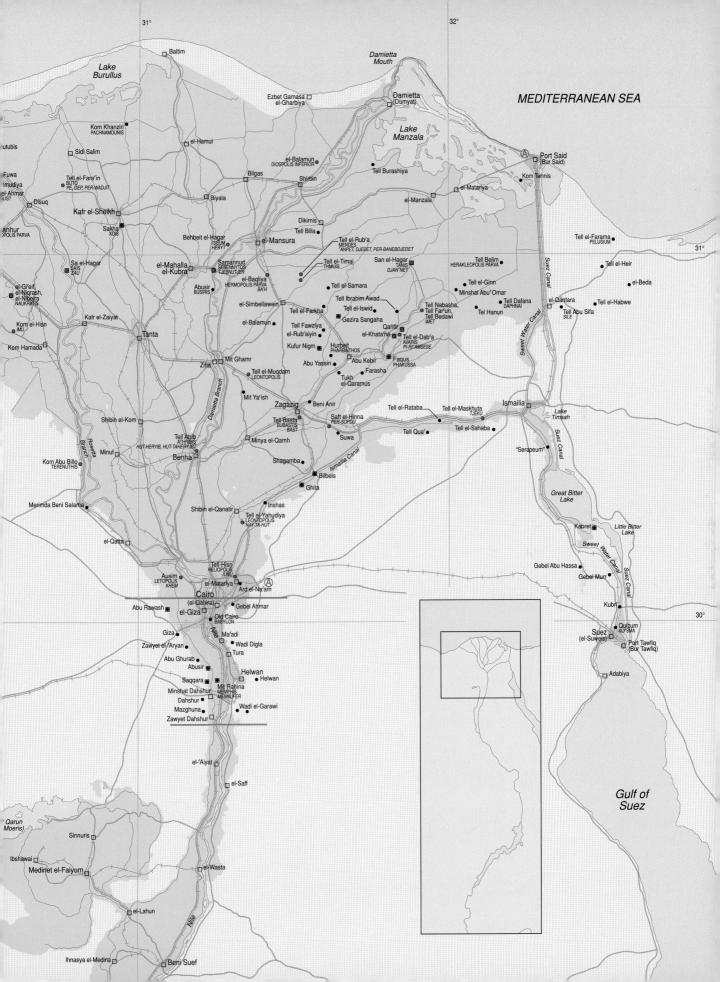

Lake Burullus

Baltim

MEDITERRANEAN SEA

Damietta Mouth

Ezbet Gamasa el-Gharbiya

Damietta (Dumyat)

Lake Manzala

Kom Khanziri PACHNAMOUNIS

utubis

el-Hamul

el-Balamun DIOSPOLIS INFERIOR

Tell Burashiya

Port Said (Bur Said)

Fuwa

Sidi Salim

Bilgas

Shirbin

el-Matariya

Kom Tennis

mmudiya el-Ahmar LIS?

Tell el-Fara'in BUTO PE, DEP, PER-WADJIT

Biyala

el-Manzala

Disuq

Kafr el-Sheikh

Dikirnis

Tell Billa

Tell el-Farama PELUSIUM

anhur OPOLIS PARVA

Sakha XOIS

Behbeit el-Hagar ISEUM HEBYT

el-Mansura

Tell el-Rub'a MENDES 'ANPET, DJEDET, PER-BANEBDJEDET

Tell Belim HERAKLEOPOLIS PARVA

Tell el-Heir

Sa el-Hagar SAIS ZAU

Samannud SEBENNYTOS TJEBNUTJER

Tell el-Timai THMUIS

San el-Hagar TANIS DJAN'NET

el-Beda

el-Mahalla el-Kubra

el-Bagliya HERMOPOLIS PARVA BA'H

Tell el-Samara

Tell el-Ginn

el-Gi'eif, el-Nigrash, el-Nibeira NAUKRATIS

Abusir BUSIRIS

Tell Ibrahim Awad

Minshat Abu'Omar

Tell Dafana DAPHNAI

el-Qantara

el-Simbellawein

Tell el-Farkha

Tell el-Iswid

Tell Nabasha, Tell Far'un, Tell Bedawi IMET

Tell el-Habwe

Kom el-Hisn IMU

Kafr el-Zaiyat

el-Balamun

Gezira Sangaha

Tel Hanun

Tell Abu Sifa SILE

Kom Hamada

Tanta

Tell Fawziya

Qantir

el-Rub'aiyin

el-Khata'na

Tell el-Dab'a AVARIS PI-RI'AMSESE

Mit Ghamr

Kufur Nigm

Hurbeit PHARBAITHOS

Zifta

Tell el-Muqdam LEONTOPOLIS

Abu Yassin

Abu Kebir

Faqus PHAKUSSA

Shibin el-Kom

Mit Ya'ish

Tukh el-Qaramus

Farasha

Rosetta Branch

Damietta Branch

Zagazig

Beni Anir

Tell el-Rataba

Tell el-Maskhuta TJEKU

Ismailia

Lake Timsah

Tell Atrib ATHRIBIS HUT-HERYIB, HUT-TAHERYABT

Tell Basta BUBASTIS BAST

Saft el-Hinna PER-SOPDU

Tell Qua'

Tell el-Sahaba

Minuf

Minya el-Qamh

Suwa

"Serapeum"

Kom Abu Billo TERENUTHIS

Benha

Shagamba

Suez Canal

Merimda Beni Salama

Bilbeis

Ghita

Great Bitter Lake

el-Qatta

Inshas

Ismailia Canal

Shibin el-Qanatir

Tell el-Yahudiya LEONTOPOLIS NAY-TA-HUT

Kabret

Little Bitter Lake

Sweet Water Canal

Tell-Hisn HELIOPOLIS IUNU

Gebel Abu Hassa

Ausim LETOPOLIS KHEM

el-Matariya

Ard el-Na'am

Gebel Murr

Abu Rawash

Cairo (el-Qahira)

Gebel Ahmar

Kubri

el-Giza

Old Cairo BABYLON

Suez (el-Suweis)

Quizum KLYSMA

Giza

Ma'adi

Port Tawfiq (Bur Tawfiq)

Zawyet el-'Aryan

Wadi Digla

Tura

Abu Ghurab

Abusir

Helwan

Helwan

Adabiya

Saqqara

Mit Rahina MEMPHIS MENNUFER

Minshat Dahshur

Dahshur

Wadi el-Garawi

Mazghuna

Zawyet Dahshur

Qarun Moeris)

el-'Aiyat

el-Saff

Gulf of Suez

Sinnuris

Nile

Ibshawai

el-Wasta

Medinet el-Faiyum

el-Lahun

Ihnasya el-Medina

Beni Suef

necropolis have been found nearby at the mound of Kom Abu Billo.

The temple of Kom Abu Billo is dedicated to Hathor "Mistress of Mefket" (ancient *Tarrana*, but *mefket* also means turquoise). Blocks decorated with exquisite low raised relief show it to be one of the few surviving works of Ptolemy I Soter, completed by Ptolemy II Philadelphus.

The large necropolis of Kom Abu Billo contains burials ranging from the 6th Dynasty to the 4th century CE. A number of New Kingdom pottery sarcophagi (called "slipper coffins"), with their lids modeled as grotesque faces, have been found. The site is famous for a type of tomb stela dating to the first four centuries CE (called "Terenuthis stelae"). The deceased, represented in un-Egyptian style, usually stands with upraised arms or reclines on a couch, with a short text in demotic or Greek below.

Kom el-Hisn

A large, low mound, measuring 545 yards (500 m) across, called Kom el-Hisn, covers the remains of the ancient town of Imu. From the New Kingdom onward, this was the capital of the 3rd Lower Egyptian nome.

Kom el-Hisn has extensive remains of occupation dating from the Old and Middle Kingdoms. The most important feature is the rectangular outline of a temple enclosure. Statues of Amenemhet III and Ramesses II found there identify the temple as belonging to Sakhmet-Hathor. Hathor was the traditional goddess of the area. The Middle Kingdom tomb of the "Overseer of Priests" Khesuwer southwest of the temple enclosure is one of the few major nonroyal tombs surviving in the delta.

Naukratis

A mound near the villages el-Gi‘eif, el-Nibeira, and el-Niqrash, in the 5th (Saite) nome of Lower Egypt, is the site of the Greek trading post of Naukratis. The Greeks (initially Milesians) settled in the area some time during the 26th Dynasty. Under Amasis, the town was granted a monopoly of Aegean trade. Naukratis contained several almost entirely lost temples of Greek gods but also an Egyptian temple, dedicated probably to Amun and Thoth, in its southern part (the "Great Mound" within the "Great Temenos").

Alexandria

The native Egyptian word for Alexandria was *Raqote*. This name occurs in an early text of Ptolemy I Soter and designated an older settlement on the site. Remains of timber works, from c. 400 BCE, prove the harbor's existence before Alexander. Native Egyptians lived in an area, Rhakotis in Greek, that may have contained monuments in an Egyptian style. Alexandria was a mixed Greek city whose most important non-Greek element was Jewish. As the Hellenistic world's chief city and port, it was vital in the dissemination of Egyptian lore.

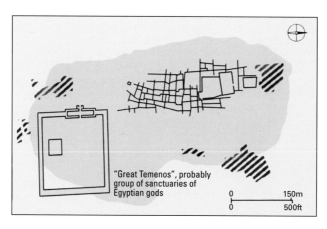

"Great Temenos", probably group of sanctuaries of Egyptian gods

0 — 150m
0 — 500ft

▶ *This plan shows the main excavated areas of Naukratis.*

The Serapeum, the main temple of the Greco-Egyptian god Sarapis, was located in Rhakotis. Bilingual plaques date its founding to Ptolemy III Euergetes I. Its foundations survive, along with remains of the Roman replacement of around 200 CE and "Pompey's pillar" of the reign of Diocletian, which still stands. It contained much older Egyptian material, notably sphinxes and other scene-setting statuary. Near the Serapeum is the 1st–2nd century CE catacomb of Kom el-Shuqafa, whose burial areas contain Egyptianizing scenes and motifs. Chambers near ground level retain painted decoration; deeper parts have only statuary and relief.

Underwater archaeology has uncovered stonework from the Ptolemaic harbor. Work there, and near Fort Qait Bey, the site of the Pharos lighthouse, has revealed hundreds of blocks from Classical columns and smaller numbers of Egyptian blocks. Important finds also include monumental Egyptian-style statues of Ptolemaic kings and their wives that had probably been erected nearby.

Abusir

About 28 miles (45 km) west of Alexandria is Abusir, ancient *Taposiris Magna,* an important town in the Ptolemaic Period, which has an unfinished temple of Osiris in native Egyptian style. The enclosure is in limestone instead of traditional mud brick but uses mud-brick building techniques. The temple is uninscribed and cannot be dated precisely. Nearby was a large animal necropolis, which is a further indication of the town's significance as a native center.

Sa el-Hagar

Sais (ancient Egyptian *Zau*) and its goddess Neith are attested from the beginning of Egyptian history. The town was the capital of

the 5th Lower Egyptian nome, which until the 12th Dynasty also incorporated the area south of it, later the 4th nome. Politically, Sais came to prominence toward the end of the 8th century BCE. Its ambitious leaders, Tefnakhte and Bocchoris (later the 24th Dynasty), clashed with the rulers of the 25th (Nubian) Dynasty. Their successors ruled over Egypt; temples, palaces, and royal tombs (all largely undiscovered) bore witness to the success of these kings of the 26th (Saite) Dynasty.

Despite the city's famous past, no monuments, except some isolated stone blocks, are visible in the area today. Even at the end of the 19th century, it was still

▲ A diorite sculpture of the head of a king dating from the 26th Dynasty (664–525 BCE). The sculpture was discovered in the undersea remains of the ancient city of Herakleion off the coastal town of Abu Qir near Alexandria.

possible to trace the remains of a huge rectangular enclosure north of the village of Sa el-Hagar, on the right bank of the Rosetta branch of the Nile. Fifty years earlier, in the middle of the 19th century, the artists of Lepsius' expedition recorded a view of the sizable remains of the walls. The relatively recent, but very quick, disappearance of the enclosure was due to the activities of the sabbakhin who look for old mud-brick structures as a source of cheap fertilizer. Stone blocks had already been removed to be used as building material in the Middle Ages. It has been possible to locate some of them in various towns and villages along the Rosetta branch of the Nile.

Tell el-Fara'in

Tell el-Fara'in ("The Mound of the Pharaohs"), in the 6th Lower Egyptian nome, is the site of Buto (ancient Egyptian *Per-Wadjit,* "The Domain of Wadjit;" Coptic *Pouto*). The town was important from the very beginning of Egyptian history. It was held to have consisted of two parts, called Pe and Dep, and was the home of the cobra goddess Wadjit, the tutelary goddess of Lower Egypt. In this function it was paralleled by Upper Egyptian Nekheb (el-Kab) and Nekhen (Kom el-Ahmar) and the vulture goddess Nekhbet.

Behbeit el-Hagar

Behbeit el-Hagar is the site of one of the most important temples of Isis in Egypt. It is near Samannud, the home town of the kings of the 30th Dynasty, said to have a special devotion to Isis. The foundation likely dates from that period, or the temple may be built on the site of an unimportant predecessor.

The temple seems to have been built entirely of granite. The ruins are set in an enclosure whose two sides can still be distinguished. The temple has collapsed completely, either through quarrying or after an earthquake, and its plan has not been fully recovered; all that is visible is a disorderly mass of relief blocks and some architectural elements. The reliefs are very fine work of Nectanebo I–II and of Ptolemy II Philadelphus and III Euergetes I, much more delicate than that of the Greco-Roman temples of Upper Egypt. Reliefs in this style and material played an important part in formulating the Classical image of Egypt.

Tell Atrib

Tell Atrib, north of the town of Benha on the right bank of the Damietta branch of the Nile, derives its name from ancient Egyptian *Hut-(ta-)hery(t)-ibt* (Coptic *Athrebi;* Greek Athribis). It was the capital of the 10th Lower Egyptian nome, and the name *Kem-wer* ("The Great Black One," or bull) could equally be applied to the local god, the nome, and its capital. In the Dynastic Period, the crocodile (or falcon) god Khentekhtai became the most prominent local deity.

Egyptian texts show that the history of Tell Atrib goes back at least to the early 4th Dynasty. The remains of the earliest temple found there are dated by foundation deposits to the reign of Amasis. A town, temples, and necropolis of the Greco-Roman Period have also been located. Isolated monuments of various dates are known from, or have been ascribed to, the site on the basis of their inscriptions; none is earlier than the 12th Dynasty. As with all delta sites, caution is required when dealing with objects that might have been brought from elsewhere and reused. In 1924, the sabbakhin, whose activities have seriously affected the site, discovered a large cache of silver treasure, including ingots, amulets, rings, and earrings dating to the 25th–30th Dynasties.

Tell el-Muqdam

Some of the most extensive human-made mounds in the delta used to be on the right bank of the Damietta branch of the Nile, about 6¼ miles (10 km) southeast of Mit Ghamr, at Tell el-Muqdam. This is the site of ancient Leontopolis, an important town in the 11th Lower Egyptian nome and its capital during the Ptolemaic Period. There are indications that Tell el-Muqdam was the seat of a line of kings of the 23rd Dynasty and perhaps their burial place, but only the tomb of Queen Kamama, the mother of Osorkon IV, has been found so far.

The temple of the local lion god Mahes/Mihos (Greek Miysis), situated in the east part of the ruins, suffered the fate of many similar buildings in the delta: most of its stone blocks have been removed and reused, leaving even the date of the structure uncertain. Another tell in the neighborhood, Mit Ya'ish, has produced material of the 22nd Dynasty (a stela of Osorkon III) and of the Ptolemaic Period.

Samannud

Ancient *Tjebnutjer* (Coptic *Djebenoute/ Djemnouti*, Greek Sebennytos), now on the left bank of the Damietta branch of the Nile, was the capital of the 12th Lower Egyptian nome and a town of some importance toward the end of the Dynastic Period: according to Manetho, himself a native of Sebennytos, the kings of the 30th Dynasty came from there.

A large mound west of the modern town marks the remains of the temple of the local god Onuris-Shu. The granite blocks bear the names of Nectanebo II, Philip Arrhidaeus, Alexander IV, and Ptolemy II Philadelphus.

Some earlier monuments are said to have come from Samannud or its neighborhood, including an Old Kingdom false door of a certain Sesni, an altar of Amenemhet I, a statue dated to Psammetichus I, a fragment of a shrine of Nepherites (probably I), and statuary of the reign of Nectanebo I.

el-Baqliya

South of the modern village of el-Baqliya, three low mounds, rising only a few yards above the cultivated land, marked the site of the ancient Ba'h (Hermopolis Parva of the Greco-Roman Period), the capital of the 15th Lower Egyptian nome and a city of considerable importance. In the late 20th century, this site was leveled completely and nothing is now to be seen there.

Tell el-Naqus probably covered the town and the temple of the local god Thoth. The necropolis belonging to the town, including a cemetery of ibises, was probably situated at Tell el-Zereiki.

Tell el-Rub'a and Tell el-Timai

Two mounds several hundred yards apart, northwest of the modern town of el-Simbellawein in the central delta, were in turn the site of the capital of the 16th Lower Egyptian nome: the northern Tell el-Rub'a (ancient Egyptian *Per-banebdjedet*, "The Domain of the Ram Lord of Djedet;" Greek Mendes) was in the Greco-Roman Period replaced in this role by the southern Tell el-Timai (Greek Thmuis). The earlier names of Tell el-Rub'a were *'Anpet* and *Djedet*. Originally, the fish goddess Hatmehyt was the local deity; in the Dynastic Period the most prominent local cult was that of the Ram (*Ba*) of Mendes (*Djedet*). A cemetery of sacred rams, with large sarcophagi in which the rams were buried, can be seen in the

northwest corner of the enclosure of Tell el-Rub'a. The 29th Dynasty kings were said to have come from Mendes, and the city probably functioned as the royal residence.

Heliopolis

Ancient Egyptian *Iunu* (Coptic *On*), the capital of the 13th Lower Egyptian nome, is at and around Tell Hisn, northwest of the modern el-Matariya (a Cairo suburb, north of Misr el-Gedida). The temples of the Sun god Re', Re'-Atum or Re'-Harakhty at Heliopolis were some of the most important and influential religious institutions in the land. The Heliopolitan doctrine with the creator god Atum and the Sun god Re' (hence the Greek name of the town, from *helios,* meaning "Sun") at its center was crucial to the shaping of Egyptian religious and political history. The benu bird (phoenix) and the Mnevis bull were worshiped as manifestations of the god, and Hathor "Mistress of Hetpet" and Ius'as were the goddesses connected with Heliopolis.

No spectacular monuments can be seen in the area nowadays, except a standing obelisk of Senwosret I. Obelisks were particularly characteristic of the temples at Heliopolis, and "Cleopatra's Needles" in London and New York, although removed from Alexandria in the second half of the 19th century, originally stood in Heliopolis.

The history and topography of the site are not clear. Many isolated monuments such as statues, reliefs, and obelisks, dating between the 3rd Dynasty (Djoser) and the Ptolemaic Period, have been found. Excavations have revealed religious and other buildings built by New Kingdom kings: Amenhotep III (restored by Ramesses II), Sety I, several kings Ramesses, and Merneptah.

Tell el-Yahudiya

Tell el-Yahudiya ("The Mound of the Jews")—ancient Egyptian *Nay-ta-hut;* Greek Leontopolis—lies 1¼ miles (2 km) southeast of the village of Shibin el-Qanatir, within the 13th (Heliopolitan) nome of Lower Egypt.

The most puzzling feature of the site is the remains of an earthwork enclosure called "Hyksos Camp," dating from around the late Middle Kingdom or 2nd Intermediate Period. Inside the enclosure, in its northeastern part, the discovery of colossal statues of Ramesses II suggests that this was the site of a temple of that date. In its western part there stood a temple of Ramesses III.

Outside the enclosure are remains of a temple and town built by the exiled Jewish priest Onias. The settlement flourished for more than 200 years, but the temple was closed in 71 CE by the Roman emperor Vespasian. Cemeteries of various dates, starting with the Middle Kingdom, extend to the east of the enclosure.

Tell Basta

Tell Basta, southeast of Zagazig, is the site of the ancient *Bast* (classical Bubastis, from *Per-Bastet,* "The Domain of Bastet"), the town of the lioness goddess Bastet (Bubastis), and the capital of the 18th Lower Egyptian nome during the Late Period. The town gained prominence very early, at least partly because of its strategically important location controlling the routes from Memphis to Sinai (Wadi Tumilat) and to Asia. Politically, its influence peaked during the 22nd Dynasty, the kings of which came from Bubastis.

The main temple, dedicated to Bastet, was excavated by Edouard Naville between 1887 and 1889. The edifice consisted of a court of Osorkon II, *sed*-festival gate and hypostyle hall of Osorkon III, and shrine of Nectanebo

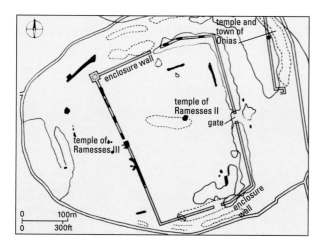

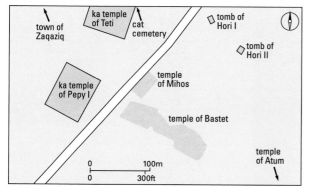

Few inscribed monuments have been found at Saft el-Hinna: statue fragments of Ramesses II are among the earliest, but the remains of a granodiorite naos dedicated to Sopd by Nectanebo I, now in the Cairo Museum, are the most impressive.

El-Khata'na, Tell el-Dab'a, and Qantir

El-Khata'na and Qantir are villages some 3¾ and 5⅔ miles (6 and 9 km) north of Faqus, respectively, in the northeastern delta. Many sandy mounds reveal settlements of the Middle Kingdom and indicate the area's increased importance during the 2nd Intermediate and Ramessid Periods. Avaris, the Hyksos center during the 2nd Intermediate Period, is at Tell el-Dab'a, and Pi-Ri'amsese, the delta residence of the Ramessids and Raamses of the Book of Exodus, near Qantir.

The occupation at Tell el-Dab'a probably goes as far back as the Herakleopolitan (1st Intermediate) period. Monuments of Queen Nefrusobk and Kings Harnedjheriotef (Hetepibre') and Nehesy were among the finds of the late 12th and 13th Dynasties. In the Middle Kingdom and 2nd Intermediate Period Tell el-Dab'a witnessed a large influx of migrants from Asia, leading up to the rise of the 15th (Hyksos) Dynasty. In the 1960s, an excavation unearthed a town and cemeteries of a local variant of the Palestinian Middle Bronze culture.

Excavations conducted in the vicinity of Qantir have uncovered the remains of a city, which was at its peak during the Ramessid

II. A birth house of Mihos (the lion god and son of Bastet) dedicated by Osorkon III, stood to the north of the main temple.

The earliest tombs date from the late Old Kingdom. Several burials of important officials have been found. Extensive cemeteries of sacred animals, particularly cats (associated with Bastet from the 3rd Intermediate Period onward), have also been located. The site has been excavated by the University of Zagazig since the 1970s.

Saft el-Hinna

The village of Saft el-Hinna, east of Zagazig, stands on the site of ancient *Per-Sopdu* ("The Domain of Sopd"), the earlier capital of the 20th nome of Lower Egypt. In 1885, E. Naville partly uncovered the mud-brick enclosure walls of the local temple as well as a number of uninscribed basalt blocks.

▲ *The imposing figure of the Sphinx of the 12th Dynasty king Amenemhat III was subsequently "usurped" by kings who added their names to it, including Merneptah, Ramesses II, and Psusennes I. The sphinx had been moved several times before it ended up at San el-Hagar. Now on display at the Egyptian Museum, Cairo.*

period, Pi-Ri'amsese. The city flourished from the 18th until the 21st Dynasty.

Tell Nabasha

A large mound, some 1 mile (1·5 km) across, but now mostly built over, in the northeastern delta, is the site of ancient Egyptian *Imet*. During the New Kingdom this was the capital of a district that was later divided into two Lower Egyptian nomes, the 18th (capital: Bubastis) and 19th (capital: Tanis). The modern names of the locality are Tell Nabasha, Tell Far'un, or Tell Bedawi.

The earliest finds are late Predynastic and Early Dynastic. The outlines of mud-brick temple enclosure of the goddess Wadjit were still discernible in the 20th century. Reused

Middle Kingdom monuments were also discovered here. Remains of a town of the Greco-Roman Period were located southeast of the temple enclosure, and a cemetery, mostly of the Late Period, lies in the plain farther to the east.

San el-Hagar

Situated in the northeastern part of the Nile delta, ancient *Dja'net* (Greek Tanis, modern San el-Hagar) was the residence and burial place of the kings of the 21st and 22nd Dynasties. In the Late Period, it became the capital of the 19th Lower Egyptian nome. It is easily the most impressive ancient site of the Delta, and the largest.

The salient feature of San el-Hagar is a large rectangular mud-brick enclosure. Inside this precinct there are remains of another, inner enclosure, with stamped bricks dating it to Psusennes I. This contains the great temple of Amun.

Today, the temple is a mass of inscribed and decorated blocks, columns, obelisks, and statues of various dates, some of which bear the names of rulers of the Old and Middle Kingdoms (Khufu, Khephren, Teti, Pepy I and II, Senwosret I) and many connected with Ramesses II. The Ramessid and earlier monuments were brought from other places as building material (a near-universal Egyptian practice—in the delta stone monuments often traveled considerable distances). The main royal builders who contributed to the temple of Amun were Siamun, Osorkon III, and Shoshenq III.

Other kings who built in the larger enclosure were Osorkon III ("The East Temple") and Nectanebo II with Ptolemy II Philadelphus (temple of Horus). Outside the enclosure, near its southwest corner, there was a precinct of A'nta (Mut), built mainly by

Siamun and Apries and rebuilt by Ptolemy IV Philopator.

In 1939, Pierre Montet found six royal tombs of the 21st and 22nd Dynasties near the southwest corner of the great temple. They belonged to Psusennes I, Amenemope, Osorkon III, and Shoshenq III—the owners of the two remaining tombs are unknown.

Apart from the 18th Dynasty tomb of Tut'ankhamun, the royal tombs of San el-Hagar are the only ones that have been discovered almost intact. The underground parts, in most cases consisting of several rooms, were built of limestone (much reused material of an earlier date), granite, or mud brick and were entered through a shaft. The walls of the tombs of Psusennes I, Osorkon III, and Shoshenq III were decorated with reliefs and inscriptions. Some of the tombs contained several burials, with sarcophagi made of granite. Two additional royal burials were found: the sarcophagus used by Takelot II was found in the tomb of Osorkon III, while the silver falcon-headed coffin of Shoshenq II was placed in the tomb of Psusennes I. The tomb of Osorkon III may have been used as a cache for other royal burials. The sarcophagus and coffin of Amenemope were discovered in the tomb of Psusennes I. Silver coffins and gold

mummy masks and jewelry, such as pectorals, collars, and bracelets, are some of the most spectacular finds.

Tell el-Maskhuta

In 1883, Edouard Naville excavated a large mud-brick enclosure with a badly damaged temple at Tell el-Maskhuta, in Wadi Tumilat. Tell el-Maskhuta is generally identified with ancient Egyptian *Tjeku,* the capital of the 8th Lower Egyptian nome, and also often with Pithom (probably from *Per-Atum,* "The Domain of Atum") of the biblical Book of Exodus.

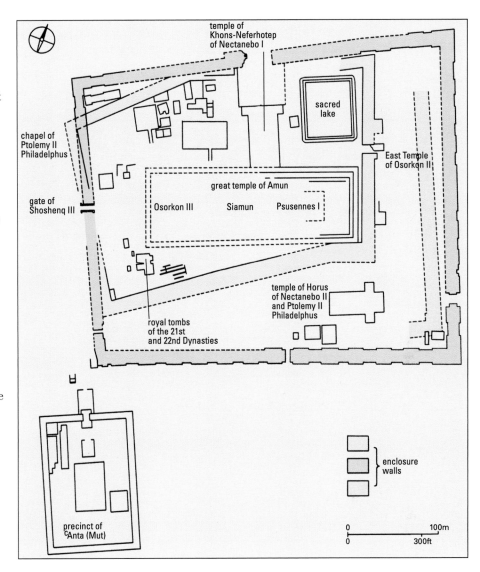

temple of
Khons-Neferhotep
of Nectanebo I

sacred
lake

chapel of
Ptolemy II
Philadelphus

East Temple
of Osorkon II

gate of
Shoshenq III

great temple of Amun

Osorkon III   Siamun   Psusennes I

temple of Horus
of Nectanebo II
and Ptolemy II
Philadelphus

royal tombs
of the 21st
and 22nd Dynasties

enclosure
walls

precinct of
ʿAnta (Mut)

0   100m
0   300ft

▲ *A plan of the site at San el-Hagar—one of the most important archaeological sites in the Delta region. The mud-brick walls of the main precinct were 50 feet (15 m) thick and stood at more than 30 feet (10 m) tall. The walls enclosed the Great Temple of Amun, which today stands as a mass of crumbling columns, blocks, and other structures.*

Mighty 70-foot (21-m) tall statues, or colossi, of Ramesses II dominate the facade of the Great Temple at Abu Simbel. Smaller figures at the king's feet portray his mother, wife, and eight of his children.

Nubia

Nubia is the area south of the 1st cataract. It formed a buffer zone at the southern frontier—a region through which exotic goods from African reached Egypt. Nubia was also an important source of gold, minerals, and wood (especially hard wood) and provided valued recruits for the Egyptian army and police force.

The Early Dynastic and Old Kingdom methods of exploitation consisted of raids aimed at bringing back captives and cattle. In the Middle Kingdom, the area under direct military control, exercised through a series of strategically placed fortresses, extended to the southern end of the 2nd cataract. During the New Kingdom, Egyptian rule extended beyond the 4th cataract. In the Late Period, Nubia produced a royal dynasty, the 25th of Egypt. After an unsuccessful encounter with the Assyrians, its Napatan rulers withdrew to the 4th cataract and ceased to take an interest in Egyptian affairs, instead developing their own, Meroitic, culture. A number of temples were built in the northern part of Lower Nubia during the Ptolemaic and early Roman Periods. In the 1960s, many Nubian temples were relocated in an international cooperation unmatched in the history of archaeology.

Dabod

The early temple of Dabod was built by the Meroitic ruler Adikhalamani in the first half of the 3rd century BCE and was dedicated to Amun. In the Greco-Roman Period, several Ptolemies (VI Philometor, VIII Euergetes II, and XII Auletes) enlarged it and rededicated it to Isis. In 1960–1961, the temple was dismantled; since 1970 it has charmed visitors in lake setting in a park in Madrid.

Tafa

Two temples of Roman date used to stand at Tafa. The "North Temple" was dismantled in 1960 and rebuilt in the Rijksmuseum van Oudheden in Leiden, Netherlands, in 1978. The "South Temple" was lost at the end of the last century.

Beit el-Wali

The small rock-cut temple of Beit el-Wali, on the west bank of the Nile, was built by Ramesses II and dedicated to Amon-Re' and other gods. The temple was cut into sections and transferred to New Kalabsha, close to the new Aswan Dam, in 1962–1965.

Kalabsha

The largest freestanding temple of Egyptian Nubia was built at Kalabsha (ancient *Talmis*) during the reign of the emperor Augustus and dedicated to the Egyptian gods Osiris and Isis, and the Nubian god Mandulis. The temple contains an inscription of the Nubian ruler Silko, written in Greek, which marks the triumph of Christianity in Nubia in the 6th century CE. In the early 1960s, the temple was dismantled and rebuilt near the new Aswan Dam (New Kalabsha).

Dendur

The temple of Dendur was dismantled in 1962 to save it from the rising waters of Lake Nasser and presented by the Egyptian government to the United States. The temple was shipped across the Atlantic and rebuilt at the Metropolitan Museum of Art in New York, where it now forms the Sackler wing of the museum.

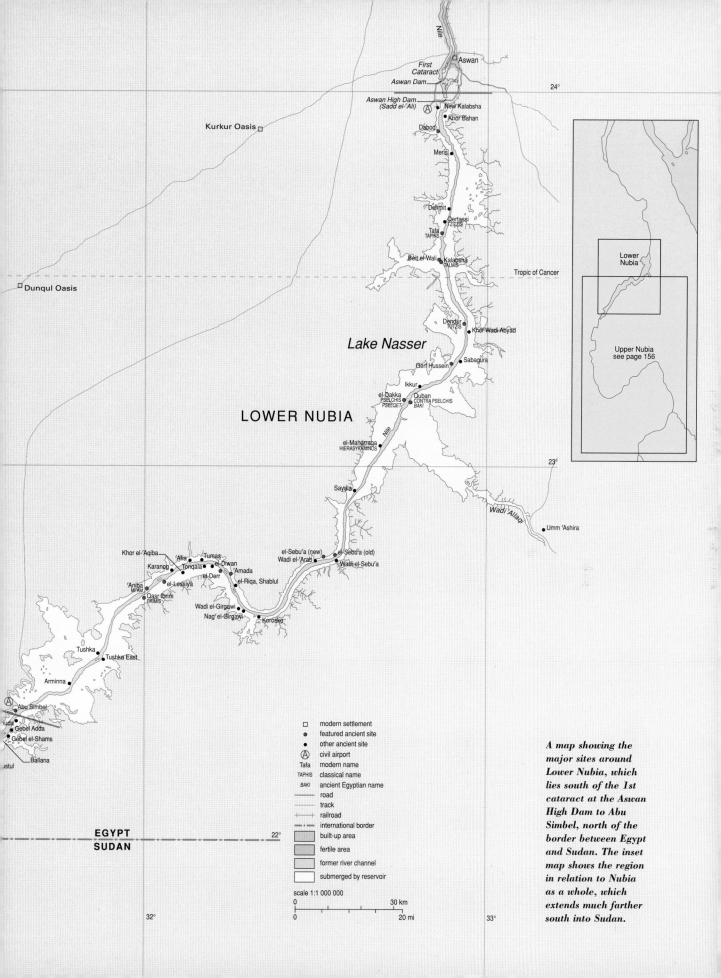

Nile

Aswan

First
Cataract

Aswan Dam

24°

Aswan High Dam
(Sadd el-'Ali)

New Kalabsha

Khor Bahan

Dabod

Kurkur Oasis

Meris

Dehmit

Qertassi
TZITZIS

Tafa
TAPHIS

Beit el-Wali

Kalabsha
TALMIS

Dunqul Oasis

Tropic of Cancer

Dendur
TUTZIS

Khor Wadi Abyad

Lake Nasser

Sabagura

Gerf Hussein

Ikkur

LOWER NUBIA

el-Dakka   Quban
PSELCHIS   CONTRA PSELCHIS
PSEEQET   BAKI

Nile

el-Maharraqa
HIERASYKAMINOS

23°

Sayala

Wadi 'Allaqi

Umm 'Ashira

Khor el-'Aqiba

Tumas

'Afia   el-Diwan
Karanog   Tonqala

el-Sebu'a (new)
Wadi el-'Arab

el-Sebu'a (old)

Wadi el-Sebu'a

'Amada
el-Derr
el-Riqa, Shablul
'Aniba
MI'AM
el-Lessiya

Qasr Ibrim
PRIMIS

Wadi el-Girgawi
Nag' el-Girgawi   Koroshko

Tushka

Tushka East

Arminna

Abu Simbel

uda
Gebel Adda

Gebel el-Shams

ustul   Ballana

□ modern settlement
● featured ancient site
• other ancient site
Ⓐ civil airport
Tafa modern name
TAPHIS classical name
BAKI ancient Egyptian name
road
track
railroad
international border
built-up area
fertile area
former river channel
submerged by reservoir

EGYPT
SUDAN

22°

scale 1:1 000 000

0   30 km

0   20 mi

32°   33°

*A map showing the
major sites around
Lower Nubia, which
lies south of the 1st
cataract at the Aswan
High Dam to Abu
Simbel, north of the
border between Egypt
and Sudan. The inset
map shows the region
in relation to Nubia
as a whole, which
extends much farther
south into Sudan.*

Lower
Nubia

Upper Nubia
see page 156

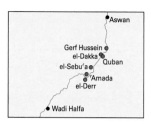

Augustus built the small temple for two local "saints," Peteese and Pihor, sons of Quper. The exact reason for their deification at Dendur is not clear; one theory is that they may have drowned somewhere near the spot. The original place of their worship was a *speos* (rock chamber) behind the temple, which may have dated back to the 26th Dynasty.

Gerf Hussein

"The Temple of Ri'amsese-meryamun [Ramesses II] in the Domain of Ptah" at Gerf Hussein was built by the viceroy of Kush, Setau, sometime between years 35 and 50 of Ramesses II. The gods to whom it was dedicated were depicted as four seated statues at the back of the sanctuary: Ptah, the deified Ramesses II, Ptah-tanen with a hawk above his head, and Hathor.

The temple, located on the west bank of the Nile, was partly free-standing and partly cut into the living rock, and its plan was remarkably similar to that of the great temple of Abu Simbel. However, most of it disappeared beneath Lake Nasser after the building of the new Aswan Dam; only fragments have been salvaged.

el-Dakka

Several rulers are recorded as having contributed to the building and decoration of the temple of el-Dakka (ancient Egyptian *Pselqet*; classical Pselchis), notably Ptolemy IV Philopator, Ptolemy VIII Euergetes II, the Meroitic King Arqamani of the turn of the 3rd century BCE, and the Roman emperors Augustus and Tiberius.

Between 1962 and 1965, the temple was dismantled and restored at a new site near el-Sebu'a. During the work, a number of reused blocks were found. These come from an earlier temple which had been built by Hatshepsut and Thutmose III for Horus of Baki (Quban), and which probably stood on the opposite side of the river.

Quban

The fort of Quban (ancient Egyptian *Baki;* classical Contra Pselchis) was built at the beginning of the 12th Dynasty, probably by Senwosret I, but may have had a precursor on the same site in the Old Kingdom. During the New Kingdom, Quban was the most important settlement in Nubia north of 'Aniba, not least because it controlled access to the gold mines of Wadi 'Allaqi.

el-Sebu'a

El-Sebu'a, on the west bank of the Nile, was the site of two temples of the New Kingdom. The earlier temple was built by Amenhotep III, and originally seems to have been dedicated to one of the local Nubian forms of Horus, but the representations were later altered to Amun. The decoration suffered during the 'Amarna persecution of images of Amun. Ramesses II restored and extended the temple by building in front of the pylon of the original plan.

The larger temple of el-Sebu'a, "The Temple of Ri'amsese-meryamun (Ramesses II) in the Domain of Amun," was built 490 feet (150 m) northeast of the temple of Amenhotep III; representations of the viceroy of Kush, Setau, show that it was built between regnal years 35 and 50 of Ramesses II.

In 1964, during the massive UNESCO campaign to save the monuments of Nubia, the temple was dismantled and moved some 2½ miles (4 km) to the west. In its new setting, and with an imposing avenue of sphinxes, it is one of the most impressive sights of Lower Nubia.

ʻAmada

The temple of ʻAmada was originally built by Thutmose III and Amenhotep II for the gods Amon-Reʻ and Reʻ-Harakhty. A hypostyle hall was later added by Thutmose IV. Various kings of the 19th Dynasty, in particular Sety I and Ramesses II, carried out minor restorations and also added to the temple's decoration. The temple as it stands today has been re-erected 1⅔ miles (2·6 km) away from where it originally stood. The inner part of the temple was transported to its new setting in one piece along a temporary railroad line between January and March 1965.

el-Derr

The only Nubian rock-cut temple built by Ramesses II on the right bank of the Nile used to stand at el-Derr. In 1965, the temple was removed to a new site near ʻAmada.

"The Temple of Riʻamsese-meryamun (Ramesses II) in the Domain of Reʻ" was built in the second half of the king's reign, and in plan and decoration resembles the Great Temple of Abu Simbel (minus the colossal seated statues against the facade). After cleaning, the temple's relief decoration is unusually bright and vivid, contrasting strongly with the more subdued color tones to which we are used from elsewhere.

▲ *The large temple at Kalabsha was built during the reign of Augustus. The temple was reconstructed at a site named "New Kalabsha" near the High Dam in the early 1960s.*

153

▲ *Four giant seated colossi of Ramesses II are carved into the rock façade of the Great Temple at Abu Simbel. In the 1960s, the temple was relocated a few hundred yards away from its original site to protect it from the rising waters of Lake Nasser, following the construction of the High Dam.*

el-Lessiya

A small chapel was cut at el-Lessiya, on the right bank of the Nile, during the reign of Thutmose III. The plan consists of a single room with a niche. The niche once contained statues of Thutmose III between Horus of Mi'am ('Aniba) and Satis, but they were damaged during the 'Amarna Period, and Ramesses II restored them to represent himself between Amon-Re' and Horus of Mi'am. The chapel was rescued from Lake Nasser and is in the Museo Egizio in Turin.

Qasr Ibrim

Parts of the fortress of Qasr Ibrim ("The Castle of Ibrim" in Arabic) were constructed during the short stay of the Roman garrison under the prefect Gaius Petronius in the reign of Augustus, and from then on Qasr Ibrim remained occupied until the beginning of the 19th century. Rock-cut shrines (chapels) dedicated to the reigning king and various gods were made by viceroys of Kush of the 18th and 19th Dynasties at the bottom of the cliff. After the completion of the new Aswan Dam, the site has become a low island in the middle of Lake Nasser.

'Aniba

'Aniba, ancient *Mi'am*, was prominent in the New Kingdom, when it served as the administrative center of *Wawat* (Lower

Nubia, between the 1st and 2nd cataracts). The town contained a fort, probably of Middle Kingdom origin, and the temple of Horus of *Mi'am*. The temple may go back to the 12th Dynasty (Senwosret I), but most of the evidence dates to the 18th Dynasty (Thutmose III and later kings).

Abu Simbel

Of the seven temples in Nubia built by Ramesses II, the rock temples at Abu Simbel (Ibsambul), on the west bank of the Nile, are the most impressive. The Great Temple, "The Temple of Ri'amsese-meryamun (Ramesses II)," was probably completed by the king's 24th regnal year. The Great Temple of Abu Simbel bears witness to the deification of Ramesses II during his lifetime, including scenes showing the king performing rites before the sacred bark of his deified self. A gateway leads into a forecourt, and on to a terrace. There the visitor is confronted by the temple's rock-cut facade, some 98 feet (30 m) high and 115 feet (35 m) wide, with four colossal seated statues of Ramesses II about 69 feet (21 m) tall, accompanied by smaller standing statues of relatives by his legs, including his wife Queen Nofretari, his mother Queen Muttaya, and various of his children.

The temple was precisely oriented so that twice a year, when the rising Sun appeared above the horizon on the east bank of the Nile, its rays

penetrated the temple entrance, shot through the great hall with eight pillars in the form of colossal statues of the king, the second pillared hall, the vestibule, and the sanctuary, and rested on the four statues in the niche at the back, which they illuminated fully. The statues represented the three most important state gods of the Ramessid Period: the Memphite Ptah (first on the left), the Theban Amon-Re' (second), and the Heliopolitan Re'-Harakhty (fourth). The third figure was the Ramesses II himself.

The Small Temple of Abu Simbel, contemporary with the Great Temple, was dedicated to Hathor of Ibshek and Queen Nofretari. In its plan the Small Temple is an abbreviated version of the Great Temple. The facade is formed by six colossal standing statues cut in the rock. Four represent the king and two the queen, each being flanked by princes and princesses.

Between 1964 and 1968, both temples were moved away from the river. They have become popular with visitors to the Egyptian part of Nubia and, partly because of their spectacular rescue, are among the best-known sights of ancient Egypt.

▼ *A plan of the original site of the temples at Abu Simbel before they were relocated away from the river.*

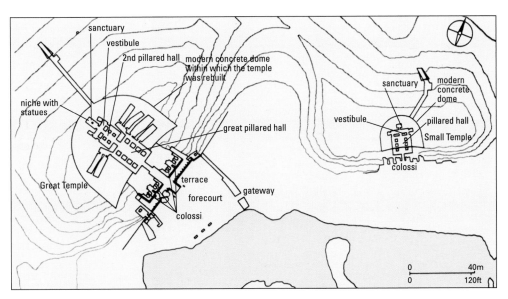

Peripheral Regions

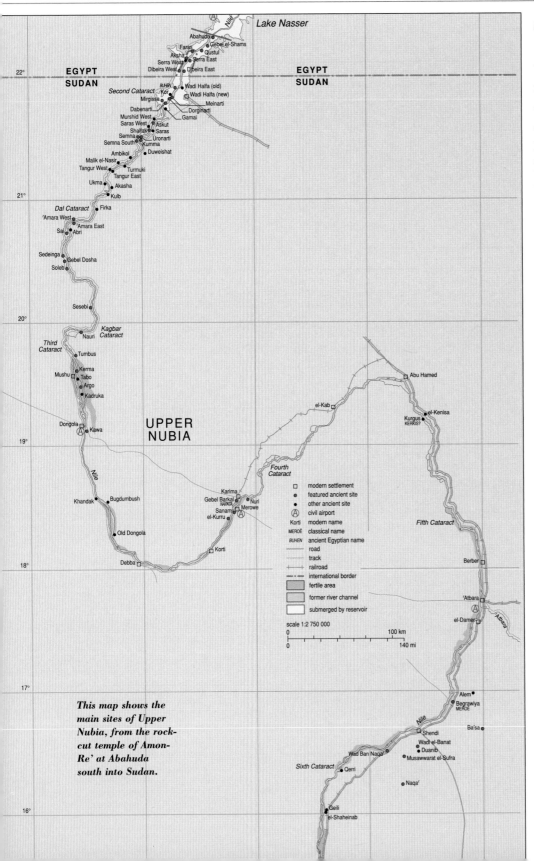

Lake Nasser

EGYPT
SUDAN

EGYPT
SUDAN

22°

Abahuda
Faras
Aksha
Serra West
Dibeira West
Gebel-el-Shams
Qustul
Serra East
Dibeira East

21°

BUHEN
Kor
Mirgissa
Second Cataract
Wadi Halfa (old)
Wadi Halfa (new)
Meinarti
Dorginarti
Dabenarti
Murshid West
Saras West
Shalfak
Semna
Semna South
Askut
Saras
Uronarti
Kumma
Gamai
Ambikol
Duweishat
Malik el-Nasir
Tangur West
Ukma
Turmuki
Tangur East
Akasha
Kulb

Dal Cataract
Firka
'Amara West
Sai
Abri
'Amara East
Sedeinga
Gebel Dosha
Soleb

Sesebi

20°

Kagbar
Cataract
Nauri
Third
Cataract
Tumbus
Kerma
Mushu
Tabo
Argo
Kadruka

Abu Hamed

el-Kab
Kurgus
KERKIS?
el-Kenisa

19°

Dongola
Kawa

UPPER
NUBIA

Fourth
Cataract

Khandak
Bugdumbush

Karima
Gebel Barkal
NAPATA
Sanam
el-Kurru
Nuri
Merowe

Fifth Cataract

Old Dongola

Korti

18°

Debba

Berber

'Atbara

el-Damer

17°

*This map shows the
main sites of Upper
Nubia, from the rock-
cut temple of Amon-
Re' at Abahuda
south into Sudan.*

Alem
Begrawiya
MEROE

Ba'sa

Nile

Shendi
Wadi el-Banat
Duanib
Musawwarat el-Sufra

Wad Ban Naqa'

Naqa'

Sixth Cataract
Qerri

16°

Geili
el-Shaheinab

□ modern settlement
● featured ancient site
• other ancient site
Ⓐ civil airport
Korti modern name
MEROE classical name
BUHEN ancient Egyptian name
— road
— track
+—+ railroad
—·—·— international border
▨ fertile area
▨ former river channel
□ submerged by reservoir

scale 1:2 750 000
0   100 km
0   140 mi

The western oases consist of a series of wind-eroded depressions in the Libyan desert, containing natural springs and wells that are bored up to ⅔ mile (1 km) below the surface. The water can support agriculture, but wells are scattered and may fail. The population (more than 100,000 for el-Dakhla in 1999) is spread over wide areas, with barren tracts, often formerly inhabited, between settlements.

The oases have been inhabited since Paleolithic times. The Western Desert has produced traces of early pastoralism and agriculture, and sites comparable to, but earlier than, Egyptian Predynastic cultures have been found in el-Dakhla. The area was important both as a staging post and for its specialized mineral and agricultural produce, such as wine. The economy of the area fluctuated with that of the Nile valley, with which the oases traded.

Early history is poorly known. For the Old–New Kingdoms, all the main oases except for Siwa are mentioned in Egyptian texts and archaeological finds have been made notably in el-Dakhla. They were probably all administered by Egypt. From the Late Period, the remains are more frequent and show that prosperity increased until the Roman Period, when Greeks and members of new religious communities settled. Siwa was annexed permanently in the 26th Dynasty; its population, now Berber-speaking, was probably always more Libyan than Egyptian.

Late antiquity brought widespread depopulation in the Western Desert. The oasis economy did not recover fully, so that the naturally good conditions for preserving sites are enhanced.

Sinai

Commercial and military routes connecting Egypt with Western Asia followed the Mediterranean coast or traversed north Sinai. The Egyptians were attracted by the mineral deposits of the valleys of southwest Sinai no later than the 3rd Dynasty. The objective of the expeditions regularly sent out to work the mines during the Old to New Kingdoms was to bring back turquoise and to acquire copper; the copper workings over much of Sinai are mostly not associated with Egyptian finds. Egyptian activities in Sinai ceased at the end of the New Kingdom.

The mines of Maghara were the first to be exploited, with the earliest rock inscriptions and reliefs dating to Djoser, Sekhemkhet, and Zanakht. The last known Old Kingdom expedition was that of Pepy II in the "year of the 2nd census" (around his 3rd year); although Middle and New Kingdom rulers are attested (Amenemhet III and IV, Hatshepsut and Thutmose III, and perhaps

Ramesses II), the site did not regain its former significance.

The most important site of Egyptian activities in Sinai is Serabit el-Khadim with its temple of Hathor. The temple's earliest part, the rock-cut "Cave of Hathor" preceded by a court and a portico, goes back to the early 12th Dynasty. In the New Kingdom, a shrine for Sopd, the god of the eastern desert, was built, and the temple of Hathor was enlarged (mainly by Hatshepsut and Thutmose III); thousands of votive offerings have been recovered from the site. Thoth was also worshiped locally, together with several deified kings, notably Snofru. Ramesses VI is the last ruler whose name has been encountered. There is a Middle Kingdom rock inscription at Rud el-'Air, some 1 mile (1·5 km) to the west.

A rock text of Sahure' and a large stela of Senwosret I date the third important center of turquoise mining in the Wadi Kharit. Nearby, in the Wadi Nasb, were found a rock stela of year 20 of Amenemhet III and Middle Kingdom and Ramessid texts.

▶ *This series of maps shows the location of important sites at the oases of the western desert in present-day Libya (from top to bottom): the monuments at Aghurmi, Umm el-'Ebeida, and Gebel el-Mawta at the Siwa Oasis; the sites near el-Qasr and el-Bawiti at Bahriya; the prehistoric remains at Farara; the prehistoric to Old Kingdom and Greco–Roman Period settlements and cemeteries around el-Dakhla; and the sites at 'Ain Amur, 'Ain Manawir, Hibis, Qasr el-Ghueida, Gebel el-Teir, Nadura, Aqsr Zaiyan, and Dush, which lie around the oasis at el-Kharga.*

ASPECTS OF EGYPTIAN SOCIETY

There is no one method of studying the everyday life and culture of the ancient Egyptians; instead, a mosaic of different approaches is usually adopted. Tomb reliefs and paintings provide a wealth of material. Although only members of the top stratum of society were buried in large decorated tombs, subsidiary scenes afford glimpses of the life of ordinary people. For example, agricultural scenes in the 18th Dynasty Tomb of Unsou show workers plowing the fields, sowing seeds, reaping grain, threshing with cattle, and carrying ears of grain to granary. But it would be a mistake to accept this evidence alone. Small wooden figurines ("models") and objects of daily use often form part of funerary equipment; less common but more trustworthy are those found in excavations of settlements. Texts on papyri and ostraca are invaluable because they provide details not available from elsewhere. Biographical accounts of observers such as the Greek scholar who is often known as the "father of history," Herodotus of Halicarnassus (c. 484 BCE–c. 425 BCE), also provide a rich source of information about Egyptian life and culture from the later Greco-Roman period.

Scribes and Writing

The spread of writing to record year names around 3000 BCE defines the beginning of Egyptian history more than any other single development. Similarly, literacy set the civilizations of the ancient Near East apart from their contemporaries, from the cuneiform tablets that emerged from Sumer in the 30th century BCE to Chinese script of a similar period in history. The emergence of these new forms of communication opened up new possibilities in social organization and in the transmission, and occasionally criticism, of growing bodies of knowledge. But they were complex, and literacy was confined to a small elite. Only relatively recently has writing spread much more widely in societies.

In Egypt, it seems that there was no separate, nonliterate class of nobility, as a landed aristocracy might be. All high-ranking people had scribal careers in officialdom, army, or priesthood; kings, too, were literate. Among administrative titles, the highest do not allude to writing, but representations show that such people claimed also to be scribes; they had surpassed the level of achievement at which writing was the main occupation, not bypassed it. In all spheres of society, writing formed the basis of official organization.

Learning to read and write

In most cases, learning to read and write formed part of training for administration. Sons of important people could begin their careers from a very early age, perhaps as young as 12. Literary references to schools survive, but no materials from basic instruction in writing are known. Secondary education was provided by a scribe's official superior on his first job—normally another scribe. At Deir el-Medina, the only place at which detailed evidence survives, apprentices at work studied under their superiors by copying passages from a cursive hieroglyphic text called *Kemyt* and from classic literature, as well as contemporaneous miscellanies of model letters, satirical compositions, religious and secular poems, and panegyrics, some of which superiors set as daily exercises. Numerous papyri of the miscellanies have been preserved, mainly from Memphis; their preservation suggests that they were ultimately deposited in their owners' tombs.

Two features of training are noteworthy. First, it was mainly in cursive writing, which was from the beginning the commonest form. Further instruction was probably needed for proficiency in the monumental hieroglyphic script, which was comprehensible to rather fewer people, although many may have known the meaning of a few salient signs; in the Late Period, the two forms diverged rather sharply. Second, although the Egyptians analyzed their script into something like a syllabary and had an "alphabetical" order into which lists were sometimes arranged, learning was by copying sentences or words, not by starting from individual signs. Writing was perceived in groups of signs, and there was little stimulus to minute subdivision of the script.

Writing and literature

Apart from the purposes of administration and correspondence, cursive writing was used for nonessential purposes, the most interesting of which, from a modern

◀ (previous pages) This tomb painting shows a procession of people and animals, including cattle which the Egyptians raised on farms and deer which they hunted for food.

perspective, was in works of literature, which are preserved in school copies and from other contexts. These works include narrative fiction, instructions and discourses, cult and religious hymns, love poetry, some royal inscriptions and other texts used secondarily as literature, and various genres that are not literary in a narrow sense of the word, for example in medical and mathematical texts, rituals, and some mortuary books. The chief center of production was the "house of life," a scriptorium attached to temples, which made copies of the entire range of traditional writings, not only of religious texts. The tradition continued almost without a break into the 3rd century CE, although few texts were transmitted from hieratic to demotic. Some literary works became generally familiar and were alluded to in later texts, playing on a lettered culture common to writer and reader. One classic example is *The Tale of Sinuhe*, written around the early 20th century BCE, which tells the tale of Sinuhewho finds out about a plot to assassinate King Senusret I before he can ascend the throne.

▲ *A seated scribe holds a papyrus in his lap, preparing to read it. The statue dates from the 5th Dynasty, c. 2400 BCE. On display at the Egyptian Museum, Cairo.*

The Army

One of the advantages Egypt derived from its unique geographical position was relative safety. Nomadic tribes in the deserts on either side of the Nile valley soon ceased to pose a serious threat to the highly organized and much more powerful Egyptian civilization; only during periods of instability and weakened central rule did they become a force to be reckoned with.

Colonial expansion in the 12th Dynasty led to intensive campaigning and the building of huge fortresses in Nubia in the south, but it was not until the 18th Dynasty, under the reign of Thutmose III, that the Egyptians encountered real opposition, when they entered the regional military arena of West Asia by contending for Syria and Palestine. Widely considered to be Egypt's greatest military campaigner, Thutmose III succeeded in creating an Egyptian superpower by conquering a vast area that stretched from Syria to Nubia.

Military organization

The word *mesha'*, or "army," originally described both military forces and peaceful expeditions sent to quarry minerals—"task force" would be the most fitting translation. During the Old Kingdom, when an emergency arose, a body of men was mustered to back the small specialized permanent units. The situation changed in the 1st Intermediate Period: this time of instability and unrest brought about the creation of private armies led by nomarchs and the more extensive use of non-Egyptian mercenary troops.

The Middle Kingdom was characterized by well-organized standing military units, supplemented when needed by local militia.

The force consisted mainly of infantry, into which was integrated boat personnel. The 2nd Intermediate Period and the 18th Dynasty saw unprecedented advances in the development of weapons, organization of military units (such as the appearance of chariotry and the organization of infantry into companies of some 250 men led by a standard-bearer), strategy, and tactics. The standing army and professional army officers began to play an important part in internal politics.

In the Late Period, foreign mercenaries, especially from ancient Greece, formed the core of Egyptian military power.

Ancient Egyptian weapons

Various ancient Egyptian weapons are known from contemporary representations and models, as well as archaeological finds.

The bow, the most important long-range weapon, was used in all periods: either the archaic compound horn-bow, or the wooden, slightly double-convex "self" bow. During the 2nd Intermediate Period, the composite bow was introduced from Asia. It was made of laminated strips of various materials and had a much improved range and power. When strung, the bow acquired a characteristic triangular shape. The quiver was in use from the Old Kingdom onward.

The spear was employed throughout Egyptian history.

The mace with a stone mace-head of varying form was the most powerful weapon of close combat in the Predynastic Period.

In historic times, the mace was replaced by the **battle-ax** with a copper ax-head. Some of the early semicircular ax-heads

differed little from contemporary tools of woodworkers and other craftsmen, but already during the Old Kingdom a specialized shallow type appeared. This, and the scalloped ax-head, were characteristic of the weapons of the Middle Kingdom.

In the 2nd Intermediate Period, a new type with a narrow ax-blade and therefore much-improved power of penetration appeared, probably an indigenous development.

The scimitar (sickle sword), an Asiatic weapon used in much the same way as the Egyptian battle-ax (as a cutting or piercing, rather than thrusting, weapon), is also met in the New Kingdom. **Cudgels, clubs,** and **throwing-sticks** of various types remained in use as side arms at all times. The **dagger** was used in the same way.

Personal protection was afforded by the shield, already attested during the late Predynastic Period. Light **body armor** was known from the New Kingdom but its use remained limited.

The two-wheeled horse-drawn **chariot**, which was introduced to Egypt from Asia in the 2nd Intermediate Period, was a light vehicle, made of wood with some leather and metal elements. It was manned by two soldiers: the charioteer and the chariot-warrior, who was armed with a bow and spear and carried a protective shield. The chariot's main contribution to the art of warfare

▲ *These illustrations from temple reliefs show Egyptian soldiers and their enemies armed with various types of weapons and, at bottom, first right, a standard bearer.*

163

was rapid mobility and the element of surprise connected with it. In attack, the chariots approached at full speed, and the chariot-warriors delivered their arrows while passing the massed enemy ranks. The chariot was not armored in any way and therefore was not suitable for a direct attack. Once the enemy lines were broken, the chariotry was ideally suited for pursuing and harassing the scattered foot soldiers. To judge from the appearance of special titles within the military, the chariotry formed a separate arm of the Egyptian army from the reign of Amenhotep III onward. The chariotry was the military elite: on occasion, it was led into battle by the king himself.

▼ *This stylized illustration of the Battle of Qadesh is based on reliefs in temples built by Ramesses II to commemorate the battle.*

The earliest battle in human history that can be reconstructed in detail took place near the city of Qadesh on the Syrian River Orontes late in May 1274 BCE. The protagonists were the Egyptian king Ramesses II and the Hittite king

1. The Egyptian army consisted of four divisions, with a smaller unit operating independently. Through false information planted on them, the Egyptians were misled into believing that the Hittite host had retreated. The Egyptian divisions advanced northward along the Orontes, unaware that the Hittites lay concealed beyond Qadesh.

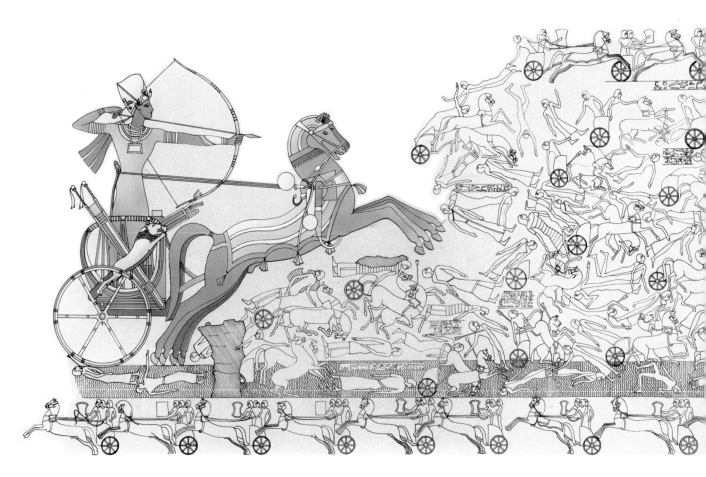

Muwatallis—at stake was the control of Syria and, for Egypt, the confirmation of dominance throughout much of the West Asia region. Both armies suffered heavy losses, but the encounter was indecisive.

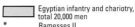
Egyptian infantry and chariotry, total 20,000 men

Ramesses II

Egyptian camp

Hittite chariotry, 3,500 chariots with 10,500 men

Hittite infantry, 8,000 men

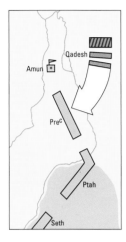

2. The Egyptian van, the division of Amun led by the king himself, reached the rendezvous point northwest of the city and set up camp. When the division of Pre', suspecting no danger, approached, its right flank was subjected to a devastating charge of Hittite chariotry.

3. The division of Pre' was broken and scattered. Survivors of the Hittite ambush were fleeing northward in the direction of the Egyptian camp, with Hittite chariots in pursuit. The division of Ptah was still emerging from the Robaui forest and crossing to the west bank of the river, and was too far away to assist the attacked unit.

4. The Egyptian camp was overrun and the division of Amun suffered heavy losses. The king and his guard tried to fight their way to meet the advancing division of Ptah. Muwatallis committed his chariot reserve to bring the battle to a quick conclusion.

5. By his gallant, though forced, action, the Egyptian king gained enough time: the special task force appeared at last, and with the division of Ptah now reaching the scene, crushed the Hittite chariotry.

165

Women and Men

The position of women in Egyptian ideology is exemplified by their presentation in Old Kingdom tomb decoration and statue groups. At the top of the female hierarchy is the elegantly dressed wife, or sometimes mother, of the tomb owner, who stands by him or sits at leisure with the owner at a table of offerings. Unlike the elite man, who engages actively in hunting in the marshes, his women are shown uniformly inactive. Men stand with feet apart in a pose of potential movement, while women's legs are statically together. The wife sometimes accompanies her husband when he watches scenes of work but is more often shown when offerings are presented to them; this distinction may signify that she would normally stay at home. At the other extreme are scenes or statuettes of serving women engaged in domestic tasks, such as making bread and beer, spinning, and weaving. These activities were probably conducted in a house or estate compound. The female flesh color is yellow, which indicates among other things less exposure to the Sun than the male red, and therefore a more enclosed existence—as it also does on successful male bureaucrats.

It may have been unsafe for women to go out. In a posthumous text, Ramesses III says: "I enabled the woman of Egypt to go on her journey, which was made easy, to where she wanted, without anyone assaulting her on the road"—implying that this was not always so.

While women are not shown in the most important work and diversions, they are not employed in the heaviest tasks. For example, men make wine, which is more strenuous than brewing. Women are present in the fields, for example, harvesting flax. Apart from scenes of musicians and of athletic girls' dances, women's roles in early periods are at least superficially decorous. In New Kingdom scenes, women are more frequently shown and their clothing is more elaborate. A number of scenes with women have heavily coded erotic content (Old Kingdom scenes may have had such meanings, but they are difficult to identify). The Late Period mostly returned to earlier decorum.

Women did not hold important titles except for some religious ones. Apart from a few members of the royal family and female kings, they had little political power. Their commonest title, "Mistress of the House," is a term of respect that may mean little more than "Mrs." Almost all were illiterate and therefore excluded from the bureaucracy—to which they probably did not aspire—and from the most intellectual high culture. A symptom of this is that age and wisdom were respected in men, who could be represented as corpulent elders, but not in women. Even a man's mother is indistinguishable from his wife in tomb depictions: both are youthfully beautiful. The way women are shown is part of men's definition of them and is a public display of an ideal. In reality, their influence may not have been so circumscribed, and their roles more varied than might at first appear. Funerary monuments of women, which are known especially from the 1st millennium, are suggestive here; a Middle Kingdom stela from the Faiyum even belonged to a Nubian elite woman.

Family structures as presented are simplified. The norms of decoration hardly give room to the widow or widower, the divorcee, homosexuals, or deviations from monogamy, all of which are attested. A tale recounts an affair between a king and a military officer, and the myth of Horus and Seth includes homosexual activity. There was a limited amount of polygyny in the Old and Middle Kingdoms—kings could have many wives, although only the queen mother and one other bore the title "Great King's Wife."

Marriage, family, and social relations

Egyptians were mostly monogamous. Inheritance passed from father to child, but followed no rigid pattern. Family property was defined by a marriage settlement, of which examples on papyrus are known from the 3rd Intermediate Period onward, and by deeds of transfer made either between the living or as wills. The woman's role was important, but not equal to that of her husband. She brought a proportion of property into marriage and had some rights over it in a divorce. At least among property owners, marriage constituted a new household, not an extension of a parental one. A woman

▼ *A brightly colored tomb painting of a court official named Nebamun, his wife, and daughter on board a skiff during a hunting trip. The image illustrates the marked contrast between the roles of man and woman in Egyptian society.*

▲ *A mural in the Tomb of Horemheb depicts the king with the goddess Nephthys.*

could make a will and leave her own property to some extent as she wished. No evidence has been identified either for marriage ceremonies or for judicial processes in divorce. Even so, the legal status of a couple living together was different from that of a married pair. In one case, a man is accused of having sex with a woman who is living with another man, but not married to him, something that might seem unlikely to constitute an offence. Despite relatively free institutions, adultery by a woman was a serious matter.

Apart from complications of these types, general mortality, and the seeming frequency of divorce, led to involved patterns of property holding and inheritance. Life expectancy was low, and it was not unusual to be widowed more than once. A Middle Kingdom deed illustrates the complexity of inheritance. A man retires and hands over his office to his son while disinheriting the son's mother, perhaps because she is deceased, and leaving his remaining property to his children (perhaps not yet born) by another woman; neither woman is stated to be his wife, although both probably were.

The definition of permitted and prohibited marriage partners is not known, but it was possible to marry close blood relatives, including on occasion half-siblings. In the royal family, there were some brother and sister marriages, but this practice may have deviated deliberately from the norm. From Roman period Egypt, such marriages are well attested among the ethnic Greek population. One difficulty in understanding the social framework lies in Egyptian kinship terms, of which there were very few. A single word could cover brother, mother's brother, and many more besides. Reconstructed genealogies are therefore difficult to verify.

The age of either partner at marriage is unknown. Genealogies show that some men had children before they were 20, but the clearest royal cases may be atypical. Long-term generation spans were 25–30 years. At first marriage, women were no doubt younger than their husbands, but this may not have been true of subsequent marriages.

Sexuality, fertility, and succession

Men, who produced the evidence, will have wished to enhance women's sexuality for their own ends, which were religious as well as pleasurable, while limiting its potential as an independent and subversive force. Their attitude toward it was ambivalent. In tales, the evil seductress is a common motif, while love poetry of the New Kingdom is often written in the words of the ardent woman, without the same moralistic overtones. Although the tales use religious motifs, both these sources give a secular view. In religious terms, however, sexuality was important because of its relationship with creation and, by association, with rebirth in the hereafter. It was also significant for the character of such deities as Hathor among goddesses and Min among gods. The covert erotic references in tomb scenes could have three purposes: to ensure rebirth through potency in the next life, to enable the deceased to lead an enjoyable otherworldly existence, and to

enhance his standing in this world through the ambiance he could display around him. Scenes with an erotic content include ones of hunting in the marshes, where the deceased is accompanied by his wife, who is implausibly dressed in her most elaborate costume, wears a heavy wig, and holds two symbols of Hathor. Heavy wigs, especially when associated with nudity, could be erotic signals. In a New Kingdom tale, an evil wife accuses her husband's young brother of

▼ *This relief from her temple at Deir el-Bahri at Luxor shows Queen Hatshepsut wearing a false beard to resemble a male king. Although it was unusual for a woman to rule Egypt, it was by no means unknown; Hatshepsut ruled for longer than any other indigenous queen of Egypt.*

attempting to seduce her by reporting him as saying: "Come, let us spend an hour lying down. Put on your wig."

An example of a comparable motif in an earlier period is a scene in the 6th-Dynasty tomb of Mereruka at Saqqara, where the owner and his wife sit facing each other on a bed, and she plays the harp to him. In part, the scene created a perpetual erotic ambiance for him. A spell or a female statuette placed in a tomb could have a similar purpose but was less conjugal in its reference. A Middle Kingdom spell in the Coffin Texts has the simple title "Having sex by a man in the necropolis." On a mythological plane, the same concerns are seen in the Book of the Dead, where Osiris complains to the creator god Atum that after the end of the world: "There will be no sexual gratification there," to which Atum replies: "I have given transfiguration in place of water, air, and gratification"—here the three preconditions of life—"and peace of heart in place of bread and beer"—physical nourishment.

Evidence of sexuality

Only one sexually explicit document of any size survives, dating from the late New Kingdom. This is a set of drawings with brief captions on a papyrus, showing a variety of sexual encounters between a fat, priapic man (or perhaps men) and a woman (or women) dressed in a wig, necklace, armlets, bracelets, and a belt. The papyrus also contains humorous sketches of animals in human roles—a well-known motif—suggesting that the sexual part is also humorous. From about the same time, there is a case of apparent prudery, where tomb paintings of nude dancing girls and lightly clothed women in the style of the 18th

Dynasty were painted over with drapery by a later owner. On Late Period dwelling sites, erotic objects, mostly statuettes of men with enormous penises, are common. These are under-represented from earlier periods in the archaeological record because of the scarcity of finds from settlements—as well as the moral qualms of earlier excavators of such material. They probably served as potency charms.

If potency was a man's worry, with a high death rate throughout society, fertility was important both to women and to men. In all but the wealthiest families, the labor of children was vital to the family's economic success, particularly in agriculture. On another plane, children carried on the family line, whose most obvious feature was the common practice of giving a son the name of his grandfather. The eldest surviving son was expected to perform funerary rituals and maintain a funerary cult, as well as managing his father's inheritance; one inscription is a lament of a childless man that he cannot look forward to a proper afterlife.

In keeping with this concern for fertility, gynecological texts are known, including prescriptions for reproductive disorders, birth prognoses, contraception, and abortion. It is unlikely that any of these were very effective. Shrines of Hathor, dwelling sites, and tombs have produced figurines of women in forms that emphasize the genitals. These, many of which do not conform to the norms of Egyptian representation, probably had a special status outside the canon and were used by a wider range of social groups than most statuary. Some were offered by women who wished the deity to grant them fertility. Until modern times, such offerings were probably as effective a way of helping to conceive a child as visiting a doctor.

◀ *A wall painting in the Tomb of Nakht shows a female guest at a banquet. Women used cosmetics to enhance their beauty. At banquets, they wore elegant dresses and beautiful jewelry.*

Religion

In Egypt, religion can be divided into the official, state aspect, about which much is known; the mortuary sphere, which is also well represented; and the everyday practices of most of the population, which were largely separate from the official cult and are very poorly known.

The king and history

In the official presentation, society consisted of the gods, the king, the dead, and humanity. The king acted as a mediator between deity and humanity. He represented humanity to the gods and vice versa. He was also the living exemplar of the creator God on Earth and re-enacted the creator God's role of setting order in place of disorder. "History" was a ritual in the cosmos, of which this re-enactment is a principal theme.

Kings sought to enhance their status before people by identifying with gods, or in some instances by deifying themselves, as is attested for Amenhotep III and Ramesses II. Finally, kings could be deified after death, more as some private individuals were deified than as if they were true gods.

Official and personal religion

Official religion consisted of cult and festivals in the main temples and of the process of "history." The basis of the cult was reciprocity. The king provided for the gods and cared for their cult images. In return, the gods took up residence in the images and showed their favor to the king and hence to humanity. But the gods had priority since they had created the world in which the king lived and endowed it with benefits; they could withdraw from it at any time.

The aim of the cult was to maintain and enhance the established order of the world. The main temples were dedicated to local deities. The cult was carried out by a hierarchy of priests. Only priests could enter the temple. The deity left the temple for festivals and could then be approached by normal people, but even then most cult images were kept hidden. Apart from the main temples there were local shrines to lesser deities throughout the country. Normal people went to these shrines, where they prayed or made offerings. There were also centers of pilgrimage, such as Abydos, whose heyday was in the Middle Kingdom.

One area of popular and official religious life was animal worship. Animals had always been kept as sacred to particular deities and buried ceremonially. In the Late Period these practices proliferated. Many species were sacred, including the Apis bull, ibises, dogs or jackals, cats, baboons, ichneumons, rams, snakes, and crocodiles.

Priesthood and temple institutions

The expansion of temples in the 18th Dynasty saw the rise of the priesthood as a group. The basic needs of the cult could be satisfied by an officiant; a ritual specialist or lector priest, who might be the same person as the officiant; and the part-time priests who saw to the practical functions.

Priests received income from temples. Offerings were laid before the god and, "after he was satisfied with them," reverted to minor shrines and statues of kings and eventually to the priests. The offerings themselves were, however, only a small

EGYPT'S LOCAL GODS

It is impossible to arrange Egyptian deities into neat categories; any attempt to do so involves simplification. However, many can be described as local deities because they were closely connected with a particular region. The gods shared the fate of their home towns, and while some of them were ultimately promoted to be Egyptian "state gods" (for example, the Theban Amon-Reʿ) whose cult spread over the whole of Egypt, others fell into obscurity and were replaced by, or assimilated with, the more vigorous gods of other localities. "Guest deities" might be worshiped in local temples.

This page illustrates important local gods with three types of information (where possible): 1. the main iconographic features by which the deity can be recognized; 2. the character and function of the deity, his or her relationship with other gods, etc…; 3. his or her main places of worship.

Reʿ (Reʿ-Harakhty) *Sun-disk on head, hawk-headed (Reʿ-Harakhty)/Sun god, identified with Harakhty and the primeval creator god Atum as Reʿ-Harakhty-Atum; linked with other gods (Amon-Reʿ)/Heliopolis*

Bastet *Lioness-headed or cat-headed/war goddess; linked with Mut and Sakhmet/Tell Basta.*

Hathor *Sun-disk, cow's horns, cow-headed, cow, "Hathor-pillar," orsistrum/goddess of women, sky goddess, tree goddess (Memphis), necropolis goddess (Thebes)/Heliopolis, Memphis, Atfih, el-Qusiya, Dendara, Thebes, Gebelein, Abu Simbel, Sinai (Serabit el-Khadim).*

Neith *Red crown or two crossed arrows and shield on her head/goddess of war and hunting; connected with Sobek; guardian deity/Sa el-Hagar, also Memphis, the Faiyum and Esna.*

Montu *Often hawk-headed, Sun-disk and two plumes/war god; connected with the Buchis bull of Armant/Armant, but also Karnak, Tod, Nagʿ el-Madamud.*

Thoth *Ibis-headed, with moon crescent/god of wisdom in general; patron of scribes; baboon another sacred animal/el-Ashmunein and el-Baqliya, and many Late Period cities.*

Khons  Mut Amun (Amon-Reʿ) *Khons: child's side-lock of hair, often with moon crescent, mummiform; Mut: vulture headdress or crowns (white or double), lioness-headed; Amun (head of triad): two plumes, often ithyphallic; also ram or goose/Mut a war goddess; Amun's female counterpart Amaunet/Theban triad (Karnak, Luxor), but Amun also important at el-Ashmunein; as state god of the New Kingdom Amon-Reʿ worshiped in many other places.*

Harsaphes *Ram-headed or ram/gained importance when Herakleopolis was Egypt's northern capital; connected with Reʿ, Osiris, and Amun/Ihnasya el-Medina.*

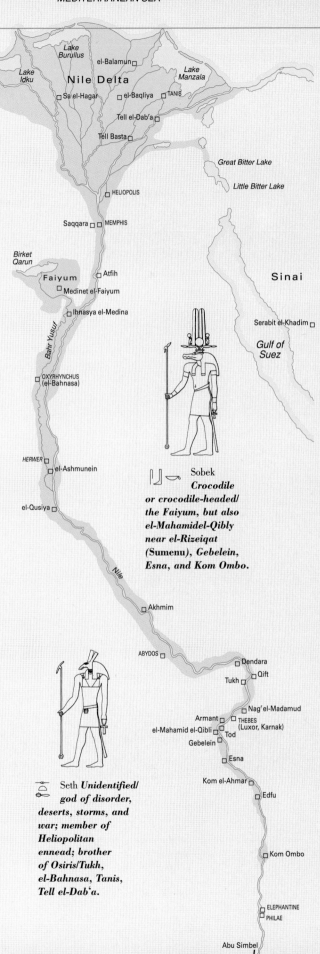

Lake Burullus
el-Balamun
Lake Idku
Lake Manzala
Nile Delta
Sa el-Hagar
el-Baqliya
TANIS
Tell el-Dab'a
Tell Basta
Great Bitter Lake
Little Bitter Lake
HELIOPOLIS
Saqqara
MEMPHIS
Birket Qarun
Faiyum
Atfih
Medinet el-Faiyum
Ihnasya el-Medina
Sinai
Serabit el-Khadim
Gulf of Suez
Bahr Yusuf
OXYRHYNCHUS (el-Bahnasa)
HERWER
el-Ashmunein
el-Qusiya
Nile
Akhmim
ABYDOS
Dendara
Qift
Tukh
Nag' el-Madamud
Armant
THEBES (Luxor, Karnak)
el-Mahamid el-Qibli
Tod
Gebelein
Esna
Kom el-Ahmar
Edfu
Kom Ombo
ELEPHANTINE
PHILAE
Abu Simbel

Sobek *Crocodile or crocodile-headed/ the Faiyum, but also el-Mahamidel-Qibly near el-Rizeiqat (Sumenu), Gebelein, Esna, and Kom Ombo.*

Seth *Unidentified/ god of disorder, deserts, storms, and war; member of Heliopolitan ennead; brother of Osiris/Tukh, el-Bahnasa, Tanis, Tell el-Dab'a.*

Horus *Hawk- headed or hawk with double crown/sky god; the earliest state god of Egypt; king was his manifestation; member of Heliopolitan ennead; son of Osiris and Isis.*

Min *Cap with two plumes and ribbon, mummiform, ithyphallic, right arm raised with flagellum/ earlier worshiped as unidentified object; fertility god; patron of eastern desert/Qift, Akhmim.*

Ptah ☐☐ Sakhmet ☐☐ Nefertem ☐☐ *Ptah: mummiform with three scepters; Sakhmet: lioness-headed; Nefertem: lotus flower on head, child on lotus flower/Ptah creator god, patron of craftsmen, merged with Sokar and Osiris, linked with Apis bull; Sakhmet linked with Mut, Bastet/ Memphite triad; Ptah also worshiped at Thebes and Abydos and as a state god of New Kingdom.*

Khnum ☐☐ Anukis ☐☐ Satis ☐☐ *Khnum: ram or ram-headed; Anukis: white crown flanked by two gazelle horns; Satis: feather headdress/triad worshiped in the 1st cataract region, hence Khnum's connection with the inundation; Khnum also ancient creator god (because of procreative powers of ram), sometimes shown molding men on a potter's wheel/Elephantine, but Khnum also at Esna and Herwer (Hur, near el-Ashmunein).*

▶ *A relief in the Temple of Kom Ombo shows Horus, god of the sky, with Hathor, protective goddess of love and joy.*

proportion of the temples' income, so that much was devoted directly to supporting staff and to barter for products the temple lacked.

Gods and myths

Some Egyptian gods are circumscribed by myth, others by location and by organization into groups. Most have a basic association with an aspect of the world but this does not exhaust their characteristics.

Presentations of creation give primacy to the Sun god Re', often in the forms Re'-Harakhty or (Re')-Atum. The most common has the creator appear from the watery chaos on a mound, the first solid matter, and create a pair of deities, Shu and Tefenet, from his own body fluids. In turn, Shu and Tefenet produced Geb and Nut, the earth and the sky, whose children were Osiris, Isis, Seth, and Nephthys. This group of nine deities formed the ennead of Heliopolis; other centers had comparable groups.

The organization of gods into sets is comparable in its variety and occasional seeming arbitrariness. The commonest grouping is the triad, consisting of two "adult" deities and one youthful one. The triads are, however, only selections, with which other deities may have a connection or may interchange position. Thus, the Theban triad consists of Amon-Re', Mut, and Khons, the deities of the three main temples at Karnak. It has the form of a family group, but Mut is not the "wife" of Amon-Re', nor is Khons their son. Rather, three deities with different origins are associated using a family model, whose lack of realism is clear from the fact that there is only one "child." The symbolic importance of the number three and a principle of economy may together account for this simplification. Amaunet, a female Amun, is another Theban deity, who

sometimes occurs in place of Mut, while Montu, probably the original chief god of the Theban nome, had his own temple complex immediately north of the main enclosure at Karnak. At Memphis, the four chief deities, Ptah, Sakhmet, Nefertem, and Sokar (the god of the necropolis), were similarly varied in their association: the first three form a triad, while Sokar was frequently fused with Ptah. Hathor and Neith, whose cults were also very important in Memphis, are not part of the main group.

A further important means of associating deities is termed *syncretism* by Egyptologists. A deity acquires a multiple name, mostly by taking on the name and some of the attributes of a more important deity. Amon-Re' is thus Amun in his aspect as Re', and this can be expanded to form Amon-Re'-Atum, Amun as Re' and Atum, the aged aspect of the Sun god. Re' is by far the commonest part of the multiple name; this reflects the Sun god's central importance.

Almost all major deities had a cult and an area in which they were sovereign. Some cosmic deities, such as Geb, had no local cult. There were also minor deities found only in restricted contexts. The best known of these are probably Bes and Taweret, "household" figures associated particularly with childbirth. In addition, a large number of demons with diverse names and often grotesque forms are attested in magical and underworld texts.

The world of the dead

The tomb was the starting point for ideas about the afterlife and the world of the dead. The Egyptians' unparalleled expenditure on burial evidently served in part to enhance the tomb owner's prestige while he was alive, but this was a sideline to the ultimate purpose.

The deceased might continue to exist in and around the tomb, or could travel through the afterworld. The aim was to identify with gods, in particular Osiris, or to become a transfigured spirit and participate in the solar cycle as a member of the "bark of millions." The bark is never shown with its vast complement, possibly because human beings were excluded from the type of pictorial material in which it occurs.

Between death and incorporation in the divine world came judgment, a theme that is less prominent for kings than for the rest of humanity. From the New Kingdom on, the judgment was often depicted in tombs, on papyri, coffins, and shrouds. Its central motif is the weighing of the deceased's heart in a balance against Ma'at, the Egyptian conception of right order, which is mostly shown as a hieroglyph, either an ostrich feather or a figure of the personification Ma'at, a goddess with the feather inserted in a band around her wig. Thoth, the scribe god of wisdom and justice, performs the weighing before Osiris, who presides over a judgment hall with 42 judges. If the heart and Ma'at are in equilibrium, the test is successful, and the deceased is presented to Osiris in triumph. The judgment is of conformity to Ma'at; that is, both order and correct conduct in life. Everyone naturally wished to avoid the judgment, and the deceased had ready a declaration of innocence from all manner of misdeeds. Both the declaration and the depiction of a successful outcome were magical ways around the judgment, just as funerary texts and other provisions in the tomb were magical aids to success in the hereafter.

Judgment scenes show a female hybrid monster called "Eater" or "Eater of the Dead." Her role was to consume those who failed the test; a unique Roman Period example shows this happening. For Egyptians, departure from this life was a first stage; the second death, which brought complete annihilation, was what had to be avoided. Here, however, Egyptian categories are unfamiliar to others. Annihilation did not remove victims entirely, but the "dead;" that is, second dead, are shown being punished in the lower registers of the underworld books. They entered a mode of "nonexistence," which was itself a threat to order and had to be combated.

Scenes on tomb walls were part of the provision for life after death. In addition to wall decoration, burials contained material possessions in great variety, including (in very early periods) enormous quantities of food, statues presenting the deceased in a variety of roles that could be inhabited by his person—as a cult statue was by a god—and the mummy itself, elaborately wrapped, protected with amulets, placed in a coffin or nest of coffins, and magically brought to life in a ritual called the "opening of the mouth." Grave goods repeated the motif of rebirth in myriad symbolic forms, while some objects provided for particular needs in the hereafter.

The most extensive and varied provision preserved is that for Tut'ankhamun, whose funerary equipment was no doubt modest in comparison with that for such kings as Amenhotep III or Ramesses II. Among the nonroyal, the intact 18th Dynasty tomb of Kha' from Deir el-Medina exhibits an extraordinary level of provision for a relatively low-ranking member of the elite. By contrast, intact Old Kingdom tombs contained quite modest grave goods. In death, as in other contexts, Egyptian practices varied significantly over time and among social groups.

◀ *A relief showing the goddess Isis holding a sistrum. The sistrum was an important instrument in ancient Egypt used in dances and religious ceremonies, particularly in the worship of the goddess Hathor.*

Glossary

abacus Rectangular block placed on top of a column capital in order to support the **architrave**.

ambulatory Roofed colonnaded walkway, often running around the outside of small New Kingdom temples and bark stations, and of Greco-Roman **birth houses**.

architrave Horizontal stone beam between columns, or between a column and a wall, which supports a ceiling.

ba One of many Egyptian words for aspects of the personality, often translated "soul." The *ba* is associated with divinity and with power; gods have many *bas*. It also describes the ability to take on different manifestations, which are themselves bas, as the Apis bull is of Ptah. The *ba* of the deceased is able to move freely in the underworld and return to earth. See also **ka**.

Badarian From el-Badari, the type site of the earliest certainly identified Neolithic culture of the Nile valley (c. 4500 BCE).

bark shrine Deities were carried in model barks when they went out from temples in procession at festivals; larger divine barks were used on the river. The model barks were kept in shrines in the temples; those at Karnak and Luxor are sizable structures.

birth house Type of small temple (also called mammisi), attached to the main temples of the Late and Greco-Roman Periods. These were where the god of the main temple was born, or, if the main temple was dedicated to a goddess, where she bore her child.

Book of the Dead A collection of spells mostly written on papyrus and placed with the mummy in a burial, attested from the New Kingdom to the Greco-Roman Period. The texts continue the tradition of the **Pyramid Texts** and **Coffin Texts** The choice of spells, of which about 200 are known, some very long, varies from copy to copy.

cartouche Circle with a horizontal bar at the bottom, elongated into an oval within which kings' names are written from the 4th Dynasty on. Detailed examples show that the sign represents a knot of rope, looped so that it is never-ending; it thus symbolizes cyclical return. Kings had two cartouche names, the first a statement about the god Re' (*praenomen*) and the second their birth name.

cataract Stretch of rapids interrupting the flow of the Nile, caused by areas of granite interspersed in the Nubian sandstone belt. There are six numbered and several minor cataracts between Aswan and Khartum. All

are hazards to navigation. The 2nd Cataract, the most formidable, was impassable except during the annual inundation. Cataracts 1–4 and the Dal Cataract were political frontiers at different times.

cavetto cornice Crowning element of walls, doorways, flat-topped **stelae**, and false doors, consisting of a semicircular forward flaring, with a scalloped decoration, often with a winged disk in its middle; probably derived from reed or other plant architectural forms, it was much imitated outside Egypt.

cenotaph Symbolic tombs or mortuary cult places additional to the owner's burial place.

Chief Steward New Kingdom and Late Period title of the administrator of an estate of the temple of a god, the king or his mortuary temple, of a member of the royal family (e.g. a *Divine Adoratrice*) or even a private individual. Because of the economic importance of the function. Chief Stewards were very influential.

Coffin Texts Texts written inside coffins of the Middle Kingdom to aid the deceased in his passage to the hereafter. The texts continue the tradition of the **Pyramid Texts** but are used by private individuals. More than 1,000 spells are known.

colossus Over-lifesize statue, usually of a king, but also of private individuals and gods; typically set up outside the gates or pylons of temples, and often receiving some sort of cult or mediating between men and gods.

contrapposto The depiction in sculpture in the round of the organic adjustment of the human body to asymmetrical poses; very rare in Egyptian art.

count Conventional translation of a **ranking title** of the old and Middle Kingdoms. As with many titles, modern translations are conventional rather than precise. In the New Kingdom the same title was used for a local administrative function and is better rendered "mayor."

cuneiform The Mesopotamian script, written with a stylus on clay tablets, with characteristic wedge-shaped (cuneiform) strokes. The script wrote many different languages, the most widespread being Akkadian, which was the diplomatic language of the late second millennium BCE. Cuneiform texts have been found in Egypt at el-'Amarna, and on various objects of the Persian Period. In the Near East cuneiform tablets from Egypt have been found at Bogazkoy in Anatolia and Kamid el-Loz in Syria.

cursive Rapid, handwritten forms of the script, chiefly **hieratic** and **demotic.** Cursive **hieroglyphs** are special simplified sign forms, similar to hieratic, written in ink and used for religious texts and for the initial training of scribes; the form died out in the first millennium BCE.

demotic From Greek "popular," a further elaboration of hieratic, developed in northern Egypt in the 7th century BCE; the normal everyday script of the Late and Greco–Roman Periods. Latest dated text 452 CE.

Divine Adoratrice Chief priestess of Amun in Thebes, an office known from the New Kingdom–Late Period. The priestess was celibate. In the 23rd–26th Dynasties princesses held it, notionally "adopting" their successors, and acting as important vehicles of political control.

ennead Group of 9 deities. Enneads are associated with several major cult centers. The number 9 embodies a plurality (3) of pluralities (3, i.e. 3 x 3). and so stands for large numbers in general; hence some enneads have more than 9 members. The best-known, the great ennead of Heliopolis, embodies two myths within its composition. It consists of Re'-Atum, Shu, Tefenet, Geb, Nut, Osiris, Isis, Seth, and Nephthys.

Fan-Bearer on the Right of the King Court title, probably purely honorific or ranking, of high officials of the New Kingdom. The right was the prestigious side.

fecundity figure Type of offering bearer shown at the base of temple walls bringing offerings into the temple; mostly personifications of geographical areas, the inundation, or abstract concepts. The male figures have heavy pendulous breasts and bulging stomachs, their fatness symbolizing the abundance they bring with them.

funerary cones Pottery cones found mostly in Theban tombs of the Middle Kingdom to Late Period, with a flat circular or rectangular base bearing an impression of a stamp with the titles and name of the tomb owner. The cones, some 12 inches (30 cm) long, were originally inserted in the brick-built tomb facade or tomb pyramid to form horizontal rows.

God's Father Common priestly title of the New Kingdom and later, usually further extended by the name of a god (e.g. God's Father of Amun). God's Fathers mostly ranked above ordinary *wa' eb*-priests ("the pure ones") but below "prophets."

Herald Middle and New Kingdom title borne by an official whose function was probably to report to the king and make his commands known, both at court and, for example, on the battlefield.

hieratic From Greek "sacred," the normal form of the script, mostly written on **papyrus** or **ostraca** and used throughout Egyptian history. In later periods hieratic was restricted to religious texts, hence its name. Hieratic signs lost the pictorial character of hieroglyphs and are often joined together.

hieroglyph Sign in the Egyptian script, from Greek "sacred carving"; used only for the monumental form of the script, in which most signs are identifiable pictures, and no signs are joined together.

High Priest Conventional translation of the title of the head of the local priesthood. The Egyptian forms of the most important among them were as follows: Amun (Thebes): "The First **Prophet** of Amun"; Ptah (Memphis): "Greatest of the Directors of Craftsmen"; Re' (Heliopolis): "Greatest of the Seers"; Thoth (el-Ashmunein): "Greatest of the Five."

Horus name The first name in a king's titulary, normally written inside a *serekh*, and consisting of an epithet that identifies the king as a manifestation of an aspect of Horus.

hypostyle hall Term for columned halls, from the Greek for "bearing pillars." The halls are the outermost, and grandest, parts of the main structures of temples, frequently added after the rest, and exhibit an elaborate symbolism. Many temples have two hypostyle halls.

ka Obscure conception of an aspect of the personality, perhaps associated originally with sexual fertility. The *ka* was horn as a "double" of the living person, but came into its own in the afterlife, when it received mortuary offerings and ensured the deceased's survival. See also **ba**.

kiosk Small, open temple structure used as a way station for statues of gods during festivals when they left their main temples, or in the **sed festival**

Lector Priest (literally "One who bears the ritual book") whose function was to declaim the ritual texts in funerary and temple cult. He wore a distinctive broad white sash diagonally across the chest. "Chief Lector Priest" was a higher rank.

logogram Sign in the script that writes an entire word, often with the addition of a stroke and/or the feminine ending *-t*.

mastaba Arabic word for bench, used as the term for free-standing tombs of the Early Dynastic Period and Old Kingdom (and some later ones). The basic form of a mastaba's superstructure is a rectangle with flat roof and vertical (mud-brick) or slightly inclined (stone) walls.

Mistress of the House Housewife, title given to married ladies from the Middle Kingdom onward.

naos Shrine in which divine statues were kept, especially in temple sanctuaries. A small wooden naos was normally placed inside a monolithic one in hard stone; the latter are typical of the late Period, and sometimes elaborately decorated. Also used as a term for temple sanctuary.

necropolis Greek word for cemetery. "Necropolis" normally describes large and important burial areas that were in use for long periods, "cemetery" smaller and more homogeneous sites; cemeteries may also be subdivisions of a necropolis.

Nilometer Staircase descending into the Nile and marked with levels above low water; used for measuring, and in some cases recording, inundation levels. The most famous are on Elephantine island and on Roda island in Cairo.

nomarch The chief official of a **nome**. In the late old Kingdom–early Middle Kingdom nomarchs became local, hereditary rulers, who governed their nomes more or less independently of the central authority; the kings of the 11th Dynasty began in this way. During the 12th Dynasty the office ceased to have political importance.

nome Administrative province of Egypt, from Greek *nomos*; the ancient Egyptian term was *sepat*. The nome system seems to have been elaborated in the Early Dynastic Period, but did not reach final form until the Ptolemies. During some periods of highly centralized administration (e.g. late Middle Kingdom) the nomes had little real importance.

obelisk Monolithic tapering shaft, mostly of pink granite, with a **pyramidion** at the top; from a Greek word for a spit. Obelisks are solar symbols, probably similar in meaning to pyramids, and associated with an ancient stone called *benben* in Heliopolis. They were set up in pairs outside the entrances to some Old Kingdom tombs, and outside temples; a single obelisk in east Karnak was the object of a cult.

ogdoad The group of 8 deities (four male–female pairs) linked with Hermopolis, who symbolize the state of the world before creation. The group's composition varies, but its classic form is: Nun and Naunet, the primeval waters; Huh and Hauhet, endless space; Kuk and Kauket, darkness; Amun and Amaunet, what is hidden.

orthogram Sign in the script whose function is to elucidate the function of another sign or to write a dual or plural.

Osirid pillar Pillar, mostly in an open court or portico, with a colossal statue of a king

forming its front part; unlike caryatids in Classical architecture, the statues are not weight-bearing elements. Most are mummiform, but not all; the connection with Osiris is doubtful.

ostracon Flake of limestone or potsherd used for writing (from the Greek for potsherd); also fragment from an inscribed jar (e.g. a wine jar inscribed with the details of a vintage). Ostraca are known from all periods, but 19th and 20th-Dynasty examples are commonest (up to 20,000 have been found). Most texts are in **hieratic** or **demotic** but there are also **cursive hieroglyphic** texts and numerous pictures, including drafts of hieroglyphic inscriptions.

Overseer of Sealers Typical administrative title of the 12th Dynasty borne by a high official of the Treasury. The "Overseer of Sealers" was responsible to the head of the Treasury ("The Overseer of the Seal") and his deputies. The term derives from the fact that most containers of produce and goods were sealed when entering or leaving the Treasury magazines.

papyrus The chief Egyptian writing material, and an important export. The earliest papyrus (blank) dates to the 1st Dynasty, the latest to the Islamic Period, when the plant died out in Egypt. Sheets were made by cutting the pith of the plant into strips laid in rows horizontally and vertically, which were then beaten together, activating the plant's natural starch to form an adhesive. Separate sheets were gummed together to form rolls. The better surface of a papyrus (the normal recto) had the fibers running horizontally, but letters were normally begun on strips inscribed across the fibers.

peristyle court Court with a roof around the sides supported by rows of columns (from Greek *peristylon*) and an open space in the center.

phonogram Sign in the script that records a sound. Only consonants are precisely recorded, and phonograms may write 1–4 consonants.

praenomen A king's first cartouche name, which he adopted on his accession; also called "throne name." It consists of a statement about the god Re', later with additional epithets, e.g. Menkheprure' (Tuthmosis IV) "Re' is enduring of manifestations."

pronaos Room in front of the sanctuary (naos) of a temple, whose exact location varies with the design of individual temples; sometimes used as a term for **hypostyle hall**.

Prophet Priestly title (literally "God's Servant"), ranking above *wa' eb*-priests and God's Fathers usually extended by the name of a god (e.g. "Prophet of Montu"). The head of the local priesthood, particularly in the provinces, was often called "Overseer of Prophets." The high priest of Amun at Thebes was "The First Prophet of Amun"; below him were the Second, Third, and Fourth Prophets.

propylon Gateway that stands in front of a **pylon**.

pylon Monumental entrance wall of a temple, from the Greek for gate; consists of a pair of massifs with an opening between, mostly elaborated into a doorway. All the wall faces are inclined; the corners are completed with a **torus molding** and the top with torus and **cavetto cornice.** Pylons are the largest and least essential parts of a temple, mostly built last. Some temples have series of them (e.g. 10 at Karnak, on two axes).

pyramidion Capstone of a pyramid or top of an **obelisk**. The pyramidion was decorated and became a symbolic object in its own right, being used also as the most striking feature of the small brick pyramids of private tombs of the New Kingdom (Deir el-Medina, Saqqara) and Late Period (Abydos).

Pyramid Texts Texts on the walls of the internal rooms of pyramids of the end of the 5th and 6th Dynasties, later used by private individuals for most of Egyptian history. Some texts may relate to the king's burial ceremonies, but others are concerned with temple ritual and many other matters.

ranking title Title that indicates status but does not go with any specific function; very important in the Old and to a lesser extent the Middle Kingdom. The typical sequence of titles, in ascending order, is "Royal Acquaintance," "Sole Companion," "**Count**," "Hereditary Prince."

reserve heads Old Kingdom tomb sculptures in the round, aiming at a realistic representation of the head of the deceased (hence the alternate term "portrait heads"), and acting as its substitute. The majority have been found at Giza.

revetment Cladding of a wall surface or bastion; may be ornamental, e.g. stone covering mud brick, or structural, and intended to give stability to a core of rubble.

sabbakhin Arabic word for diggers of *sabbakh*, nitrogenous earth from ancient sites used as fertilizer; *sabbakh* may be mud brick or remains of organic refuse. Sabbakhin are among the chief agents of destruction of ancient sites.

saff tomb Arabic word for row, describing rock-cut tombs of the early 11th Dynasty that consist of a row of openings—or colonnade—in the hillside.

sea peoples Invaders of Egypt in the late 19th and early 20th Dynasties, probably associated with a wave of destruction on Near Eastern sites and more remotely with the fall of Mycenaean Greece and the Hittite empire. Their precise identity and origin are much disputed by scholars.

sed festival Ritual of royal regeneration, almost always celebrated after 30 years of a king's reign, and thereafter at three-yearly intervals, but very occasionally performed earlier; features prominently in the decoration of royal mortuary temples, reflecting the king's wish to rule long in the next world.

semogram Sign in the script that conveys meaning, not sound. Subcategories are **logograms**, **taxograms**, and **orthograms**. Also called ideograms.

serekh Image of a brick facade to a palace or enclosure, with a rectangular space above; the facade is in the style of the beginning of the Early Dynastic Period. A falcon (the sign for Horus) perches on the top horizontal of the rectangle, which encloses a king's **Horus name**.

sistrum Musical instrument—a kind of rattle—sacred to Hathor. Two types are common: (a) a **naos** shape above a Hathor head, with ornamental loops on the sides (the rattle was inside the box of the naos); (b) a simple loop with loose cross bars of metal above a smaller Hathor head; both had long handles. (a) was used from the New Kingdom on as a type of column capital, making play with the association between the rustle of aquatic plants and the joyful sound of the sistrum (plant and sistrum forms are occasionally combined). At Dendara the sistrum (mostly type (a)) was an important sacred object.

Standard Bearer of the Lord of the Two Lands Military title of the New Kingdom, borne by an officer of the infantry, chariotry, or one attached to a ship, who was in charge of a company of some 250 men. Companies of the Egyptian army had distinguishing "standards."

stela Slab of stone or sometimes wood with texts, reliefs, or paintings. Commemorative or votive stelae are placed in temples; tomb stelae function within the decoration of a tomb.

talatat Arabic word for three (handbreadths), describing the length of the typical small stone building blocks of temples of Amenophis IV/Akhenaten. They are found reused at a number of sites (some 30,000 at Karnak), and are decorated with scenes in the 'Amarna style. Some complete walls have been reassembled from scattered blocks.

Taslan From Deir Tasa, a Predynastic site in Upper Egypt; name of a Predynastic culture that may not be distinct from **Badarian.**

taxogram Sign in the script that is placed after the **phonograms** in the writing of a word, and indicates the class or area of meaning to which it belongs.

torus molding Semicircular or cylindrical band forming the edge of a stela or the corner of a stone wall. Detailed examples are decorated with a pattern that suggests lashings around a pole or reed bundle.

underworld books Mixed pictorial and textual compositions inscribed in New Kingdom royal tombs that describe the passage of the sun god through the underworld and the sky; taken over by private individuals in the Late Period.

uraeus The most characteristic symbol of kingship, a rearing cobra worn on the king's forehead or crown. The cobra is associated with the goddess Wadjit or with the sun, whose "eye" it is held to be. It is an agent of destruction and protection of the king, spitting out fire.

Viceroy of Kush Administrator of Nubia during the New Kingdom, at first called "King's Son," from the mid–18th Dynasty "King's Son of Kush." Despite the form of the title, its holder was not a real son of the king. The area governed by the viceroy extended as far north as Kom el-Ahmar (Hierakonpolis). His two deputies, one for Lower Nubia (Wawat), the other for Upper Nubia (Kush), resided at 'Aniba and 'Amara respectively.

vizier The highest official in the administration, whose post is found already in the Early Dynastic Period. In the New Kingdom there were two viziers, at Memphis and Thebes; from this period on, the most important individuals were often not viziers, and the office was less important in the Late Period. There are texts that describe the installation of a vizier and detail his functions.

winged disk A sun disk with an outspread pair of wings attached. The earliest possible example of the motif is of the 1st Dynasty. It is associated with Horus of Behdet (Edfu), and symbolizes the sun, especially in architecture on ceilings, cornices, and stelae. It was often copied outside Egypt.

zodiac The Babylonian and Greek signs of the zodiac were introduced into Egypt in the Greco-Roman Period, "translated" into Egyptian representational forms, and used in the decoration of astronomical ceilings of tombs and temples, and on coffin lids.

Further Reading

General and Reference Works
Bunson, Margaret. *Encyclopedia of Ancient Egypt*. New York: Facts on File, 2002.
Cox, Simon, *An A to Z of Ancient Egypt*. Edinburgh: Mainstream Pub., 2007.
Ikram, Salima, *Ancient Egypt: An Introduction*. New York: Cambridge University Press, 2009.
Redford, Donald B, *The Oxford Encyclopedia of Ancient Egypt*. New York: Oxford University Press, 2001.

Part One
The geography of ancient Egypt
Draper, Allison Stark, *A Historical Atlas of Egypt*. New York: Rosen Pub. Group, 2004.
Grant, Michael, *The Routledge Atlas of Classical History*. London: Routledge, 1994.
Manley, Bill, *The Penguin Historical Atlas of Ancient Egypt*. New York: Penguin, 1996.
Pemberton, Delia, *Atlas of Ancient Egypt*. New York: Harry N. Abrams, in association with the British Museum, 2005.

The study of ancient Egypt
Colla, Elliott, *Conflicted Antiquities: Egyptology, Egyptomania, Egyptian Modernity*. Durham, NC: Duke University Press, 2007.
Current Research in Egyptology Symposium, *Current Research in Egyptology 2005: Proceedings of the Sixth Annual Symposium which took place at the University of Cambridge*, 6-8 January 2005.
Daly, Okasha El, *Egyptology: The Missing Millennium: Ancient Egypt in Medieval Arabic Writings*. London: UCL, 2005.
Fagan, Brian M, *The Rape of the Nile: Tomb Robbers, Tourists, and Archaeologists in Egypt*. Boulder, CO: Westview Press, 2004.
Ray, J. D, *The Rosetta Stone and the Rebirth of Ancient Egypt*. Cambridge, Mass: Harvard University Press, 2007.
Sands, Emily. *The Egyptology Handbook: A Course in the Wonders of Egypt*. Cambridge, MA: Candlewick Press, 2005.
Thomas, Nancy (ed.), *The American Discovery of Ancient Egypt*. Los Angeles: Los Angeles County Museum of Art, 1996.
Tyldesley, Joyce A., *Egypt: How a Lost Civilization was Rediscovered*. Berkeley: University of California Press, 2005.

Wengrow, D, *The Archaeology of Early Egypt: Social Transformations in North-East Africa, 10,000 to 2,650 BC*. Cambridge, Cambridge University Press, 2006.
Wilkinson, Richard H., *Egyptology Today*. Cambridge, Cambridge University Press, 2008.

The historical background
Bierbrier, M. L., *Historical Dictionary of Ancient Egypt*. Lanham, MD: Scarecrow Press, 2008.
Brier, Bob, *Daily Life of the Ancient Egyptians*. Westport, CT: Greenwood Press, 2008.
Christensen, Wendy, *Empire of Ancient Egypt*. New York: Facts On File, 2005.
Dodson, Aidan, *The Complete Royal Families of Ancient Egypt*. London, Thames & Hudson, 2004.
Goldschmidt, Arthur, *A Brief History of Egypt*. New York: Facts on File, 2008.
Gozzoli, Roberto B., *The Writing of History in Ancient Egypt During the First Millennium B.C.: Trends and Perspectives*. London: Golden House Publications, 2006.
Hornung, Erik H et al (eds.), *Ancient Egyptian Chronology*. Boston: Brill, 2006.
Nardo, Don, *Rulers of Ancient Egypt*. Detroit: Greenhaven Press/Thomson-Gale, 2005.
Perry, Glenn E., *The History of Egypt*. Westport, CT: Greenwood Press, 2004.
Redford, Donald B., *A History of Ancient Egypt: Egyptian Civilization in Context*. Dubuque, IA: Kendall/Hunt, 2006.
Shaw, Ian, *The Oxford History of Ancient Egypt*. Oxford: Oxford University Press, 2003.
Wilkinson, Toby A. H., *Lives of the Ancient Egyptians*. New York: Thames & Hudson, 2007.
Wiltshire, Katharine. *The British Museum Timeline of the Ancient World: Mesopotamia, Egypt, Greece, Rome*. New York: Palgrave Macmillan, 2004.

Art and architecture
Applegate, Melissa Littlefield, *The Egyptian Book of Life: Symbolism of Ancient Egyptian Temple and Tomb Art*. Deerfield Beach, FL: Health Communications, 2000.
Arnold, Dorothea, *When the Pyramids were Built: Egyptian Art of the Old Kingdom*. New York: Metropolitan Museum of Art, 1999.

Bothmer, Bernard V., *Egyptian Art: Selected Writings of Bernard V. Bothmer*. New York: Oxford University Press, 2004.
Clarke, Somers and R. Engelbach, *Ancient Egyptian Masonry, Ancient Egyptian Construction and Architecture*. New York: Dover Publications, 1990.
Egyptian Art: Principles and Themes in Wall Scenes. Guizeh, Egypt: Prism, 2000.
Egyptian Art in the Age of the Pyramids. New York: Metropolitan Museum of Art, 1999.
Fazzini, Richard A., *Art for Eternity: Masterworks from Ancient Egypt*. Brooklyn, NY: Brooklyn Museum of Art in association with Scala Publishers, 1999.
Freed, Rita E., *Arts of Ancient Egypt*. Boston, MA: MFA Publications, 2003.
Hartwig, Melinda K., *Tomb Painting and Identity in Ancient Thebes*. Turnhout, Belgium: Brepols, 2004.
Hawass, Zahi A., *Hidden Treasures of Ancient Egypt: Unearthing the Masterpieces of Egyptian History*. Washington, D.C.: National Geographic, 2004.
Hawass, Zahi A., *Hidden Treasures of Ancient Egypt: Unearthing the Masterpieces of Egyptian History*. Washington, D.C.: National Geographic, 2004.
Hodge, Susie, *Ancient Egyptian Art*. Des Plaines, IL: Heinemann Interactive Library, 1998.
Jánosi, Peter (ed.), *Structure and Significance: Thoughts on Ancient Egyptian*. Vienna, Austria: Verlag der Österreichischen Akademie der Wissenschaften, 2005.
Jacq, Christian, *Fascinating Hieroglyphics: Discovering, Decoding & Understanding the Ancient Art*. New York: Sterling Pub., 1997.
Koltsida, Aikaterini, *Social Aspects of Ancient Egyptian Domestic Architecture*. Oxford: Archaeopress, 2007.
Lightbody, David I., *Egyptian Tomb Architecture: The Archaeological Facts of Pharaonic Circular Symbolism*. Oxford: Archaeopress, 2008.
Málek, Jaromír, *Egypt: 4,000 Years of Art*. London: Phaidon, 2003.
McKenzie, Judith, *The Architecture of Alexandria and Egypt*. New Haven, CT: Yale University Press, 2007.
Robins, Gay, *Egyptian Painting and Relief*. Oxford: Shire Publications, 2008.

Robins, Gay, *The Art of Ancient Egypt*. Cambridge, MA: Harvard University Press, 2008.

Rossi, Corinna, *Architecture and Mathematics in Ancient Egypt*. Cambridge: Cambridge University Press, 2007

Russmann, Edna R., *Temples and Tombs: Treasures of Egyptian Art from the British Museum*. New York: American Federation of Arts in Association with University of Washington Press, Seattle, 2006.

Smith, William Stevenson, *The Art and Architecture of Ancient Egypt*. New Haven, CT: Yale University Press, 1998.

Smith, William Stevenson, *The Art and Architecture of Ancient Egypt*. New Haven: Yale University Press, 1998.

Stocks, Denys A., *Experiments in Egyptian Archaeology: Stoneworking Technology in Ancient Egypt*. London: Routledge, 2003.

Strudwick, Nigel and Helen, T*he Encyclopedia of Ancient Egyptian Architecture*. Princeton, N.J.: Princeton University Press, 2003.

Tiradritti, Francesco, *Ancient Egypt: Art, Architecture and History*. London: British Museum, 2002.

Tiradritti, Francesco, *Ancient Egypt: Art, Architecture and History*. London: British Museum, 2002.

Tiradritti, Francesco, *Egyptian Wall painting* New York : Abbeville Press, 2008.

Vassilika, Eleni, *Egyptian Art*. Cambridge: Cambridge University Press, 1995.

Part Two: Journey On the Nile

Elephantine and Aswan

Kamil, Jill, *Aswan and Abu Simbel: History and Guide*. Cairo: American University in Cairo Press, 1993.

Philae

Dijkstra, Jitse H. F., *Philae and the End of Ancient Egyptian Religion: A Regional Study of Religious Transformation*. Dudley, MA: Peeters, Departement Oosterse Studies, 2008.

Portman, Ian, *A Guide to the Temples of Philae*. Cairo: Palm Press, 1984.

Kom Ombo

Portman, Ian, *A Guide to the Temple of Kom Ombo*. Cairo: Palm Press, 1984.

Edfu

Kurth, Dieter, *The Temple of Edfu: A Guide by an Ancient Egyptian Priest*. Cairo: American University in Cairo Press, 2004.

Armant

Ginter, Boles?aw, *Predynastic Settlement near Armant*. Heidelberg: Heidelberger Orientverlag, 1994.

Luxor

Hawass, Zahi A., *The Royal Tombs of Egypt: The Art of Thebes Revealed*. London: Thames & Hudson, 2006.

Schwaller de Lubicz. R.A., *The temple of Man: Apet of the South at Luxor*. Rochester, VT: Inner Traditions, 1998.

Weeks, Kent R., *The Treasures of Luxor and the Valley of the Kings*. Vercelli: White Star, 2005.

Karnak

Blyth, Elizabeth, *Karnak: Evolution of a Temple*. New York, NY: Routledge, 2006.

Siliotti, Alberto, *Luxor, Karnak, and the Theban Temples*. Cairo, American University in Cairo Press, 2002.

The West Bank

Holt, Terrence, *In the Valley of the Kings: Stories*. New York: W.W. Norton & Co., 2009.

Meyerson, Daniel, I*n the Valley of the Kings: Howard Carter and the Mystery of King Tutankhamun's Tomb*. New York: Ballantine Books, 2009.

Naqada and Tukh

Williams, Bruce, *Decorated Pottery and the Art of Naqada IL: A Documentary Essay*. Munich, Germany: Deutscher Kunstverlag, 1988.

Dendara

Portman, Ian, *A Guide to the Temple of Dendara*. Cairo: Palm Press, 1984.

el-Qasr Wa-' l-Saiyad

Säve-Söderbergh, Torgny, *The Old Kingdom Cemetery at Hamra Dom (El-Qasr wa es-Saiyad)*. Stockholm, Sweden: Royal Academy of Letters History and Antiquities, 1994.

Abydos

Spalinger, Anthony John, *The Great Dedicatory Inscription of Ramesses II: A Solar-Osirian Tractate at Abydos*. Boston: Brill, 2008.

Trout, Richard, *Falcon of Abydos: Oracle of the Nile*. San Antonio, TX: Langmarc Publishing, 2001.

Akhmim

Egberts , A. et al (eds.), *Perspectives on Panopolis: An Egyptian Town from Alexander the Great to the Arab Conquest*. Boston: Brill, 2002.

Hope, Colin A., *Akhmim in the Old Kingdom*. Oxford: Aris and Phillips, 2006.

Ockinga, Boyo, *A Tomb from the Reign of Tutankhamun at Akhmim*. Warminster, England: Aris & Phillips, 1997.

Asyut

Kahl, Jochem, *Ancien Asyut: The First Synthesis after 300 Years of Research*. Wiesbaden, Germany: Harrassowitz, 2007.

Deir El-Gebrawi

Kanawati, Naguib, Deir El-Gebrawi: *Southern Cliff—The Tombs of Ibi and*

Others. Warminster, England: Aris & Phillips, 2006)

el-'Amarna

Rose, Pamela, *The Eighteenth Dynasty Pottery Corpus from Amarna*. London: Egypt Exploration Society, 2007.

Stevens, Anna, *Private Religion at Amarna: The Material Evidence*. Oxford: Archaeopress, 2006.

el-Ashmunein

Spencer, A. Jeffrey, *Excavations at el-Ashmunein*. London: Trustees of the British Museum by British Museum Publications, 1983–1998.

Beni Hasan with Speos Artemidos

Garstang, John, *Burial Customs of Ancient Egypt as Illustrated by Tombs of the Middle Kingdom: A Report of Excavations Made in the Necropolis of Beni Hassan during 1902–4*. New York: Columbia University Press, 2002.

Tihna el-Gebel

Preliminary Report, *Eighth Season of the Excavations at the Site of Akoris, Egypt, 1988*. Kyoto: Paleological Association of Japan, 1989.

el-Bahnasa

Jones, Alexander, *Astronomical Papyri from Oxyrhynchus*. Philadelphia: American Philosophical Society, 1999.

Ihnasya el-Medina

Mukht?r, Mu?ammad Jam?l al-D?n, *Ihnâsya El-Medina (Herakleopolis Magna): Its Importance and Its Role in Pharaonic History*. Cairo: Institut Français d'Archéologie Orientale du Caire, 1983.

Maidum

Thomas, Susanna, *Snefru: the Pyramid Builder*. New York: Rosen Pub. Group, 2003.

el-Lisht

Arnold, Dieter, *Middle Kingdom Tomb Architecture at Lisht*. New York: Metropolitan Museum of Art, 2007.

Arnold, Dieter, *The Pyramid of Senwosret*. New York: Metropolitan Museum of Art, 1988.

Saqqara

Firth, Cecil Mallaby, *Excavations at Saqqara: The Step Pyramid*. Mansfield Centre, CT: Martino Pub., 2007.

Abusir

Verner, Miroslav, *Abusir IX: The Pyramid Complex of Raneferef: The Archeology*. Prague, Czech Republic: Czech Institute of Egyptology, 2006.

Giza

Lehner, Mark and Wilma Wetterstrom (eds), *Giza Reports: The Giza Plateau Mapping Project*. Boston: Ancient Egypt Research Associates, 2007.

Pyramid at Giza

Corteggiani, Jean Pierre, *The Great Pyramids*. New York: Abrams, 2007.

Hawass, Zahi A., *Mountains of the Pharaohs: The Untold Story of the Pyramid Builders*. New York: Doubleday, 2006.

Matthews, Sheelagh, *Pyramids of Giza*. New York: Weigl Publishers, 2007.

Kom el-Hisn

Cagle, Anthony, *The Spatial Structure of Kom el-Hisn: An Old Kingdom Town in the Western Nile Delta, Egypt*. Oxford, England: Archaeopress, 2003.

Naukratis

Möller, Astrid, *Naukratis: Trade in Archaic Greece*. Oxford, Oxford University Press, 2000.

Villing, Alexandra, and Udo Schlotzhauer (eds.), *Naukratis: Greek Diversity in Egypt: Studies on East Greek Pottery and Exchange in the Eastern Mediterranean*. London: British Museum, 2006.

Alexandria

Goddio, Franck (ed), *Egypt's Sunken Treasures*. Munich, Germany: Prestel, 2008.

MacLeod, Roy, *The Library of Alexandria: Centre of Learning in the Ancient World*. London: I.B. Tauris.

Tell el-Rub'a and Tell el-Timai

Redford, Donald B., *City of the Ram-man: The Story of Ancient Mendes*. Princeton, NJ: Princeton University Press, 2010.

Heliopolis

Scudamore, James, *Heliopolis*. London: Harvill Secker, 2009.

Abu Simbel

Siliotti, Alberto, *Abu Simbel and the Nubian Temples*. Cairo, American University in Cairo Press, 2000.

Sinai

Beit-Arieh, Itzhaq, *Archaeology of Sinai: The Ophir Expedition*. Tel Aviv: Emery and Claire Yass Publications in Archaeology, 2003.

Part Three: Aspects of Egyptian Society

Scribes and writing

Bagnall, Roger S., *The Oxford Handbook of Papyrology*. Oxford: Oxford University Press, 2009.

McBrewster. John, *Egyptian Hieroglyphs: Ancient Egypt, Cursive Hieroglyphs, Papyrus, Hieratic, Demotic, Egyptology, Hieroglyph*. Mauritius: Alphascript Publishing, 2009.

Women and men

Bagnall, Roger S., *Women's Letters from Ancient Egypt*. Ann Arbor: University of Michigan Press, 2006.

Manferto de Fabianis, Valeria, *The Queens of Ancient Egypt*. Vercelli, Italy: White Star Pub., 2008.

Sharp, Anne Wallace, *Women of Ancient Egypt*. Detroit: Thomson/Gale, 2005.

Religion

Baines, John, *Religion and Society in Ancient Egypt*. London: Continuum International Publishing Group, 2010.

Guilhou, Nadine, *The Legacy of Egyptian Mythology: Cosmogony and Netherworld*. Cairo, Farid Atiya Press, 2009

Kanawati, Naguib, *The Tomb and Beyond: Burial Customs of the Egyptian Officials*. Warminster, England, Aris & Phillips Ltd, 2001.

Riggs, Christina, *The Beautiful Burial in Roman Egypt: Art, Identity, and Funerary Religion*. Oxford: Oxford University Press, 2005.

Original Bibliography

The bibliography compiled for the original edition of this book remains a valuable summary of Egyptian scholarship in the 20th century.

Much of the work of Egyptologists is published in specialist journals, of which a dozen are devoted exclusively to the subject. These are listed in the *Lexikon der Ägyptologie* (see below). The presentation in this book is often based on material in journals, and may differ from that in other books. This applies especially to "The Historical Setting."

General and Reference Works
British Museum, *An Introduction to Ancient Egypt*. London 1979.
F, Daumas, *La Civilisation de l'Egyptepharaonique*. Paris 1965.
A. Erman and H. Ranke, *Ägypten and ägyptisches Leben im Altertum*. 2nd ed. Tubingen 1923.
W. C. Hayes. *The Scepter of Egypt*. New York 1953, Cambridge (Mass.) 1959.
W. Helck and E. Otto, *Kleines Wörterbuch der Ägyptologie*. 2nd ed. Wiesbaden 1970.
W. Heick et al. (eds.), *Lexikon der Ägyptologie* (6 vols. planned). Wiesbaden 1972–.
E. Hornung, *Einführung in die Ägyptologie*. Darmstadt 1967.
H. Kees, *Ägypten*. Munich 1933.
S. Moscati (ed.), *L'alba della civiltà*, i-iii. Turin 1976.
C. F. Nims, *Thebes of the Pharaohs*. London 1965.
E. Otto, *Wesen und Wandel der ägyptischen Kultur*. Berlin etc. 1969.
G. Posener et a., *Dictionnaire de la civilisation Cgyptienne*. Paris 1959
J. A. Wilson, *The Burden of Egypt/The Culture of Ancient Egypt*. Chicago (Ill.) 1951.

Part One: The Cultural Setting—The geography of ancient Egypt
W. Y. Adams, *Nubia: Corridor to Africa*. London 1977.
K. W. Butzer, *Early Hydraulic Civilization in Egypt*. Chicago (Ill.) and London 1976. H. Kees, *Das alte Ägypten, eine kleine Landeskunde*. 2nd ed. Berlin 1958
A. Lucas and J. R. Harris, *Ancient Egyptian Materials and Industries*. 4th ed. London 1962.
P. Montet, *Géographic de l'Égypte ancienne*, i-ii. Paris 1957-61.
B. Trigger, *Nubia under the Pharaohs*. London 1976.

The study of ancient Egypt
W. Dawson and E. P. Uphill, *Who was who in Egyptology*. 2nd ed. London 1972.
L. Greener, *The Discovery of Egypt*. London 1966. Works of travellers to Egypt are also available; many are collected in "*Voyageurs occidentaux en Égypte.*" Cairo 1970

The historical setting
E. Bevan, *A History of Egypt under the Ptolemaic Dynasty*. London 1927.
J. H. Breasted, *A History of Egypt*. 2nd ed. New York 1909.
Cambridge Ancient History, i-iv. 3rd ed. Cambridge 1970–.
A. H. Gardiner, *Egypt of the Pharaohs*. Oxford 1961.
W. Helck, *Geschichte des alten Ägypten*. Leiden and Cologne 1968.
E. Hornung. *Grundzüge der ägyptischen Geschichte*. 2nd ed. Darmstadt 1978.
F. IC. Kienitz, *Die politische Geschichte Ägyptens von 7 bis zum 4. Jahrhundert vorderZeitwende*. Berlin 1953.
K. A. Kitchen, *The Third Intermediate Period in Egypt (1100-650 B.C.)*. Warminster 1973.
I. G. Milne, *A History of Egypt under Roman Rule*. 3rd ed. London 1924.

Principles of art and architecture
A. Badawy, *A History of Egyptian Architecture*, i-iii. Giza 1954, Berkeley (Cal.) 1966-68.
S. Clarke and R. Engelbach. *Ancient Egyptian Masonry*. London 1930.
J.-L. de Cenival, *Égypte. Époquepharaonique*. Fribourg 1964.
E. Iversen, *Canon and Proportions in Egyptian Art*. 2nd ed. Warminster 1975.
K. Lange and M. Hirmer. *Ägypten*. 4th ed. Munich 1967.
H. Schafer, *Von agyptischer Kunst*. 4th ed. Wiesbaden 1963.
W. S. Smith. *The Art and Architecture of Ancient Egypt*. Harmondsworth 1958.
—— *A History of Egyptian Sculpture and Painting in the Old Kingdom*. 2nd ed. London and Boston (Mass.) 1949.
C. Vandersleyen et al., *Das alte Ägypten*. Berlin 1975.

Stelae
J. Vandier, *Manuel d'archdologie égyptienne*, ii(1). Paris 1954.

Part Two: A Journey down the Nile
Complete bibliographical data are given by B. Porter and R. L. B. Moss, *Topographical Bibliography of Ancient Egyptian Hieroglyphical Texts, Reliefs, and Paintings* (Oxford 1927), quoted here as PM. Regular reports on current archaeological work in Egypt and Nubia are published by J. Leclant in *Orientalia* (since 1950).

Elephantine and Aswan (PM v. 221-44)
E. Bresciani and S. Pernigotti. *Assuan. Il tempio tolemaico di Isi. I blocchi decorati e iscritti*. Pisa 1978.
E. Edel, *Die Felsengrdber der Qubbet elHawa bei Assuan*, i-. Wiesbaden 1967-.
Philae (PM vi.203-56)
H. Junker and E. Winter, *Philä*, i-. Vienna 1958-.
H. G. Lyons. *A Report on the Island and Temples of Philae*. [London 1897].
S. Sauneron and H. Stierlin. *Die letzten Tempel Ägyptens.*
Edfu und Philae. Zürich 1978.
Kom Ombo (PM vi.179203)
J. de Morgan *et al.*, *Kom Ombos*, i-ii. Vienna 1909.
Gebel el Silsila (PM v.20818. 22021) R. A. Caminos and T. G. H. James, *Gebel es-Silsilah*, i-. London 1963-.
Edfu (PM v.200-05; vi. 119-77)
M. de Rochemonteix and É. Chassinat, *Le Temple d'Edfou*, i-xiv. Paris 1892, Cairo 1918-.
Kom el Ahmar (PM v.191-200)
B. Adams, *Ancient Hierakonpolis, with Supplement*. Warminster 1974.
W. A. Fairservis, Jr. et al., "Preliminary Report on the First Two Seasons at Hierakonpolis," *Journal of the American Research Center in Egypt*, ix (1971), 768.
J. E. Quibell (vol.ii with F. W. Green). *Hierakonpolis*, iii. London 1900. 1902.
el Kab (PM v.171-91)
P. Derchain, *Elkab, i. Les Monuments religieux à l'entrée de l'Ouady Hellal*. Brussels 1971.
Esna (PM v.165-67; vi. 110-19) D. Downes, *The Excavations at Esna 1905–1906*. Warminster 1974.
S. Sauneron, *Esna*, i-. Cairo 1959.
el-Mo'alla (PM v.170)
J. Vandier, *Mo'alla, la tombe d'Ankhtifi et la tombe de Sébekhotep*. Cairo 1950.
Gebelein (PM v.162–64)
Tod (PM v.167–69)
F. Bisson de la Roque, *Tôd (1934 à 1936)*. Cairo 1937.
Armant (PM v.15161)
R. Mood and O. H. Myers, *Temples of*

Armant. A Preliminary Survey. London 1940.

——*The Bucheum*, i-iii. London 1934.

Luxor (PM ii. ²301-39)

H. Brunner. *Die südlichen Räume des Tempels von Luxor*. Mainz 1977.

A. Gayet. *Le Temple de Louxor*. Cairo 1894.

Karnak (PM ii. ²l-301)

P. Barguet, *Le Temple d'Amon-Rê a Karnak. Essai d'exégèse*. Cairo 1962.

Reliefs and Inscriptions at Karnak, i-, by the Epigraphic Survey. Chicago (Ill.) 1936

The West Bank (PM i² and ii.²339-537)

H. Carter and A. C. Mace, *The Tomb of Tutankh.amen*, i-iii. London etc. 1923-33.

E. Hornung and F. Teichmann. *Das Grab des Haremhab im Tal der Könige*. Bern 1971.

Medinet Habu, i-viii, by the Epigraphic Survey. Chicago (Ill.) 193070.

E. Navulle, *The Temple of Deir el Bahari*, Introductory Memoir and i-vi. London 1894-1908.

J. Osing. *Der Tempel Sethos' I. in Gurna. Die Reliefs und Inschriften*, i-. Mainz 1977-.

G. Thausing and H. Goedicke, *Nofretari. Eine Dokumentation der Wandgemälde ihres Grabes*. Graz 1971.

Nag' el-Madamud (PM v.137-50)

F. Bisson de la Roque. J. J. Clère *et al.*, *Rapport sur les fouilles de Medamoud (1925-32)*. Cairo 1926-36.

Naqada and Tukh (PM v.117-19)

J. de Morgan, *Recherches sur les origines de l'Égypte*. ii. 147–202. Paris 1897.

Qua (PM v.135-6)

Qift (PM v.123-34)

W. M. F. Petrie, *Koptos*. London 1896.

Dendara (PM v.109-16; vi.41-110)

E. Chassinat and F. Daumas, *Le Temple de Dendara*, i. Cairo 1934-.

F. Daumas. *Dendara et le temple d'Hathor*. Cairo 1969. A. Mariette, *Denderah*, i-iv. Paris 1870-73.

el-Qasr Wa-' l-Saiyad (PM v.119-22)

Hiw (PM v.107-09)

W. M. F. Petrie, *Diospolis Parva: the Cemeteries of Abadiyeh and Hu, 1898-9*. London 1901.

Abydos (PM v.39105; vi. 14-1)

A. M. Calverley et al., *The Temple of King Sethos I at Abydos*, i. London and Chicago (Ill.) 1933

A. Mariette. *Abydos*, i-ii. Paris 1869-80.

W. M. F. Petrie, *The Royal Tombs of the First Dynasty/Earliest Dynasties*. London 1900-01.

Beit Khallaf (PM v.37)

J. Garstang, *Mahâsna and Bêt Khallâf*. London 1903.

Akhmim (PM v.17-26)

Wannina (PM v.31-34)

W. M. F. Petrie, *Athribis*. London 1908.

Qaw el-Kebir (PM v.9-16)

H. Steckeweh. *Die Fürstengräber van Qaw*. Leipzig 1936.

Asyut (PM iv.259-70)

F. L. Griffith, *The Inscriptions of Siut and Der Rifeh*. London 1889.

Deir el-Gabrawi (PM iv.242-46)

N. de G. Davies, *The Rock Tombs of Deir el Gebrawi*, iti. London 1902.

Meir (PM iv.247-58)

A. M. Blackman, *The Rock Tombs of Meir*, i-vi. London 1914-53.

el-'Amarna (PM iv. 192-237)

N. de G. Davies, *The Rock Tombs of El Amarna*, i-vi. London 190308.

G. T. Martin. *The Royal Tomb at el-'Amarna*, i. London 1974

T. E. Peet, C. L. Woolley, J. D. S. Pendlebury et al., *The City of Akhenaten*, i-iii. London 1923, 1933, 1951

el-Sheikh Sa'id (PM iv. 187-92)

N. de G. Davies, *The Rock Tombs of Sheikh Said*. London 1901.

Deir el-Bersha (PM iv.177–87)

P. F. Newberry and F. L. Griffith, *El Bersheh*, i-ii. London 1893.

el-Ashmunein (PM iv. 165–69)

G. Roeder, *Hermopolis 1929-1939*. Hildesheim 1959.

Tuna el-Gebel (PM iv. 169-75)

S.Gabra and E. Drioton. *Peintures à fresques et scènes peintes à Hermoupolis ouest (Touna el-Gebel)*. Cairo 1954.

G. Lefebvre, *Le Tombeau de Petosiris*, i-iii. Cairo 1923-24.

el-Sheikh 'Ibada (PM iv. 175-77)

Antinoe (1965-1968). *Missione archeologica in Egitto dell' Università di Roma*. Rome 1974.

Beni Hasan with Speos Artemidos (PM iv.140-65)

P. E. Newberry, F. L. Griffith et al., *Beni Hasan*, i-iv. London 18931900.

Zawyet el-Amwat (PM iv. 134-39)

A. Varille. *La Tombe de Ni-Ankh-Pepi à Zdouyet el Mayetîn*. Cairo 1938.

Tihna el-Gebel (PM iv. 127-33)

R. Holthoer and R. Ahlqvist, "The 'Roman Temple' at Tehna elGebel, *Studia Orientalia*, xliii.7 (1974).

el-Bahnasa (PM iv. 124)

W. M. F. Petrie. *Tombs of the Courtiers and Oxyrhynkhos*. London 1925.

The Oxyrhynchus Papyri, i-. London 1898-.

el-Hiba (PM iv. 124-25)

H. Ranke, *Koptische Fried hofe bei Kardra und der Amontempei Scheschonks I bei ci Hibe*. Berlin and Leipzig 1926.

Dishasha (PM iv. 121-23)

W. M. F. Petrie, *Deshasheh 1897*. London 1898.

Ihnasya el-Medina (PM iv. 118-21)

E. Naville, *Ahnas ci Medineh (Heracleopoiis Magna)*. London 1894.

W. M. F. Petrie, *Ehnasya 1904*. London 1905.

Kom Medinet Ghurab (PM iv. 112-15)

L. Borchardt. *Der Porträtkopf der Königin Teje*. Leipzig 1911.

el-Lahun (PM 1v. 107-12)

W. M. F. Petrie, *Kahun, Gurob, and Hawara*. London 1890.

——*Iliahun, Kahun and Gurob 1889-90*. London 1891.

The Faiyum (PM iv.96-104)

E. Bresciani, *Rapporto preiiminare delle campagne di scavo 1966 e 1967*. Milan and Varese 1968.

A. Vogliano, *Rapporto degii scavi… Madinet Madi*, i-ii. Milan 193637.

Maidum (PM iv.89-96)

W. M. F. Petrie, *Medum*. London 1892.

el-Lisht (PM iv.77-85)

H. Goedicke, *Re-used Blocks from the Pyramid of Amenemhet 1 at Lisht*. New York 1971.

Mit Rahlna (PM iii.217-27)

R. Anthes et al., *Mit Rahineh 1955 and 1956*. Philadelphia (Pa.) 1959 and 1965.

W. M. F. Petrie et al., *Memphis*, iv. London 190913.

Dahshur (PM iii.228-40)

J. de Morgan, *Fouiiies a Dahchour*, i-ii. Vienna 1895-1903.

A. Fakhry, *The Monuments of Sneferu at Dahshur*, i-ii. Cairo 1959-61.

Saqqara (PM iii.83-215 and iii.²393-776)

P. Duell et al.. *The Mastaba of Mereruka*, i-ii. Chicago (111.) 1938.

M. Z. Goneim, *Horus Sekhem-khet. The Unfinished Step Pyramid at Saqqara*, i: Cairo 1957.

J.-P. Lauer. Saqqara. *The Royal Cemetery of Memphis*. London 1976.

Le Tombeau de Ti, i-iii (i by L. Epron and F. Daumas, ii and iii by H. Wild). Cairo 1939-66.

A. M. Moussa and H. Altenmilller, *Das Grab des Nianchchnum und Chnumhotep*. Mainz 1977.

Abusir (PM iii.²324-50) .

L. Borchardt, *Das Grabdenkmal des Königs Sa3hu-re'*, iii. Leipzig 191013.

H. Ricke et al., *Das Sonnenheiligtum des Königs Userkaf*, i-ii. Cairo 1965, Wiesbaden 1969.

Abu Ghurab (PM iii.²314-24)

E. Edel and S. Wenig, *Die Jahreszeitenreliefs aus dem Sonnenheiligtum des Königs Ne-user-Re*. Berlin 1974.

Zawyet el-'Aryan (PM iii.²312-14)

D. Dunham, *Zawiyet el-Aryan. The Cemeteries Adjacent to the Layer Pyramid*. Boston (Mass.) 1978.

Giza (PM iii.²103-l2)

D. Dunham and W. K. Simpson, *The Mastaba of Queen Mersyankh Ill*. Boston (Mass.) 1974.

H. Junket, *Giza*, i-xii. Vienna and Leipzig 1929-55.

G. A. Reisner. *Mycerinus. The Temples of the Third Pyramid at Giza*. Cambridge (Mass.) 1931.

——*A History of the Giza Necropolis*, i-ii. Cambridge (Mass.) 1942-55.

W. K. Simpson, *The Mastabas of Kawab, Khafkhufu I and II*. Boston (Mass.) 1978.

C. M. Zivie, *Giza au deuxième millénaire*. Cairo 1976.

Abu Rawash (PM iii.²1-10)

F. Bisson de la Roque, *Rapport sur iesfouilies d'Abou Roasch (1922-1923) and (1924)*. Cairo 1924-25.

Ausim (PM iv.68)

Kom Abu Billo (PM iv.67-68)

Kom el-Hisn (PM iv.51-52)

Naukratis (PM iv.50)

D. G. Hogarth, H. L. Lorimer and C. C. Edgar. "Naukratis, 1903, "*Journal of Hellenic Studies*, xxv (1905), 105-36.

Alexandria (PM iv.2-6)

A. Adriani, *Repertorio d'arte dell'Egittogrecoromano*, series C, i-ii. Palermo 1966.

P. M. Fraser, *Ptolemaic Alexandria*, iiii. Oxford 1972.

Sa elHagar (PM iv.46-49)

R. el-Sayed, *Documents reiatifs à Sais et ses divinités*. Cairo 1975.

Tell el-Fara'in (PM iv.45)

Behbelt el-Hagar (PM iv.40-42)

Tell Atrib (PM iv.65-67)

P. Vernus, *Athribis*. Cairo 1978.

Tell el-Muqdam (PM iv.37-39)

E. Naville, *Ahnas el Medineh* (Heracleopolis Magna). London 1894, 27-31.

Samannud (PM iv.43-44) G. Steindorff, "Reliefs from the Temples of Sebennytos and Iseion in American Collections," *Journal of the Walters Art Gallery*, vii-viii (1944-45), 38-59.

el-Baqliya (PM iv.39-40)

A.-P. Zivie. *Hermopolis et le nome de l'Ibis*. Cairo 1975.

Tell el-Rub'a and Tell el-Timai (PM iv.35-37) H. De Meulenaere and P. MacKay, *Mendes II*. Warminster 1976.

Heliopolis (PM iv.59-65)

W. M. F. Petrie and B. Mackay, *Heliopolis, Kafr Ammar and Shurafa*. London 1915.

H. Ricke, "Eine inventartafel aus Heliopolis im Turiner Museum," *Zeitschrift für ägyptische Sprache und Altertumskunde*, lxxi (1935), 111-33.

Tell el-Yahudiya (PM iv. 5658)

B. Naville. *The Mound of the Jew and the City of Onias*. London 1890.

G. R. H. Wright. "Tell elYehüdiyah and the Glacis," *Zeitschrift des Deutschen Palästina-Vereins*, lxxxiv (1968), 11-7.

Tell Basta (PM iv. 27-35)

Labib Habachi, *Tell Basta*. Cairo 1957.

Saft elHinna (PM iv.10-11)

E. Naville, *The Shrine of Saft ci Henneh*

and the Land of Goshen 1885. London 1887.

District of el-Khata'na and Qantlr (PM iv.9-1O) M. Bietak, Tell elDab'a II. Vienna 1975.

Tell Nabasha (PM iv.79) W. M. F. Petrie, *Tanis II, Nebesheh (Am) and Defenneh (Tahpanhes)*. London 1888.

San el-Hagar (PM iv. 13-26)

P. Montet, *La Nécropole royale de Tanis*, i-iii. Paris 1947-60.

——*Les Énigmes de Tanis*. Paris 1952.

Tell el-Maskhuta (PM iv.53-55) B. Naville, *The Store City of Pithom and the Route of the Exodus*. London 1903.

el-Dakka (PM vii.40-50) G. Roeder and W. Ruppel, *Der Tempel von Dakke*, i-iii. Cairo 1913-30.

Quban (PM vii.82-83)

'Amada (PM vii.65-73) H. Gauthier. *Le Temple d'Amada*. Cairo 1913-26.

el-Sebu'a (PM vii.5364) H. Gauthier. *Le Temple de Ouadi es-Sebouâ*. Cairo 1912.

el-Derr (PM vii.84-89) A. M. Blackman, *The Temple of Derr*. Cairo 1913.

el-Lessiya (PM vii.90-91) S.Curto, *Ii tempio di Ellesija*. Turin 1970.

Qasr Ibrim (PM vii.92-94) R. A. Caminos, *The Shrines and Rock-inscriptions of Ibrim*. London 1968.

Dabod (PM vii.1-5)

M. Almagro. *El templo de Debod*. Madrid 1971.

Tafa (PM vii.8-10)

H. D. Schneider, *Taffeh. Rond de wederopbouw van een Nubische tempel*. The Hague 1979.

Beit el-Wall (PM vii. 21-27)

H. Ricke, G. R. Hughes and B. F. Wente, *The Beit el-Wali Temple of Ramesses II*. Chicago (Ill.) 1967.

Kalabsha (PM vii.10-21)

K. G. Siegler. *Kalabsha. Architektur und Baugeschichte des Tempels*. Berlin 1970.

Dendur (PM vii.27-33)

C. Aldred. "The Temple of Dendur," *Metropolitan Museum of Art Bulletin*, xxxvi (1) (Summer 1978).

Gerf Hussein (PM vii.33-37)

'Anlba (PM vii.7581)

G. Steindorfl *Aniba*, i-ii. Glückstadt etc. 1935-37.

Abu Simbel (PM vii.95-119)

C. Desroches-Noblecourt and C. Kuentz, *Le Petit Temple d'Abou Simbel*, i-ii. Cairo 1968. W. MacQuitty, *Abu Simbel*. London 1965.

Sinai

A. H. Gardiner, T. B. Peet, and J. Cerny, *The Inscriptions of Sinai*, i-ii. London 195255.

Boats

B. Landström, *Ships of the Pharaohs. 4000 Years of Egyptian Shipbuilding*. London 1970.

M. Z. Nour *et al.*, *The Cheops Boats*, i. Cairo 1960.

Pyramids

I. E. S. Edwards, *The Pyramids of Egypt*. London. Various editions.

A. Fakhry, *The Pyramids*. Chicago (Ill.) and London 1969.

J.P. Lauer, *Le Mystère des pyramides*. Paris 1974.

Part Three Aspects of Egyptian Society

Women In society

P. W. Pestman, *Marriage and Matrimonial Property in Ancient Egypt*. Leiden 1961.

S. Wenig, *Die Frau im aiten Ägypten*. Leipzig 1967.

Scribes and writing

There are grammars of different stages of the language by: J. B. Callender; J. Cerny and S. I. Groll; E. Edel; A. H. Gardiner; H. Junker; G. Lefebvre; F. Lexa; W. Spiegelberg; and dictionaries by: W. Erichsen; A. Erman and H. Grapow; R. O. Faulkner. The terminology used in the description of the script is that of W. Schenkel.

The army

A. R. Schulman, *Military Rank, Title, and Organization in the Egyptian New Kingdom*. Berlin 1964.

W. Wolf, *Die Bewaffnung des altägyptischen Heeres*. Leipzig 1926.

Y. Yadin. *The Art of Warfare in Biblical Lands in the Light of Archaeological Discovery*. London 1963.

Religion

H. Frankfort. *Ancient Egyptian Religion*. New York 1948

E. Hornung. *Der Eine und die Vielen*. Darmstadt 1971.

S. Morenz, *Ägyptische Religion*. Stuttgart 1960.

E. Otto, *Osiris und Amun. Kult und heilige Stätten*. Munich 1966.

Burial customs

J.-F. and L. Aubert, *Statuettes égyptiennes, chaouabtis, ouchebtis*. Paris 1974.

M.-L. Buhl, *The Late Egyptian Anthropoid Stone Sarcophagi*. Copenhagen 1959.

W. R. Dawson and P. H. K. Gray, *Mummies and Human Remains*. London 1968.

A. M. Donadoni Roveri. *I sarcofagi egizi dalle origini alla fine dell'Antico Regno*. Rome 1969.

J. Hamilton Paterson and C. Andrews, *Mummies: Death and Life in Ancient Egypt*. London 1978.

H. Schneider, *Shabtis*, i-iii. Leiden 1977.

Index